D0201266

Mountain Biking the San Francisco Bay Area

Help Us Keep This Guide Up to Date

Every effort has been made by the author and editors to make this guide as accurate and useful as possible. However, many things can change after a guide is published—trails are rerouted, regulations change, techniques evolve, facilities come under new management, etc.

We would love to hear from you concerning your experiences with this guide and how you feel it could be improved and kept up to date. While we may not be able to respond to all comments and suggestions, we'll take them to heart and we'll also make certain to share them with the author. Please send your comments and suggestions to the following address:

> The Globe Pequot Press
> Reader Response/Editorial Department
> P.O. Box 480
> Guilford, CT 06437

Or you may e-mail us at:

> editorial@GlobePequot.com

Thanks for your input, and happy travels!

A FALCON GUIDE®

Mountain Biking the San Francisco Bay Area

A Guide to the Bay Area's Greatest Off-Road Bicycle Rides

Lorene Jackson

FALCON®

GUILFORD, CONNECTICUT
HELENA, MONTANA
AN IMPRINT OF THE GLOBE PEQUOT PRESS

Λ FALCONGUIDE ®

Maps by XNR Productions Inc. © The Globe Pequot Press

Photos by Lorene Jackson

ISSN 1548-1638
ISBN 0-7627-2715-2

Manufactured in the United States of America
First Edition/First Printing

To each of my children,
Aaron, Anna, Alex, and Jeffrey,
who inspire me daily

Contents

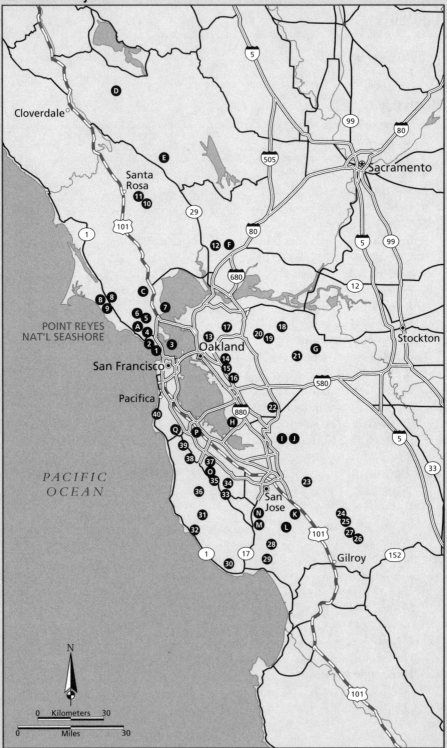

Acknowledgments

It takes many people to breathe life into a book like this. To begin, thanks from the bottom of my heart to the best betties and friends, Jill Nickels, MaryLyn Bondlow, and Donna Spinelli. I would never have done this without you. Big thanks to Deb and Mark Swigert for the rides and showing me new trails.

I am grateful for the patience and support of all my trail mates: Frank Jackson (sorry for the wrong turn, bro), Alan Urena (thanks for coming back for more rides), Paul Smail, D. J. Campagna, Ford Nickels, Hunter Morgan, Taylor Peterson, both Tai Williamses, and all the others who joined me in testing these trails.

Special thanks to Joe Breeze, Blair Lombardi, and Jacquie Phelan for their contributions and inspirations. I received valuable trail advice from many folks but especially from Randy Berthold, Karl Vavrek, Jim Jacobson, Danny Foyer, Dave Ambrose, and Paul Nam.

I offer gratitude to Debra Hunter for planting the seed and to Scott Adams for giving me the chance to write this book. Who would imagine a mandate to go forth and ride? Credit goes to everyone at The Globe Pequot Press who had a hand in moving this guidebook through the pipeline, especially Julie Marsh and Joanna Beyer. To Lynn Larson and Melodee Kistner, thanks for your constant encouragement. Much appreciation goes to my field scouts, Tamara Williams and Pat Bracewell: Got to have the facts. And of course to Mom and Dad, thanks for sending me outside to play.

We all share indebtedness to the forward-thinking souls who have worked so hard to avert the paving of paradise throughout the Bay Area. May we repay them with our stewardship. Likewise, special thanks go to the trail builders, bicycle trail councils, and mountain bike advocates who enable us to keep riding the dirt. To all the park rangers, land managers, and staff who reviewed this guide, thanks for your time and input. I wish I had space to list every one of you.

Big kudos go to the pit crew at Mike's Bikes of San Rafael for ensuring that I didn't break down on the trail. You guys are great.

My love to Aaron, Alex, and Jeffrey for being my riding companions, for sharing the load, and for your patience throughout this project. You have lived this book with me.

Thank you all.

Introduction

Welcome home, mountain biking souls. The San Francisco Bay Area is where legends are born, the riding is year-round, the trails are impressive, and the access is easy. Let this guide take you away from the urban landscape to enjoy spectacular views, solitude, and some wild rides. Within minutes you will forget there are nearly seven million people living nearby. There is still wilderness out here where you can ride all day and barely see another person.

There are trails for every rider: from beginner to expert, quick fixes to epic rides, and rugged singletrack to smooth dirt roads. There are new trails and the old classics. You may know the trails in your backyard; you may have tested a few trails across the bay. Now ride them all—more than 700 miles. You will be a different person at the end of the journey.

With all the options and honorable mentions, this guide offers more than eighty of the best rides in the Bay Area. Still, there are more trails out there that don't fit in a handy book. Some trails can't handle much more traffic, and some are better left to the locals. Look around and you will find them. Contact the local bicycle trail council, join a bike club, connect with a group ride, and talk to the folks at the bike shops. They know where the remaining gems are.

Now a quick bit of business about bike odometers: Some people don't like them. Why find out you have gone only 15 miles when it felt like 20 miles? However, mileage cues have their place in a guidebook. Some riders may find that these published distances don't agree precisely with their readings. Sorry, but the book is correct—and that's that. Do not get hung up about small differences. Readings will vary depending on the calibration of your odometer, the line you ride, whether you backtrack, or if you take any side trips. Use these mileage cues as guides. Armed with the maps, directions, and descriptions, you should stay on track.

Weather

Overall, the Bay Area enjoys a temperate marine climate of mild weather throughout the year. Average temperatures range from 50 to 70 degrees Fahrenheit. Sounds great, and it is. The qualifier here is variability, as in dramatic changes in temperature around the corner.

Offshore breezes along the coast and over the coastal mountains affect temperatures throughout the region. The darling Golden Gate acts as a wind funnel. From June to mid-August, morning and evening coastal fog rolls into the bay. Once it hits Berkeley and Oakland, it fans out over the inland waters and low-lying communities, corralled by the East Bay Hills. Meanwhile, summer temperatures can climb as you move inland to 90 degrees and rising.

How many betties does it take to fix a chain? A little trailside repair takes place along the Coyote Ridge Trail on the Tennessee Valley–Green Gulch Loop ride.

Even without fog, these coastal breezes (aka winds) can create temperature differences of 25 degrees on a single ride. It may be warm and sunny at the trailhead, yet a fog bank may greet you over the next hill. Unexpected cloud cover can chill the unprepared rider to the bone. Just as likely, you may start your ride in the damp fog and watch it clear away to a warm day.

If you count ridable days, you'll be pleased that the average rainfall in the Bay Area is only 20 inches and there is no snow to speak of. Actually, that's wrong; if it snows, *everyone* talks about it and runs around in it. Typically, most rain falls from November to March, with January's rainfall being the heaviest. Again, the weather varies dramatically. Annual rainfall can range from 49 inches at the base of Mount Tamalpais to 20 inches in nearby San Francisco or 15 inches in Palo Alto.

As a mountain biker, you will quickly learn the subtleties of the local microclimates. Knowing and planning for this will be your advantage. For local weather conditions and forecasts, check out www.sfgate.com/weather or www.wrh.noaa.gov/monterey.

Yes, the first challenge for Bay Area riders is what to wear. The key to comfortable riding is to dress in layers. Lightweight windbreakers, vests, and arm and leg warmers pack easily. Sometimes it is handy to have a change of dry clothing on long rides, especially when your clothes get soaked and you start to chill. You can handle cooler temperatures and wind with a dry layer next to your skin.

Flora and Fauna

The Bay Area offers classic California landscapes: Coarse chaparral and coastal scrub cover the bluffs overlooking the Pacific Ocean. Lush redwood forests thrive in the deep canyons along the coastal fog belt. Rolling grass-covered hillsides are studded with oak trees. Canyons are shaded in woodlands of oak, madrone, bay laurel, buckeye, and Douglas fir. More chaparral, manzanita, and pine withstand the rugged peaks and craggy outcroppings along ridgetops. In spring and early summer, wildflowers pop up throughout the region, with the grassy hillsides making a particularly brilliant show.

The diversity of the landscape brings a wealth of wildlife. You may catch glimpses of deer, fox, coyote, bobcat, rabbit, raccoon, squirrel, skunk, and wild turkey. During winter watch out for banana slugs and salamanders crossing the trails in the damp redwood forests. Along the ridges and opens hillsides, you'll be accompanied by an array of raptors. You may also spot gray whales migrating along the coast.

Not all the flora and fauna are benign. Be aware of these trailside hazards:

Poison oak is pervasive on way too many trails in the region. For the sensitive it can lead to irritating rashes, blisters, and a general crawling-out-of-your-skin discomfort. It doesn't affect everyone; but while it may not bother you today, you may become sensitized next time. Distinguishing features of poison oak are clusters of three leaves with gently lobed edges: "Leaves of three let it be." In fall the bright red leaves are easy to spot. In spring the waxy green leaves are often camouflaged. In winter only a trained eye can identify the bare sticks. Preexposure products are available if you know you are heading for infested trails. The best defense is a careful eye, protective clothing, and a wide trail. Be careful how you handle any clothing that touches poison oak; you can still pick up the oil. If you are exposed, wash your skin as soon as possible. Over-the-counter Technu scrub can be effective.

Ticks have become an increasing concern now that Lyme disease has moved west. The Bay Area has more than its share of these nasty hitchhikers. Do some spot-checking while on the trail, and have a careful look-see when you finish your ride. If you get a bite, watch for a distinctive ring appearing around the site. It may appear within a day or up to a month, but not all Lyme disease sufferers exhibit a ring. Seriously, save the tick for lab testing if necessary.

Rattlesnakes are polite poisonous snakes and usually sound an alarm when you are in their space. They are not aggressive, but they do take a stand if startled. The best advice is to be on the alert for them. Chances are you will be a long way from help should you be bitten.

Mountain lions also call the hills and mountains of the Bay Area home. You will see warnings posted at many trailheads. Although sightings are rare, take the warnings seriously. Mountain lions do not take well to surprises. If you encounter one, do not turn your back and ride away from it. Make yourself *big;* don't bend over or crouch down. Stare them down as you slowly back away. Rear your bike up as a shield if necessary. Act like a predator or risk becoming prey.

Wilderness Restrictions and Regulations

A slew of city, county, regional, state, and federal agencies manage the wilderness, greenbelts, and open trails of the Bay Area. Each agency is watching out for its respective interests, be it recreation, open space, watershed management, ecological protection, private property, or multipurpose uses. One ride may traverse land owned by several different entities. Each has its own regulations and enforcement personnel, with rules often posted at trailheads. Helmets are becoming a requirement in more and more areas, but you should always wear one anyway for safety's sake. Some places are more bike-friendly than others are. It is encouraging to see an increased emphasis on the sharing of trails among mountain bikers, hikers, and equestrians. The Bay Area seems to be recovering from a dark period of antibiking sentiment. At the same time, more and more public land is becoming accessible through acquisitions from land trusts. New trails are opening to bicycles!

Mountain bikers are a closely watched group. So, my dear fat-tire enthusiasts, consider every person you meet as a potential lobbyist for or against mountain biking. Make sure your encounter will convince them that we belong on these trails.

Now go out and ride.

How to Use This Book

Each region begins with an introduction where you're given a sweeping look at the lay of the land. After this overview specific rides within that region are presented.

Each ride begins with a short summary that gives you a taste of the terrain and what surprises the route has to offer. Just below this you'll find the quick, nitty-gritty details of the ride: where the trailhead is located, the nearest town, ride distance, approximate riding time, difficulty rating, best riding season, type of trail terrain, if dogs are permitted, what other trail users you may encounter, trail contacts (for updates on trail conditions), trail schedules, and any fees or permits required. (Fees and permit requirements can change. Check before you ride.) The **Finding the trailhead** section gives you dependable directions from a nearby city or town right down to where you'll want to park your car. **The Ride** is the meat of the chapter. Detailed and honest, it's the author's carefully researched impression of the trail. In **Miles and Directions** mileage cues identify all turns and trail name changes, as well as points of interest. The **Ride Information** section at the end of each ride contains more useful information, including local resources for learning more about the area, where to stay, where to eat, and what else to see while you're riding in the area.

The **Honorable Mentions** section details additional rides that will inspire you to get out and explore. Short descriptions of each ride are included that cover the rides' length, directions on how to get to the trailhead, and contact information. The Honorable Mention rides, designated by letters, are located after the numbered rides in each region.

How to Use These Maps

Elevation profile: This book uses elevation profiles to provide an idea of the length and elevation of hills you will encounter along each ride. In each of the profiles, the vertical axes of the graphs show the total distance climbed in feet. In contrast, the horizontal axes show the distance traveled in miles. It is important to understand that the vertical (feet) and horizontal (miles) scales can differ between rides. Read each profile carefully, making sure you read both the height and distance shown. This will help you interpret what you see in each profile. Some elevation profiles may show gradual hills to be steep and steep hills to be gradual. Elevation profiles are not provided for rides with little or no elevation gain.

Route map: This is your primary guide to each ride. It shows all the accessible roads and trails, points of interest, water, towns, landmarks, and geographical features. It also distinguishes trails from roads and paved roads from unpaved roads. The selected route is highlighted, and directional arrows point the way.

Map Legend

══(84)══	Interstate
══(26)══	U.S. highway
──(1)──	State highway
──────	Paved road
▬▬▬▬▬	Featured gravel/dirt road
═════	Gravel/dirt road
▪▪▪▪▪▪▪	Featured unimproved/doubletrack
═ ═ ═ ═	Unimproved road/doubletrack
▬ ▬ ▬ ▬	Featured singletrack trail
--------	Other singletrack trail
············	Ferry route
⊨⊣	Tunnel
⊨	Bridge
▲	Campground
†	Cemetery
○ ◉	City
—	Dam
•—•	Gate
⌕	Golf Course
🄷	Hospital
◘	Overlook/viewpoint
🄿	Parking
)(	Pass
▲	Peak/elevation
⛲	Picnic area
■	Point of interest
▮	Ranger station
⛶	School
⚲	Spring
START 🚴	Trailhead
🄸	Visitor information
//	Waterfall

North Bay

The Golden Gate Bridge makes a fitting entryway to the North Bay. Heading north across the bridge, you arrive on the dramatic coastal cliffs of the Marin Headlands. Continuing north around the corner, you pass through a rainbow-painted tunnel above Sausalito. At the other end of the tunnel is the pot of gold. There stands Mount Tamalpais, with its deep-seeded roots in mountain biking history. If you look carefully, you will see up-and-coming legends alongside Hall of Famers cruising through the maze of mountain trails running between the San Francisco Bay and the Pacific Ocean.

For all that is said about the folks of Marin, they deserve credit for their tenacious passion for preserving the land. While a no-growth mind-set has driven up housing prices, it also has preserved miles of open space and trails. An array of local, state, and federal agencies managing parks, preserves, monuments, and seashores combines to define the Marinscape: the Marin Headlands, Point Reyes, Mount Tamalpais, China Camp, Angel Island, watershed lands, and county open-space preserves. The brilliant part is the interconnecting network of trails. The permutation of rides is limitless. You can ride all day over hills, along ridges, to the tops of mountains, and to the ocean. Dirt trails will take you from the Golden Gate Bridge to Point Reyes. Awesome.

This has not been accomplished without Herculean effort. Some of the resolve to preserve open space has failed to embrace mountain biking. Staunch stewardship has come back to bite mountain bikers in their chamois pads. With time we will hopefully arrive at a balance among all trail users. For our part mountain bikers need to follow the rules.

Aside from the amazing terrain, the North Bay is legendary for year-round riding. The ridability factor is big here. Coastal fog keeps it cool in summer, to say nothing of the shade of the redwood forests. Then there is the dirt. The North Bay has some of the best in the winter. Okay, some trails are off-limits, some are just no fun to ride, and you don't want to trash the trails by riding right after a rain. But the soil drains. This is where the East Bay folks head in winter.

The North Bay is not all about Marin County; it extends to Sonoma, Napa, and Solano Counties, encircling the northern part of San Pablo and Suisun Bays. The rolling hills overlooking the wine country offer something that is hard to find in the bastion of Marin: miles of sweet singletrack. Those twisty, never-boring paths are waiting in Annadel State Park, Skyline Wilderness Park, Boggs Mountain Demonstration State Forest, and a city playground called Rockville. Go, while you still can.

1 Tennessee Valley–Golden Gate Loop

Skip the parking lot overlooks; see the Golden Gate Bridge and feel the Pacific Coast from this vantage. Just north of San Francisco, this ride takes you on fire roads through the open grassland and chaparral-covered hills of the Marin Headlands. Savor the spectacular views. Bird-watchers will want to linger near Hawk Hill, Bird Island, and Rodeo Lagoon. History buffs will want to explore historical sights in Forts Baker, Barry, and Cronkhite. However, true mountain bikers will reride the sweet single-track at the end of this ride a couple of times.

Start: From the parking lot at the end of Tennessee Valley Road, Mill Valley.
Distance: 14-mile figure eight.
Approximate riding time: 1.5 hours.
Difficulty: Moderate; nontechnical ride with some steady climbing, suitable for hardy beginners.
Trail surface: 60 percent dirt fire road, 30 percent paved road, and 10 percent single-track.
Terrain: Smooth coastal hills, steep coastal cliffs.
Seasons: Good year-round. Exceptional in spring with all the wildflowers, not as nice when cold fog blocks the view.
Other trail users: Hikers, equestrians, and cars.

Canine compatibility: Dogs not permitted.
Land status: Golden Gate National Recreation Area.
Nearest town: Mill Valley.
Fees and permits: No fees or permits required.
Schedule: Open year-round, 24 hours a day.
Maps: USGS maps: Point Bonita, CA; San Francisco North, CA.
Marin County Bicycle Coalition, *Marin Bicycle Map for Road, Mountain, and Transit Biking,* available at most bike shops.
Trail contact: Marin Headlands Visitor Center, Fort Barry, Sausalito, CA 94965; (415) 331-1540; www.nps.gov/goga/mahe.

Finding the trailhead: Tennessee Valley Trailhead from Mill Valley: Exit U.S. Highway 101 onto California Highway 1 toward Stinson Beach/Mill Valley. Follow signs to Stinson Beach. About half a mile from the freeway, turn left onto Tennessee Valley Road. The road ends in less than 2 miles at the parking lot and trailhead. Although there are other places to access this route, there are restrooms, picnic tables, and a phone here.

Golden Gate Bridge Trailhead Option

From San Francisco: Head north across the Golden Gate Bridge on US 101. Take the Alexander Avenue exit. Turn left and go under the freeway, following signs to the Marin Headlands. Turn right onto Conzelman Road. The Headlands parking lot is immediately on the left. You can park here and ride up the steep narrow road. Alternatively, you can drive up and park at any of the turnouts near the convergence of McCullough Road and Coastal Trail. Trailhead GPS: N 37 50.013, W 122 29.389.

The Ride

The ride begins with a steady climb out of Tennessee Valley on Marincello Trail and a section of the Bay Area Ridge Trail. Great views of Richardson Bay open up on

The Golden Gate Bridge welcomes you to San Francisco.

the left as you climb. Developers built portions of this road in the 1960s with hopes of leading over the hill to the proposed city of Marincello in Gerbode Valley. Think high-rise offices, hotels, and apartments. With a fierce battle, conservationists stopped development plans in the courts and further ensured that this area would remain open space forever. The land was initially preserved as part of The Nature Conservancy, which later led to the formation of the Golden Gate National Recreation Area (GGNRA).

Past the first summit is a singletrack trail on the right to Hawk Camp, one of two hike- or bike-in campsites in the Headlands. Bikes are allowed on the trail to the camp. The long descent down Bobcat Trail makes up for the first climb and usually perks up fledgling bikers. Gerbode Valley, on the right, is the site of one of the former Portuguese dairies that covered the Headlands from the 1860s to 1960s. Eucalyptus, Monterey cypress, fruit trees, and roses remain today.

Near the bottom of Bobcat Trail, you cut across Bunker Road and climb up Coastal Trail. This brings you to narrow, paved Conzelman Road. On a clear day this is the picture-postcard view of the Golden Gate Bridge and San Francisco. Ride uphill to the lookout near Battery Construction No. 129. This road is very popular on weekends and holidays, so watch out for drivers who may be more intent on the view than on you. Along the way notice the dramatic swirls of sediment layers in the

Tennessee Valley–Golden Gate Loop

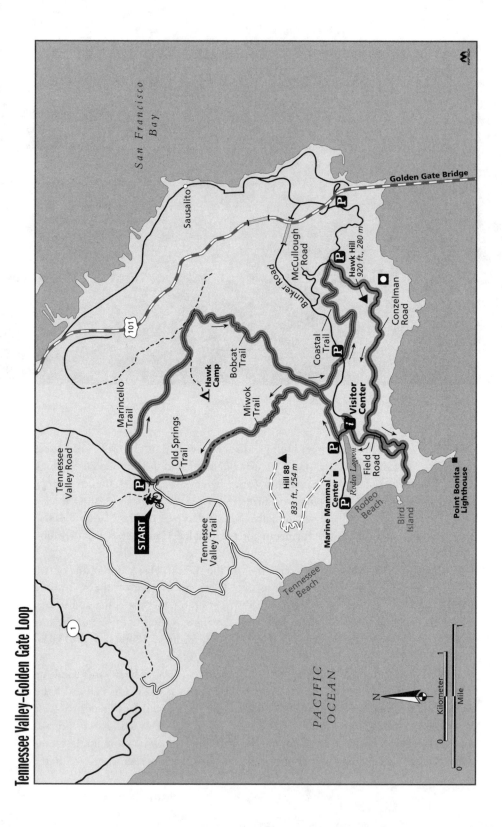

right road cuts, evidence of an uplifted ocean floor. These ribbons of radiolarian chert are part of the Franciscan formation. Radiolarians are single-celled plankton whose skeletons accumulate on the ocean floor.

Past the lookout, the road becomes one-way and makes a fast drop toward the Point Bonita Lighthouse. Never mind that this is not mountain biking, the view of the coast is worth it. You weave past more batteries, an eerie reminder of the Nike Missile days. Interpretive signs give explanations at each site. There are several scenic picnic areas and campgrounds along the way. The turnaround is at the overlook for Bird Island and Rodeo Beach. Depending on the season, you may find brown pelicans, cormorants, and gulls.

Heading back, ride up Rodeo Valley and past the Marin Headlands Visitor Center. Then jog around Rodeo Lagoon—another great bird-watching spot. The dirt trail picks up again past the lagoon for an easy ride up Rodeo Valley on the lower section of Miwok Trail. You can also take side trips down to the beach and visit the California Marine Mammal Center. This is a rescue, rehabilitation, and research center for sick and injured sea otters, seals, sea lions, dolphins, and whales. For the energetic there is a ride north on a spur of the Coastal Trail to the top of Hill 88.

TIDBIT: The Golden Gate National Recreation Area (GGNRA) is one of the largest urban national parks in the world. Although not all the land is contiguous, the total park area is nearly 75,400 acres of land and water. That is nearly two and a half times the size of San Francisco. In addition to the Marin Headlands, other popular sites include Alcatraz Island, Fort Funston, Fort Mason, Muir Woods National Monument, Fort Point National Historic Site, and the Presidio of San Francisco.

Miwok Trail takes you back to a junction with Bobcat Trail, completing one loop. The next mile is a steady grind to the summit. Try to enjoy the view of the valley as you climb. The reward is the best and last section of the ride. Old Springs Trail is a fun and wide singletrack back to the stables. Walk bikes through the stables and finish up at the parking lot.

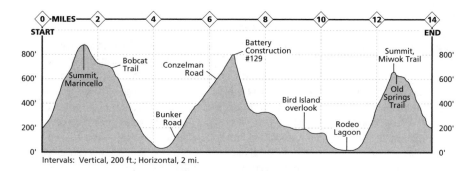

Intervals: Vertical, 200 ft.; Horizontal, 2 mi.

Throughout the ride keep your eyes up for hawks, eagles, falcons, and vultures. These hills are one of the best places in the country to watch raptors. The Golden Gate Raptor Observatory carefully studies their migration from atop Hawk Hill, above Conzelman Road.

Miles and Directions

0.0   **START** from the parking lot at the end of Tennessee Valley Road. Follow the sign to Miwok Trail North, although you actually face south toward Miwok Stables and Livery. At the gate on the left, take the wide dirt road—Marincello Trail. Trailhead GPS: N 37 51.38, W 122 32.09.

1.5   Stay left at the junction with Bobcat Trail.

1.8   Pass the trail to Hawk Camp on the right. There is no through access to Miwok Trail here.

2.2   Stay right on Bobcat Trail at the junction. A left turn would take you south on the Alta Trail—a hiking-only section of the Bay Area Ridge Trail.

2.3   Stay right at the Rodeo Valley Cutoff Trail on left—no bikes allowed.

4.2   Turn left onto Rodeo Valley Trail. The trail splits just before a NO BICYCLES sign. Turn right here onto the singletrack. When you get to the dirt parking lot, turn right. **Shortcut:** You can cut off the second loop by going straight for the short remainder (0.1 mile) of Bobcat Trail. Turn right up Miwok Trail, picking up directions at 11.4 miles.

4.7   Cross paved Bunker Road onto Coastal Trail. Stay on Coastal Trail all the way up the hill, ignoring any side trails on the left.

6.2   Turn right onto Conzelman Road and ride up the narrow paved road.

6.8   At first this appears to be the end of the road. However, continue on the paved road past Battery Construction No. 129 for a steep descent along the coast. As the road levels out, pass by Battery Rathbone-McIndoe.

8.7   Continue straight at stop sign toward Point Bonita. You will soon pass Battery Wallace.

9.0   Turn left at the YMCA Camp Bonita outdoor conference center. Pass Battery Mendell.

9.1   Pass the trailhead to Point Bonita Lighthouse—no bikes.

9.4   Reach the Bird Island overlook. Return down the paved road.

9. 7   Go straight at YMCA Camp Bonita.

10.1   Continue straight at the junction; pass between buildings for the Headlands Center for the Arts.

10.5   Reach the Marin Headlands Visitor Center and restrooms. Continue straight on Field Road at the junction with Bodsworth Road.

10.6   Turn left at junction onto Bunker Road, following sign to Sausalito Beach. Cross the bridge over Rodeo Lagoon and ride onto the dirt parking area on the right. The trailhead for Miwok Trail is on the right here. **Option:** Stay left on Bunker Road to Rodeo Beach, passing the Marine Mammal Center on the right. Continue to the end of pavement and take Coastal Trail about 2 miles up to Hill 88, elevation 833 feet. Much of the trail is an overgrown blacktop road; sections have washed out (as in completely gone). Bits of singletrack take you around the sections of missing road. There is a steep hike-a-bike up one hundred steps. These are not steps you can ride down. At the top, if you can ignore the abandoned artillery platforms, there is a sweet 360-degree view of the Headlands. It is a fast descent back down Coastal Trail.

11.4 Veer left on Miwok Trail at the junction with Bobcat Trail. Up ahead, ignore Wolf Ridge Trail, where no bikes are allowed.

12.7 Turn left onto Old Springs for a wide singletrack ride to the finish.

14.0 Arrive back at the parking lot.

Ride Information

Local Information

Golden Gate National Recreational Area, Headquarters and General Information, Fort Mason, Building 201, San Francisco, CA 94123; (415) 561-4700; www.nps.gov/goga.
Live Weather Cam on the Golden Gate Bridge, www.kron4.com/Global/category.asp?C=21304.

Local Events and Attractions

Golden Gate National Recreational Area, Marin Headlands Visitor Center, Building 948, Fort Barry, Sausalito; (415) 331-1540; www.nps.gpv/goga.
Marin Mammal Center, Marin Headlands, 1065 Fort Cronkhite, Sausalito; (415) 289-7325; www.marinemammalcenter.org.
Headlands Center for the Arts, 944 Fort Barry, Sausalito; (415) 331-2787; www.head lands.org.
Golden Gate Raptor Observatory, Building 210, Fort Mason, San Francisco; (415) 331-0730; www.ggro.org.

Accommodations

The Golden Gate National Recreation Area operates four campgrounds in the Headlands: Hawk and Haypress Camps are hike- or bike-in only. Bicentennial and Kirby Cove Campgrounds are walk-in sites off Conzelman Road. Reservations are required. Call (800) 365-CAMP to make reservations for Kirby Cove. For the other three campgrounds, call the Marin Headlands Visitor Center at (415) 331-1540.
Marin Headlands Hostel, Building 942, Fort Barry, Sausalito; (415) 331-2777 or (800) 909-4776, ext. 168; www.headlandshostel. homestead.com.

Group Rides

Tam Valley Bike Club, Tamalpais Community Services District, 305 Bell Lane, Mill Valley, CA 94941; (415) 388-6393; www.tamvalleybike club.com. Group rides Sunday morning. Full-moon night rides in the Golden Gate National Recreational Area.

NIKE MISSILE SITES Riding the ridges of the Bay Area, you eventually come upon flat and tattered concrete pads. These pads, remnants of the cold war and the Nike Missile era, are positioned at some of the best views of the bay and coastline. During the 1950s the U.S. Army built twelve air defense sites throughout the Bay Area, armed with missiles named for the Greek winged goddess of victory. The first generation, Nike Ajax, contained conventional warheads and had a range of 25 miles. The Nike Hercules replaced these, with the capacity of delivering a nuclear device four times as powerful as the one used at Hiroshima and having a range of nearly 100 miles. No missile was ever deployed, and the program ended with the signing of the Strategic Arms Limitations Treaty (SALT I) in 1972. Today one site is maintained as a museum at Fort Barry in the Marin Headlands. It is open to the public on the first Sunday of every month. Call (415) 331-1540.

2 Tennessee Valley-Green Gulch Loop

On a clear day this is a spectacularly scenic ride through the Marin Headlands. At the peak there is a 360-degree view of the Pacific Ocean, Mount Tamalpais, and San Francisco Bay that is hard to beat. At times the ride through the grass- and chaparral-covered hill is challenging. The climbs, rapid descents, hairpin turns, water bars, and steps break up the cadence of the fire road. Obstacles are relatively short and can always be walked.

Start: From the parking lot at the end of Tennessee Valley Road, Mill Valley.
Distance: 8.8-mile loop.
Approximate riding time: 1.5 to 2 hours.
Difficulty: Moderate; some strenuous climbing, intermediate technical skills required for the singletrack and descents.
Trail surface: 80 percent dirt fire road and 20 percent wide singletrack.
Terrain: Smooth and steep coastal hills.
Seasons: Best in spring, summer, and fall. Avoid Middle Green Gulch Trail in the wet season.
Other trail users: Hikers, equestrians, and joggers.

Canine compatibility: Dogs not permitted.
Land status: Golden Gate National Recreation Area.
Nearest town: Mill Valley.
Fees and permits: No fees or permits required.
Schedule: Open year-round, 24 hours a day.
Maps: USGS map: Point Bonita, CA. Marin County Bicycle Coalition, *Marin Bicycle Map for Road, Mountain, and Transit Biking*, available at most bike shops.
Trail contact: Golden Gate National Recreation Area, Marin Headlands Visitor Center, Fort Barry, Sausalito, CA 94965; (415) 331-1540; www.nps.gpv/goga.

Finding the trailhead: From Mill Valley: Exit U.S. Highway 101 onto California Highway 1 toward Stinson Beach/Mill Valley. Follow signs to Stinson Beach. About half a mile from the freeway, turn left onto Tennessee Valley Road. The road ends in less than 2 miles at the parking lot and trailhead. There are restrooms, picnic tables, and a phone here.

The Ride

This is a classic ride through the Marin Headlands and one that offers less traffic than the Golden Gate Loop. Riders seeking a longer ride can combine the two loops.

Tennessee Valley is a popular starting point for all park users. But don't freak— many of the cars in the parking lot are for hikers and joggers heading down to the beach at Tennessee Cove. With a large stable and arena near the parking lot, this is obviously a popular spot for equestrians. As you head up to the ridge, it becomes quieter.

The ride begins with an easy coast down the paved Tennessee Valley Trail before climbing up the Coastal Trail dirt road. As you climb, look back to see the marsh, pond, and trail leading to Tennessee Beach. The grass- and chaparral-covered hillside

Riding the edge of America.

is brilliant with wildflowers in the spring. As you reach windswept Coyote Ridge, an ever more spectacular view unfolds of the rugged Pacific coastline and Muir Beach. On a clear day you may see the Farallon Islands, located 26 miles off the coast. Native Americans never set foot on those islands, calling them the Islands of the Dead. Take a moment and enjoy the view, because once you start the descent, your eyes will focus only on the deeply rutted trail ahead.

At the bottom you can opt for a quick side trip to Muir Beach. Otherwise, ride up the Green Gulch Trail and quietly pass through the Green Gulch Farm Zen Center. The trail narrows for a singletrack climb back to Coyote Ridge. This is a pleasant trail; peacefulness seems to rise from the valley below. Try to hold on to that feeling through the switchbacks; water bars; and short, steep climbs. Bridge crossings here can be very slippery. Be careful not to slide off into the poison oak! Look back now and then to enjoy the coastal view. Most maps say no bike traffic *down* this trail

TIDBIT: The S.S. *Tennessee,* a side-paddle steamer, went aground here in 1853, having missed the Golden Gate in the fog. Fortunately all 551 aboard survived. During certain times of year, the sand washes out to reveal parts of the ship's engine on the left side of the beach.

Tennessee Valley–Green Gulch Loop

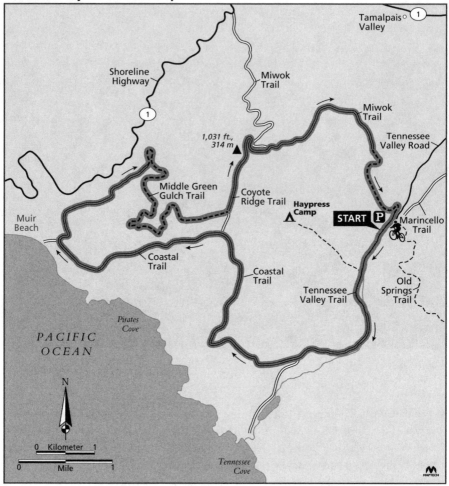

(it's okay to ride up), although there may not be a trail sign providing this warning. Do not ride the Green Gulch Trail during the wet season; it is too muddy. Riding under these conditions will ruin the trail.

Once back on the ridge fire road, there is more climbing to the highest point of the ride. Although the small peak is not on the fire road, take a short 30-foot detour up the rise for a full 360-degree view of Mount Tamalpais, the coast, San Francisco Bay, and the south tower of the Golden Gate Bridge. Nice—there are no abandoned Nike Missile sites on this loop. Return to the fire road for a quick drop to Miwok Trail, which weaves through a dense eucalyptus grove. As you may now perhaps appreciate, early dairy ranchers planted these nonnative trees as windscreens from the harsh coastal winds. The lower part of Miwok Trail is narrow, steep, and fun. Watch for ruts, water bars, and stairs at the switchbacks. The ride ends with a short jog back to the parking lot along Tennessee Valley Road.

While there are some steep climbs along this ride, they are manageable. Inexperienced riders may want to skip the drop down to Muir Beach; instead stay on Coyote Ridge Trail and be content to ride down Miwok Trail. This misses the more technical backside of the loop but still has some challenges of its own. This is also a good option in winter while the north-facing trails are taking forever to dry.

Miles and Directions

0.0 **START** from the parking lot at the end of Tennessee Valley Road. Head west through the gate on Tennessee Valley Trail. You will be heading down the main paved road toward the ocean. Trailhead GPS: N 37 51.38, W 122 32.09.

0.6 Continue straight where the road becomes dirt.

1.2 Turn right onto Coastal Trail and begin the climb to the ridge. Stay on Coastal Trail fire road past Pirates Cove hiking trail (formerly the hiking-only Coastal Trail). At the junction with Fox Trail, continue to the left, following signs to stay on Coastal Trail.

2.6 Turn left down Coastal Trail fire road toward Muir Beach. The trail is steep, rutted, and extremely muddy in winter. **Shortcut:** Turn right onto Coyote Ridge Trail and ride the ridge all the way to the highest point; continue ride as described below at Mile 6.7.

4.0 At the T junction turn right onto wide singletrack Middle Green Gulch Trail. **Option:** Turn left and take a quick side trip to Muir Beach. It is only about 300 yards away. Up ahead, the trail makes a 90-degree turn to the left and takes you to a back entrance of Green Gulch Farm Zen Center.

4.3 Pass through the gate into Green Gulch. Be sure to close it behind you. Quietly ride along a dirt road past the fields of the Zen Center.

4.6 Turn right at the bike trail sign to Middle Green Gulch Trail and Coyote Ridge. Ride along a row of cypress and pass through a gate exiting the Zen Center. Turn left onto the singletrack leading through a thicket of anise, thistle, and chaparral. It is a steady climb back to the ridge.

6.4 Turn left onto Coyote Ridge Trail.

6.7 Arrive at the highest point of the ride. Take a quick left up to a rocky lookout with the last and perhaps best view on this ride. Drop back down and continue left down the other side (southern) of Coyote Ridge.

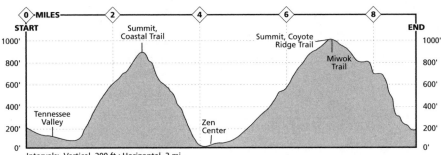

Intervals: Vertical, 200 ft.; Horizontal, 2 mi.

7.0 Continue straight as the road becomes Miwok Trail. Be careful where the trail drops down through a thick eucalyptus grove. There can be loose gravel in summer and debris and mud in winter. Bear right to stay on the main fire road.

7.7 Continue right on Miwok Trail where the road splits. No bikes are allowed on the trail to the left. The fire road becomes a wide singletrack and gets technical. At the bottom, turn right and follow the trail back along the road.

8.8 Arrive back at the parking lot.

Easy Option

Take an easy 3.6-mile round-trip out-and-back on Tennessee Valley Trail. Start from the same west gate as above, but continue straight at Mile 1.2 all the way to the beach at Tennessee Cove. This can be a good family ride. There is one hill near the beach that appears bigger on the ride back. This climb may be more than some kids want to deal with. Not to worry; your kids will be learning one of the first tenets of mountain biking—it's okay to walk.

Ride Information

Local Information

Golden Gate National Recreation Area: Headquarters and General Information, Fort Mason, Building 201, San Francisco, CA 94123; (415) 561-4700; www.nps.gov/goga.

Accommodations

The Golden Gate National Recreation Area operates four campgrounds in the Headlands. Haypress Camp is hike- or bike-in only off Tennessee Valley Road. For reservations call the Marin Headlands Visitor Center at (415) 331-1540.

Marin Headlands Hostel, Building 941, Fort Barry, Sausalito; (415) 331-2777 or (800) 909-4776, ext. 168; www.headlandshostel. homestead.com.

Green Gulch Farm Zen Center, 1601 Shoreline Highway, Sausalito; (415) 383-3134; www.sfzc.org.

Restaurants and Java Jolts

Dipsea Cafe, 200 Shoreline Highway, Mill Valley; (415) 381-0298.

Pelican Inn (includes an English pub); CA 1, Muir Beach; (415) 383-6000; www. pelicaninn.com.

Group Rides

Tam Valley Bike Club, Tamalpais Community Services District, 305 Bell Lane, Mill Valley, CA 94941; (415) 388-6393, ext. 19; www. tamvalleybikeclub.com. Group rides Sunday morning; full-moon night rides in the Golden Gate National Recreation Area.

3 Angel Island Double Loop

This is a great family ride with stunning views of San Francisco, Mount Tamalpais, and the Golden Gate Bridge. The Perimeter Road loop is paved, but the upper Fire Road is dirt and much less traveled. There are a few short climbs, but overall the grade is easy. The island is rich in history and landmarks. It is a perfect place for a picnic. Bring layers of clothing; temperatures can vary dramatically from one side of the island to another. If you're unprepared, it can be miserable in the fog and wind. Bring a bike lock if you want to hike one of the trails to the peak.

Start: Ayala Cove on Angel Island, arriving by ferry or private boat.
Distance: 9.8-mile double loop.
Approximate riding time: 1 to 1.5 hours.
Difficulty: Easy; that does not mean flat; some hills require moderate effort, nontechnical.
Trail surface: 51 percent paved road, 42 percent dirt road, and 7 percent paved/dirt bike path.
Terrain: Hilly, grass- and forest-covered island.
Seasons: Good year-round, but can be bitterly cold in a windy summer fog.
Other trail users: Hikers, Park Service vehicles, and an occasional sight-seeing tram on the Perimeter Road.
Canine compatibility: Dogs not permitted.

Land status: Angel Island State Park.
Nearest town: Tiburon.
Fees and permits: Contact ferry service for ticket fees. There is also a fee for taking bikes on the ferry. Unless you park outside Tiburon, be prepared to pay for parking.
Schedule: Open daily 8:00 A.M. to sunset. Ferry service to the island changes throughout the year. Contact the ferry companies for current schedules and fares. Be sure to allow enough time to catch the last ferry home.
Map: USGS map: San Francisco North, CA.
Trail contact: Angel Island Association, P.O. Box 866, Tiburon, CA 94920; (415) 435-3522; www.angelisland.org.

Finding the trailhead: From Mill Valley: From U.S. Highway 101 take the Tiburon Boulevard exit and drive east about 4 miles. Turn right onto Main Street and take the walkway on the left to the Angel Island Ferry dock at 21 Main Street. There is a parking lot down Main Street on the right, but it is very expensive for the day. The Tiburon Boulevard parking lot is cheaper; it is on the left just past Tiburon Town Hall as you come into town. Another option is the free parking lot at Blackie's Pasture. This is on the right heading toward Tiburon, 1.5 miles from the highway. From here you can ride the paved bike path 2.5 miles into town and the ferry dock.

    Ferry Service from Tiburon: Angel Island Ferry, 21 Main Street, Tiburon; (415) 435-2131; www.angelislandferry.com.

    Ferry Service from San Francisco Fisherman's Wharf and the Oakland/Alameda Ferry Terminal: Blue and Gold Fleet, Pier 41 Marine Terminal, San Francisco; (415) 773-1188; www.blueandgoldfleet.com.

The Ride

Angel Island is a 740-acre jewel with a rich and varied history. For thousands of years it was a hunting and fishing site for the Coast Miwok Indians. In 1775 Spanish

Ayala Cove on Angel Island—another lap before the next ferry?

explorer Juan Manuel de Ayala anchored in what is now Ayala Cove. Here he prepared the first charts of San Francisco Bay. Ayala named the island "Isla de los Angeles," Island of the Angels. In the early 1800s Russians used the island for sea otter hunting expeditions. By 1859, after a dispute over a Mexican land grant, the U.S. government declared ownership. The island has since served as a military installation during the Civil War, Spanish-American War, and World War I, as well as a quarantine station. From 1910 to 1940 it served as a U.S. Immigration Station processing immigrants, the majority of whom were Asian. The entire island became a state park in 1963, after the hard-won efforts of conservationist Caroline Livermore. That is the nutshell history.

The ride begins at the main ferry terminal in Ayala Cove. At the dock there is a good display map for bike routes. This map reappears at several places along the Perimeter Road. There are also restrooms, a gift shop, a cafe, and seasonal bike rentals. The ride quickly leaves the cove, passes the visitor center, and heads up a dirt bike path to the paved Perimeter Road—the first and outer loop. The road winds around the island through woodlands of eucalyptus, bay, and madrone. There are several side trips off the Perimeter Road to explore historical buildings and beaches. The route is well marked with plenty of signs explaining points of interest. Watch out for hikers, service vehicles, and the occasional tram.

Going clockwise, the first views are of Tiburon and the Richmond–San Rafael Bridge. At the North Garrison walk your bike down and see the Immigration Station. There are bike racks if you would rather leave your bike. The upper fire road loop begins shortly beyond this point and quickly becomes gravel. After a steady climb the road levels off and becomes dirt near a reservoir. As you pass through pine and manzanita woodlands, watch for deer, which at times have overpopulated the island. There are several intersecting hiking trails to the top of Mount Livermore (781 feet). None of the trails to the summit allows bikes, so lock your bike and enjoy the short but steep hike.

On the southern end of the fire road loop, the woodlands give way to grassy hillsides and panoramic views of San Francisco Bay. As the trail wraps around the island and heads north again, you pass the East Bay camping area. These sites have more protection from the wind than the other two camping areas on the island. You will soon complete the fire road loop and head back down to the Perimeter Road.

Continuing clockwise around the island, the road passes through Fort McDowell (East Garrison) and the crumbling old hospital built in 1911. Fort McDowell processed and discharged soldiers during World Wars I and II. A side road takes you down through the fort and to Quarry Point. Just beyond Fort McDowell, the road climbs steadily. Near the top of the climb is a Nike Missile site and premier view of San Francisco, Alcatraz Island, and, a little farther, the Golden Gate Bridge. In summer you can watch the fog roll in through the Gate and over the Marin Headlands.

The last chance for a side trip is Camp Reynolds (West Garrison). Originally built as an Army camp for the Civil War, this is the oldest military site on the island and location of an annual mock battle. The ride finishes up with a nice descent to the beginning of the Perimeter Loop. If you have time before the next ferry, stop at the visitor center and watch the twenty-minute video on the island's history.

Miles and Directions

0.0 **START** at the ferry dock in Ayala Cove on Angel Island. Ride along the main road, passing to the left of the historical visitor center and museum. Follow the BIKE ROUTE signs to the dirt bike path on the left, which switchbacks up to the paved Perimeter Road. Trailhead GPS: N 037 52.218, W 122 27 213 (at the dock on island).

0.5 Turn left onto the Perimeter Road. **Option:** You can go either way, but by going left you end the ride with great vistas of San Francisco and the Golden Gate Bridge and a nice spot for lunch or a snack.

1.7 Turn right onto the fire road to the upper loop. Ride between the buildings and service area. The road becomes broken pavement and gravel. Stay to the left, ignoring a steep road on the right after 200 yards.

2.0 Turn right at the fork. This is where you will complete the upper loop. The surface changes from gravel to dirt. Ride to the right past the water supply reservoir, then veer to the left following BIKE ROUTE signs. The road narrows a bit and winds around to the southern end of the island.

Angel Island Double Loop

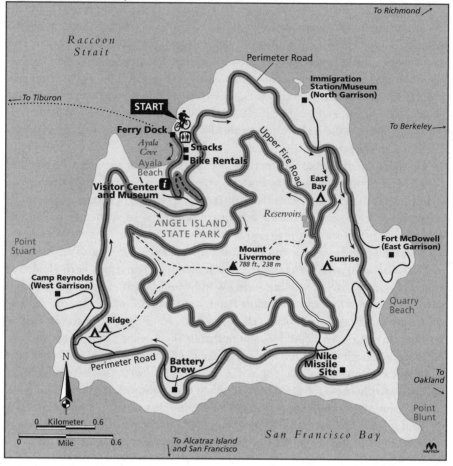

4.8 Stay to the left to continue the fire road loop. **Bailout:** Turn right for a shortcut down to the Perimeter Road (less than 0.1 mile). A posted map will help you get your bearings. Going right (clockwise) on the Perimeter Road cuts the ride in half and omits a steep grade.

5.3 This completes the upper loop. Turn right, following the sign to the Immigration Station.

5.6 Arrive back to the Perimeter Road and turn right. Ride past Fort McDowell (East Garrison) and the old hospital on the right.

6.0 Stay to the right on Perimeter Road and continue straight past the employee residence, ignoring the service road to the right.

6.2 On the left there are some steps leading down to Quarry Beach. Past these, the road begins to climb. Ignore the private road on the left to the Coast Guard Station. The road becomes gravel (this may become paved one day) until the crest of the hill. **Side trip:** Quarry Beach is a pleasant sandy spot for picnics and sunbathing in warm weather. There are no lifeguards, and swimming can be hazardous. The water quality is poor and the currents very strong.

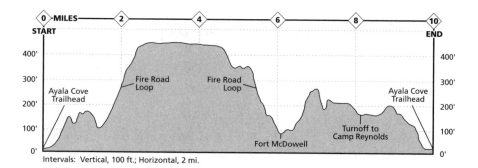

Intervals: Vertical, 100 ft.; Horizontal, 2 mi.

6.9 Turn left, staying on the Perimeter Road. You may recognize the road straight ahead that goes to the upper fire road.

7.3 Stay left on Perimeter Road, ignoring Battery Drew. There are several benches and tables along this stretch for a picnic with a view. **Side trip:** At Mile 8.1 turn left down to Perles Beach. The water here is very rough and the beach exposed to the wind and weather. However, the view is spectacular.

8.2 The Perimeter Road continues to the right at the fork to Camp Reynolds (West Garrison). This can be a side trip down to explore the military camp from the Civil War and World War II. There are restrooms up ahead.

9.2 This completes the Perimeter Loop. Take the path on the left back to Ayala Cove.

9.8 Arrive back at the ferry dock.

Ride Information

Local Information

Angel Island Association, P.O. Box 866, Tiburon, CA 94920; (415) 435-3522; www.angelisland.org.

Local Events and Attractions

Annual events on the island include a mock artillery battle, a jazz and dinner concert, and a Victorian House Tour. Check the Web site for schedule of events; for the daily weather cam from Ayala Cove, click on AngelCam.

Accommodations

Angel Island State Park; camping reservations (800) 444-7275; www.reserveamerica.com. Tip: If you can score reservations for July 4

and the sky is clear, this is a great viewpoint for fireworks.

Restaurants and Java Jolts

Paradise Hamburgers & Ice Cream, 1694 Tiburon Boulevard, Tiburon; (415) 435-8823. **Sam's Anchor Cafe,** 27 Main Street, Tiburon; (415) 435-4527; www.samscafe.com. **Sweden House Bakery & Cafe,** 35 Main Street, Tiburon; (415) 435-9767.

Local Bike Rentals

Angel Island Company, Ayala Cove; open during peak seasons; (415) 897-0715; www.angelisland.com.

4 Old Railroad Grade to East Peak Loop

This is the most popular route from the base of Mount Tamalpais (more commonly called Mount Tam) to the top at East Peak. Once an old railroad line, the grade is gradual and the trail a wide dirt road. There are many ways to modify this ride to make it longer, shorter, or more technical. Sweeping views of the East Bay, San Francisco, the Marin Headlands, and the Pacific Ocean follow you to the top. Want to ride a mountain? Ride this one.

Start: At the beginning of Old Railroad Grade fire road on West Blithedale Avenue, Mill Valley.
Distance: 12-mile loop.
Approximate riding time: 2 to 2.5 hours
Difficulty: Moderate to difficult; nontechnical ride up the mountain, somewhat strenuous if you are not used to a long ride. Eldridge Grade and Blithedale Ridge have some technical downhill, rocky and extremely steep in sections. A moderate option is an out-and-back to the top.
Trail surface: Wide dirt road.
Terrain: A mountain; steady climb from the redwood-forested base at 200 feet to the chaparral- and manzanita-covered lookout at 2,340 feet, with oak and madrone woodlands in between.
Seasons: Year-round.
Other trail users: Hikers, joggers, an occasional equestrian, and MMWD patrol and maintenance vehicles.
Canine compatibility: Leashed dogs permitted.

Land status: Marin County Open Space District, Marin Municipal Water District, and Mount Tamalpais State Park.
Nearest town: Mill Valley.
Fees and permits: No fees or permits required.
Schedule: Open daily 7:00 A.M. to sunset; may close during extreme fire-hazard conditions.
Maps: USGS map: San Rafael, CA.
Marin County Bicycle Coalition, *Marin Bicycle Map for Road, Mountain, and Transit Biking*, available at most bike shops.
Trail contacts: Marin County Open Space District, 3501 Civic Center Drive, Room 415, San Rafael, CA 94903; (415) 499-6387; www.marinopenspace.org.
Marin Municipal Water District, 220 Nellen Avenue, Corte Madera, CA 94925; Sky Oaks Ranger Station, off Bolinas Road at entrance to Lagunitas/Bon Tempe Lake; (415) 945-1195; www.marinwater.org.
Mount Tamalpais State Park, 801 Panoramic Highway, Mill Valley, CA 94941; (415) 388-2070; www.parks.ca.gov.

Finding the trailhead: From Mill Valley: Take the East Blithedale exit off U.S. Highway 101 and head west nearly 2 miles to Mill Valley. Go straight at the stop sign at junction with Throckmorton Avenue. The road narrows and becomes West Blithedale Avenue. After driving 1.1 miles park along the road. Old Railroad Grade starts at the gate on the right where the road crosses the stream. If parking is not available, *turn around at the gate;* park back at Blithedale Park or in downtown Mill Valley and ride to the trailhead. There are no restrooms or water.

Heads-up for the view as you wind down Mount Tamalpais.

The Ride

The Miwok Indians named Mount Tamalpais: *tam´-mal* (bay country) and *pi´-is* (mountain). From 1896 to 1930 San Franciscans took the ferry from Market Street to Sausalito and caught the connecting narrow-gauge train to Mill Valley. From there they took the Mount Tamalpais Scenic Railway train to the top of the mountain. With 281 curves this was known as the Crookedest Railroad in the World. The rails have long gone, but the route remains as Old Railroad Grade.

The ride up Railroad Grade is for just about anyone; stamina will determine how far a rider goes. The grade is gradual, never exceeding 7 percent. The ride begins in the cool redwood forests of Mill Valley. As you climb, there is a transition to oak, bay, and madrone (with their distinctive red bark) woodlands. The redwoods reappear in the ravines. Although the creeks are dry in the summer and fall, there are cascading waterfalls in the wet seasons. (Do not drink the water.) After a couple of miles, thick chaparral, manzanita, lupine, and toyon begin to open up the view for the remaining ride to the top.

Old Railroad Grade to East Peak Loop

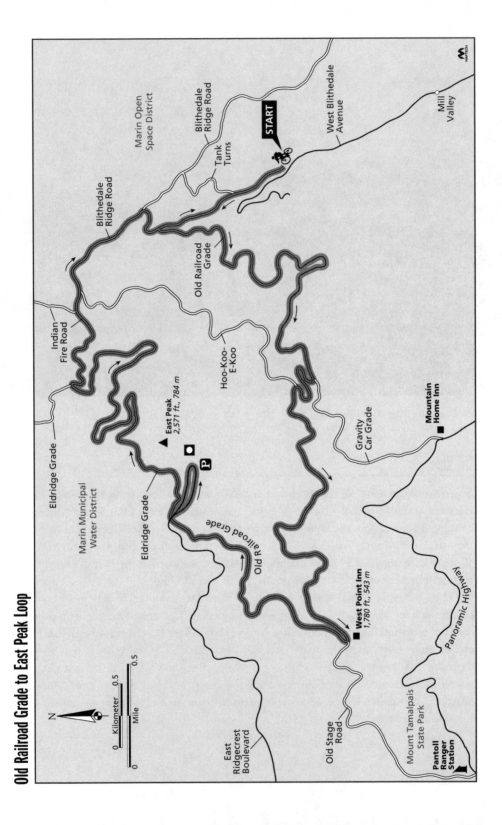

START

Marin Open
Space District

Blithedale
Ridge Road

Tank
Turns

West Blithedale Avenue

Mill
Valley

Blithedale
Ridge Road

Old Railroad
Grade

Indian
Fire Road

Hoo-Koo-
E-Koo

▲ East Peak
2,571 ft., 784 m

Eldridge Grade

P

Marin Municipal
Water District

Eldridge Grade

Old Railroad Grade

Gravity
Car Grade

Mountain
Home Inn

East
Ridgecrest Boulevard

Old Stage
Road

Old Railroad Grade

■ West Point Inn
1,780 ft., 543 m

Mount Tamalpais
State Park

Panoramic Highway

Pantoll Ranger
Station

N

Kilometer   0.5

0   Mile   0.5

0   0.5

About three-quarters of the way to the summit is the historic West Point Inn. This makes a nice stop along the way to snack and savor the panoramic view of the Pacific Ocean and San Francisco Bay. Be sure to bring your own water. There are restrooms and a pay phone here. Sometimes you can buy drinks and snacks inside the inn. Advanced reservations are required to stay overnight.

The uphill climb ends at a parking lot near the summit. During the railroad era a tavern stood here. Visitors could dine, dance, and stay the night. After burning down, the grand old tavern was rebuilt and stood until 1950. Some of the old foundation is still visible near today's restroom. There is also a drinking fountain, telephone, and vending machine for drinks. On weekends in spring and summer, a small snack bar and visitor center are open. You can lock your bike and hike 0.3 mile up the Plank Walk to the fire lookout at East Peak (2,571 feet). There is also the 0.7-mile Verna Dunshee hiking-only loop around the peak, with an amazing panorama of the Bay. On a clear day you can see Mount Diablo to the east.

You have two choices down the mountain: You can turn around and return down Old Railroad Grade the way you came or take a more technical route down Eldridge Grade. The Eldridge Grade route is rocky and very steep in sections. This way is not for beginners.

The riding is good year-round, but it can be bitterly cold in heavy fog or rain. Bring layers of clothing and a windbreaker. Although you may get hot and sweaty going up, you can become chilled riding down without another layer of clothing. The soil drains fairly well after a rain. While there can be plenty of mud, tires do not disappear. When it is hot it can be unrelenting, since most of the trail is not shaded.

Preserving bike access on Mount Tam has been a battle. At one time there were efforts to exile bikes from these fire roads. So please be courteous and ride in control. The speed limit is 15 mph (5 mph when passing). Bikes are not allowed on any singletrack on watershed land. Patrols are out there and it is a hefty fine if you are where you do not belong.

Once you get the lay of the land, there is a network of fire roads to explore on Mount Tam. This is Marin at its best; connecting one trail after another, you can ride all day.

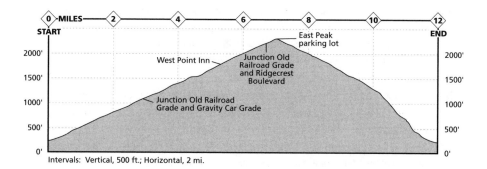

Intervals: Vertical, 500 ft.; Horizontal, 2 mi.

WEST POINT INN—MOUNT TAMALPAIS RETREAT The Mill Valley and Mount Tamalpais Scenic Railway Company built the historic West Point Inn in 1904. Up until 1930 this was a stopover and restaurant for passengers on their way to the top of the mountain and Muir Woods. It was also the place to catch the stagecoach for Bolinas. Now volunteers from the West Point Inn Association run the inn, and most visitors hike or bike in. There are picnic tables and a grand veranda from which you can rest and enjoy the open view. Coffee, tea, hot chocolate, lemonade, and energy bars are available for a donation when the inn is open. Once a month in spring and summer, volunteers host a Sunday pancake breakfast. The first breakfasts each year are on Mother's Day and Father's Day. For general information and a schedule, call (415) 388-9955. The inn is closed on Monday.

If you want to stay overnight on the mountain, this is the place. There are guest rooms in the main lodge, a living area with a fireplace, a fully equipped communal kitchen, and five rustic cabins. Accommodations are basic; guests need to bring their own food, sheets, and towels. Advance reservations are required. The twenty-four-hour reservation line is (415) 646-0702.

The closest place to park is the Pantoll Ranger Station at the junction of Panoramic Highway and Pantoll Road. There is a nominal parking fee. From the parking lot it is an easy 2.0-mile ride to the inn up the dirt Old Stage Road. Kids love this ride on Pancake Sundays.

Miles and Directions

0.0 **START** at the gate on Old Railroad Grade near West Blithedale Avenue. Trailhead GPS: N 37 55.160, W122 33.141.

0.2 Take the left fork. (For your information: The right fork is Tank Turns and climbs up to Blithedale Ridge. The road is steep, loose, and a quick way to the other side of Mount Tamalpais.)

0.7 Veer left at the fork. The road on the right is the return route from Blithedale Ridge.

1.9 The trail enters a paved residential section. Veer right up Fern Canyon Road.

2.5 Back on the dirt.

2.9 Veer right again at the next junction to continue on Old Railroad Grade. The concrete sidewalk is where passengers once boarded the gravity cars for a ride to Muir Woods. **Option:** Going straight on Gravity Car Grade fire road takes you to Mountain Home Inn and Panoramic Highway, a place to start a shorter ride.

3.3 Veer left at the fork with Hoo-Koo-E-Koo.

5.3 Reach the West Point Inn. The fire road continues up to the right behind the inn.

6.7 Turn right onto paved East Ridgecrest Boulevard. Veer right onto the paved lane for hikers and bicyclists.

7.0 Arrive at East Peak parking lot. Stop and enjoy the full view. For the return follow the directional arrows out of the parking lot and back down East Ridgecrest Boulevard.

7.3 Turn right at the gate and head down Eldridge Grade fire road for a technical descent. Look forward to lots of loose rocks and some steep downhill sections. (**Option:** If you want a smooth cruise down the mountain, stay on East Ridgecrest Boulevard another 0.1 mile, and return the way you came up on Old Railroad Grade.) Whichever way you go, the speed limit is 15 mph (5 mph when passing). Keep an eye out for hikers and other bikers, particularly on Old Railroad Grade, where there is more traffic and it is easy to go fast.

9.8 From Eldridge Grade take a sharp right onto Indian Fire Road.

10.4 Turn right onto Blithedale Ridge Road toward Mill Valley and Corte Madera.

10.5 Continue straight on Blithedale Ridge Road. **Option:** A right onto Hoo-Koo-E-Koo will take you back to Old Railroad Grade. This is a bit longer and has some more climbing, but it misses the nasty downhill coming up on Blithedale Ridge.

11.3 Take a right turn onto the unmarked trail before the steep climb.

11.4 Turn left, back onto Old Railroad Grade.

11.9 Stay to the right.

12.0 Arrive back at the gate and West Blithedale Avenue where you started.

Ride Information

Local Events and Attractions

Mountain Play—May and June: When the play is showing, shuttle buses take you to this outdoor amphitheater near the top of Mount Tamalpais. Another option is to bike to West Pont Inn, lock your bike, and hike 1.5 miles on the Theater Trail. Advance tickets required; (415) 383-1100; www.mountainplay.com.

Mill Valley Fall Arts Festival—September; (415) 381-8090.

Mill Valley Film Festival—October; (415) 383-5256.

Mill Valley Wine and Gourmet Food Tasting; (415) 454-2510.

Accommodations

Mount Tamalpais State Park Camping and Lodging:

Pantoll Campground, 801 Panoramic Highway, Mill Valley; hike or bike campsites on a first-come, first-served basis; (415) 388-2070.

Steep Ravine Cabins, located on California Highway 1; for information call (415) 388-2070. Online reservations only; access Reserve America via www.parks.ca.gov/default.asp?page_id=471.

West Point Inn, 1000 Panoramic Highway, Mill Valley; general information (415) 388-9955; reservations (415) 646-0702.

Restaurants and Java Jolts

Bonavita Coffee and Tea, 2 Miller Avenue, Mill Valley; (415) 383-8355.

The Depot Bookstore & Cafe, 87 Throckmorton Avenue, Mill Valley; (415) 388-2665.

Pearl's Phat Burgers, 8 East Blithedale Avenue, Mill Valley; (415) 381-6010; info@pearlsdiner.com.

5 The Lakes Loop

Year-round, this is a beautiful ride up the lower north side of Mount Tamalpais. The fire road passes through shaded oak woodlands and redwood stands on the protected watershed of the Marin Municipal Water District. You'll also skirt three reservoirs along the way. Near the highest point of the loop, there are great views of San Francisco Bay and East Peak of Mount Tamalpais. There are lots of spin-off options for longer and more technical rides.

Start: From the parking lot at Java Hut, 760 Center Boulevard, Fairfax.
Distance: 11.9-mile loop.
Approximate riding time: 1 to 2 hours.
Difficulty: Moderate; nontechnical but steady climb.
Trail surface: 75 percent dirt fire road and 25 percent paved road.
Terrain: Laid-back streets of town, shaded canyons and hills on the lower flanks of Mount Tamalpais, pockets of nice redwoods, scenic lakes.
Seasons: Year-round. Cool, shady ride in summer.
Other trail users: Hikers, joggers, equestrians, and MMWD patrol and maintenance vehicles.
Canine compatibility: Leashed dogs permitted.

Land status: Marin Municipal Water District and Marin County Open Space District.
Nearest town: Fairfax.
Fees and permits: No fees or permits required.
Schedule: Open sunrise to sunset; may be closed during extreme fire-hazard conditions.
Maps: USGS map: San Rafael, CA.
Marin County Bicycle Coalition, *Marin Bicycle Map for Road, Mountain, and Transit Biking*, available at most bike shops.
Trail contacts: Marin Municipal Water District, 220 Nellen Avenue, Corte Madera, CA 94925; Sky Oaks Ranger Station, off Bolinas Road at entrance to Lagunitas/Bon Tempe Lake; (415) 945-1195; www.marinwater.org.

Finding the trailhead: From San Rafael: Take the Central San Rafael exit off U.S. Highway 101 and head west on Fourth Street all the way through town. Fourth Street becomes Redhill Avenue at the San Anselmo city limits. Go straight onto Center Boulevard at the intersection with Sir Francis Drake (the Hub) in San Anselmo, and follow about 1.5 miles to Fairfax. Turn right into the parking lot past Albertson's grocery store. Java Hut Cafe stand is in the middle of the lot (about 8 miles from the freeway). This route takes you by a couple of bike shops. There is no water or restroom here, but there will be along the way. In fact, there is no shortage of restrooms on this ride, so have a cup of coffee.

Ross Trailhead Option

From Larkspur: Exit U.S. Highway 101 on Sir Francis Drake Boulevard. Head west to Ross (about 2.6 miles) and turn left onto Lagunitas Road. Follow to the end at Natalie Coffin Greene Park. There is a parking fee at this entrance. Bike up to and around the right side of Phoenix Lake (counterclockwise.) You will connect with the featured loop at Eldridge Grade. When the parking lot is full (most weekends), park back at the post office in Ross Commons. Trailhead GPS: N 37 57.28, W 122 34.21.

View of Bon Tempe Lake, should you take the Rocky Ridge option.

The Ride

This is a pleasant ride through some of Marin's most beautiful watershed. The three reservoirs along the way supply drinking water to local residents. Sorry, no swimming allowed. However, the California Department of Fish and Game periodically stocks the reservoirs with rainbow trout.

Although the directions begin with a ride through downtown Fairfax, you can start at Deer Park with its parking lot, picnic area, water, and restroom. The road to the park is rather narrow, so it is nice to keep traffic out of the neighborhood and just ride your bike there. The real ride begins behind the school and up the canyon on the Deer Park Fire Road. This is a wide shaded trail through woodlands of oak and bay laurel. The first summit is at the Five Corners crossroads. From there it is a steady descent to Phoenix Creek through patches of redwoods and ferns. Watch for uphill traffic; this trail is popular.

From Phoenix Junction it is a steady climb up Eldridge Grade. John C. Eldridge built this trail in the 1880s as a toll road for wagons heading to the summit. A quick view of Phoenix Lake peeks through the trees on the left. In the wet season cascading streams disappear under the road through culverts. Eventually the

The Lakes Loop

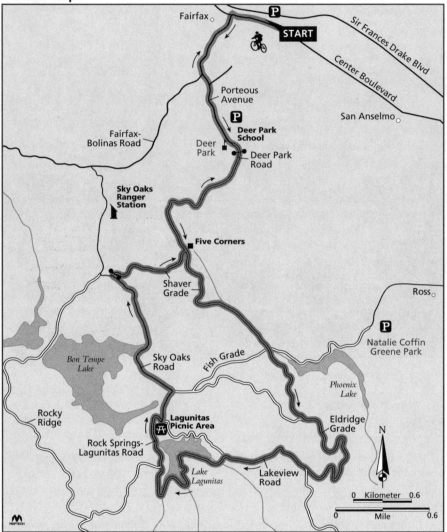

redwoods give way to madrone, oaks, bay trees, and manzanita. Breaks in the trees offer grand views of San Francisco Bay and the top of Mount Tamalpais. When Eldridge Grade makes a sharp left turn heading up to the summit, this loop drops down Lakeview Fire Road for a quick descent to Lake Lagunitas.

The ride around Lake Lagunitas is rather serene and mostly level. At one time the creek crossings were a wet challenge in winter. Now confined to crossing on bridges, riders can respect the life cycles of amphibians, fish, and other aquatic life. In winter watch for the long, orange-bellied newts slo-o-o-owly crossing the trails. Also keep an eye out for banana slugs. They are what they sound like: long yellow slugs that can grow up to 10 inches in length. You probably will not see one that long, but they are the second-largest slug in the world. Unless you want to be slimed, leave them alone. Their only defense is their thick, milky mucous, an amazing glue. Although it is a mild anesthetic, it has not been clinically tested for the treatment of road rash.

Once around Lake Lagunitas, there is a short road ride around tips of Bon Tempe Lake, the last lake on the loop. From the pavement Shaver Grade is the connecting fire road back down to Five Corners, completing the loop. The return is down Deer Park Canyon and through town.

In the heat of summer, this is a pleasantly shaded ride. The water district works hard to maintain erosion control on this road. Sometimes they layer sections of the trail with wickedly sharp blue gravel, which can be loose and unforgiving before it packs down.

The Lakes Loop is a springboard for all sorts of great rides on Mount Tamalpais and Pine Mountain. From this loop you can ride over the top of Mount Tamalpais and on to Tennessee Valley.

Miles and Directions

0.0 **START** by turning right onto Center Boulevard as you leave the parking lot. This road soon becomes Broadway, taking you into downtown Fairfax. Turn left onto Bolinas Road and then left again onto Porteous Avenue. The road forks almost immediately; bear right, following Porteous to the end. Parking lot GPS: N 37 59.114, W 22 35.028.

1.1 Arrive at Deer Park parking lot, restroom, and school. Follow the dirt path around the left side of the school, across the field, and through a gate at the beginning of Deer Park Fire Road.

2.1 Stay left on Deer Park at Boy Scout junction.

2.5 Arrive at Five Corners junction. Go straight ahead and down Shaver Grade, following the sign to Phoenix Lake.

2.6 Veer left toward Phoenix Lake at the fork with Concrete Pipe Road.

3.6 Arrive at a four-way junction. Head straight across the gravel road and uphill on Eldridge Grade. (FYI: If you start from Natalie Coffin Greene Park in Ross, you join the loop at this intersection.)

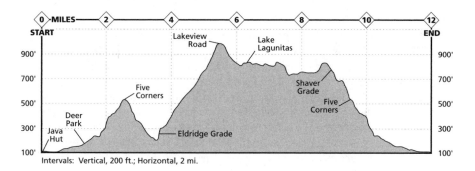

Intervals: Vertical, 200 ft.; Horizontal, 2 mi.

Lake Lagunitas awaits cyclists on the Tour de Lacs.

4.3 Turn left at the unmarked road and water spigot. A right turn takes you past a water treatment plant and yet another way to Bon Tempe Lake.

4.8 Downshift before veering right uphill at the fork. Take another right at the top of the short climb, continuing on Eldridge Grade.

5.6 Turn right onto Lakeview Road. At 1,000 feet, this is the highest point on this ride. **Option:** Go left and continue up Eldridge Grade to the top of Mount Tamalpais. At the crest of the mountain, turn right on paved East Ridgecrest Boulevard. Turn right onto Rock Springs-Lagunitas Fire Road. This will drop you down to Lake Lagunitas, where you follow the trail past the spillway and to the Lagunitas Picnic Area. Turn right, picking up the directions below at Mile 7.5. This strenuous loop adds another one to two hours and 1,500 feet of elevation to the ride.

6.2 Turn left, following the sign to Lake Lagunitas Road. Cross the bridge, heading clockwise around Lake Lagunitas.

7.2 Stay right at the fork to continue around the lake. As you approach the dam, stay left on the fire road. **Option:** For an extra grind and a technical, rocky ride, turn left at the junction and head up Rock Spring-Lagunitas Road toward Potrero Meadows. The road forks in 0.9 mile; turn right onto Rocky Ridge for a 2-mile ride to Bon Tempe Lake. Ride across the dam and along the spillway. Veer right through the parking lot; stay right on the gravel road to paved Sky Oaks Road. Turn right onto the pavement for a short distance, then turn left at the gate onto Shaver Grade fire road, picking up the loop at Mile 8.7 below.

This option adds only a couple of miles to the original loop, but it adds 600 feet of strenuous climbing and a beautiful view of Bon Tempe Lake.

7.5 Turn right onto the pavement at the Lagunitas Picnic Area, ride through a parking area, and turn left onto paved Sky Oaks Road, which is unsigned here. Stay on the main road around Bon Tempe Lake. Watch for cars on the blind corners.

8.7 Turn right through the gate onto Shaver Grade fire road.

9.4 Arrive at the Five Corners junction, completing the loop. Turn left onto Deer Park Road and follow to the gate at the end. Ride back around the school and through the parking lot.

10.8 Return to Porteus Avenue, turning right onto Bolinas Road and right on Broadway.

11.9 Arrive back at the parking lot.

Ride Information

Local Events and Attractions

Annual Biketoberfest: Fair Anselmo Plaza, 737 Center Boulevard; sponsored by the Fairfax Chamber of Commerce, P.O. Box 111, Fairfax, CA, 94978; (415) 453-5928; www.marin.org/partners (search Fairfax Chamber of Commerce).

Thanksgiving Day Group Ride: Join the stream of riders for the annual pilgrimage up the Deer Park-Pine Mountain-Repack Loop.

Fishing information: Marin Municipal Water District; (415) 945-1194. State fishing licenses are required for all fishing.

Accommodations

Samuel P. Taylor State Park Campground, P.O. Box 251, Lagunitas; (415) 488-9897; www.parks.ca.gov; reservations (800) 444-7275; www.reserveamerica.com.

Restaurants and Java Jolts

Fairfax Coffee Roasters, 4 Bolinas Road, Fairfax; (415) 451-1825.

Ross Valley Brewing Company, 765 Center Boulevard, Fairfax; (415) 485-1005; www.rossvalleybrewing.com.

Cafe Amsterdam, 23 Broadway, Fairfax; (415) 256-8020.

THANKSGIVING APPETITE SEMINAR
Bikers start gathering early on Thanksgiving Day for the traditional Deer Park–Full Pine Mountain–Repack ride. There is no set starting time, just a steady stream of bikers all morning long, including some large groups. Come solo; you will not ride alone. The normally quiet parking lot fills up early, and most rides begin between 8:00 and 9:00 A.M. Be sociable and bring snack treats to share at the top of Repack. Some kindhearted riders bring a trailer with hot chocolate to share.

If it is raining or has been for a few days prior, there is no ride. The trail gets too muddy for the crowd. Some locals are not thrilled with the ride's growing popularity and patrol the lower reaches, sometimes on horseback. So watch the speed, and skip this ride in bad weather.

6 Deer Park–Repack Loop

A steep and rutted fire road takes you down Repack, legendary trail of the first mountain bike race. Unfortunately, there is no pickup truck to take you to the top these days. You have to earn this ride. On Pine Mountain Ridge there are some equally steep and much rockier climbs to tackle before stepping back in time. Ride with a buddy; the river crossings at the end can make for a good laugh in the wet season. This is still one of Joe Breeze's favorite rides.

Start: From the parking lot at Java Hut, 760 Center Boulevard, Fairfax.
Distance: 12.2-mile loop.
Approximate riding time: 1.5 to 2 hours.
Difficulty: Moderate to difficult; some strenuous and rocky climbs, steep and rutted descents, uneven and loose dirt.
Trail surface: 63 percent fire road and 37 percent paved road.
Terrain: Steady climb up shaded canyon, paved road, and exposed, rugged ridge. Descend steep canyon, crossing a creek at the bottom.
Seasons: Best in spring, summer, and fall; avoid after periods of heavy rain. Lower Repack may be impassable in winter at the creek crossings when the water is deep.
Other trail users: Hikers, equestrians, and cars.
Canine compatibility: Leashed dogs permitted.

Land status: Marin Municipal Water District and Marin County Open Space District.
Nearest town: Fairfax.
Fees and permits: No fees or permits required.
Schedule: Open sunrise to sunset year-round; may close in extreme fire-hazard conditions.
Maps: USGS maps: San Rafael, CA; Bolinas, CA.
Marin County Bicycle Coalition, *Marin Bicycle Map for Road, Mountain, and Transit Biking*, available at most bike shops.
Trail contacts: Marin County Open Space District, 3501 Civic Center Drive, Room 415, San Rafael, CA 94903; (415) 499-6387; www.marinopenspace.org.
Marin Municipal Water District, 220 Nellen Avenue, Corte Madera, CA 94925; Sky Oaks Ranger Station, off Bolinas Road at entrance to Lagunitas/Bon Tempe Lake; (415) 945-1195; www.marinwater.org.

Finding the trailhead: From San Rafael: Take the Central San Rafael exit off U.S. Highway 101 and head west on Fourth Street all the way through town. Fourth Street becomes Redhill Avenue at the San Anselmo city limits. Go straight onto Center Boulevard at the intersection with Sir Francis Drake (the Hub) in San Anselmo. Follow about 1.5 miles to Fairfax. Turn right into the parking lot past Albertson's grocery store. Java Hut Cafe stand is in the middle of the lot (about 8 miles from the freeway.) This route takes you by a couple of bike shops. Although there is no water or restroom here, you will find both after the first mile at Deer Park.

The Ride

Eventually, all devoted mountain bikers make the journey to this piece of mountain bike history. On October 21, 1976, the first downhill bike race was staged down

A cyclist picks a line up Pine Mountain Road.

Repack. Some folks had been playing around on the old balloon-tire (2+ inches wide) bikes for years throughout the hills of Marin, the Peninsula, and who knows where else. However, it took an event to catalyze the burgeoning sport of mountain biking. With the race, folks had a place to meet, share ideas, and most of all have a good time. The word spread. Riders went home to tweak their bikes, practice their skills, and test their theories. With the right people in the right place at the right time, the technology soon followed.

These early clunkers had coaster brakes. The rear hubs would get so hot from the constant braking that the grease melted out or even vaporized into a contrail of smoke. After a run or two, many hubs would need to be—you know this—repacked.

The Repack Trail had been a popular downhill ride for two to three years when the inevitable claims of who was faster had to be tested. Fred Wolf and Charlie Kelly organized the first race, lining up the racers in a time-trial format, one at a time. Fellow race supporter Alan Bonds won that first race. There were twenty-two Repack races between 1976 and 1979, then two more in 1983 and 1984. After that, local land managers made it clear—no more races. There are many untold stories along this trail, and perhaps it is best that way. What remains are silent landmarks with names like Breeze Tree, Vendettis Face, and Danger X.

Deer Park-Repack Loop

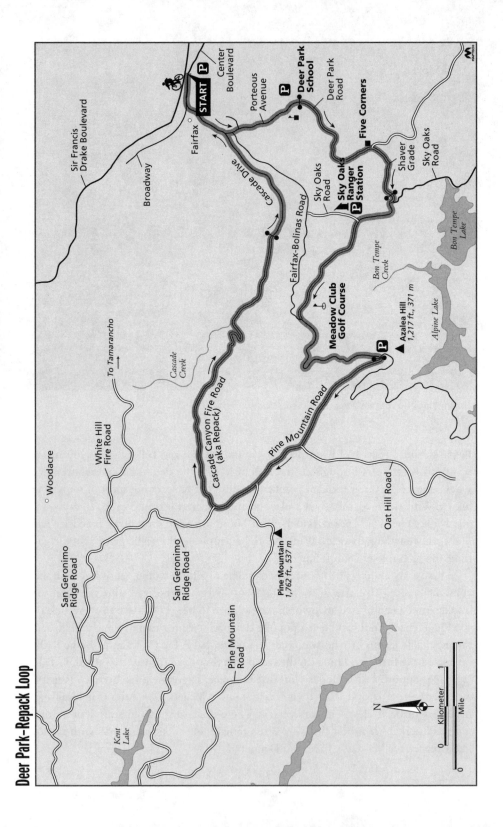

Sir Francis Drake Boulevard

Broadway

Fairfax

Cascade Drive

START

Center Boulevard

Porteous Avenue

Deer Park School

Deer Park Road

Five Corners

Fairfax-Bolinas Road

Sky Oaks Road

Sky Oaks Ranger Station

Shaver Grade

Sky Oaks Road

Bon Tempe Lake

Cascade Creek

To Tamarancho

Meadow Club Golf Course

Bon Tempe Creek

Azalea Hill
1,217 ft., 371 m

Alpine Lake

White Hill Fire Road

Woodacre

Cascade Canyon Fire Road
(aka Repack)

Pine Mountain Road

San Geronimo Ridge Road

San Geronimo Ridge Road

Pine Mountain Road

Pine Mountain
1,762 ft., 537 m

Oat Hill Road

Kent Lake

N

Kilometer

Mile

This loop begins with a ride through the streets of Fairfax, then up the wide and popular Deer Park Fire Road. This is an easy meander through the oak-lined canyon, then a steady climb to paved Sky Oaks Road. You then drop down near the ranger station, head through the meadow, and wind around the Meadow Club golf course and country club. While you have missed most of the narrow, winding Fairfax-Bolinas Road, there is still a short paved climb up this road to the Pine Mountain trailhead.

Once on Pine Mountain Road, you are on open-ridge land and have a sense of solitude. When you are not picking your line through the rocks, look up and enjoy the panoramic view of San Francisco Bay, Mount Tamalpais, and the surrounding open space. The fire road is loaded with loose rocks and buried boulders. Full suspension was made for trails like this. The crumbly blue-green rock is serpentine. Little vegetation grows on the ridge except for the hardy chaparral and manzanita. Higher up on the ridge, trees try to grow. But all that does are pockets of pygmy forest, mostly Sargent cypress.

TIDBIT: Among Repack records Gary Fisher posted the fastest time at 4:22 (nearly 30 mph). At ten wins Joe Breeze won the most races and posted the second fastest time, 4:24. Wende Cragg was the fastest woman, at 5:27. And Alan Bonds's dog won the distinction of fastest canine, although no time was given. Source: Joe Breeze; www.mtnbikehalloffame.com.

Do not expect a monument at the top of Repack; you will not even find a trail sign. On most maps this is just Cascade Canyon Road. This infamous section is steep, dropping 1,300 feet in 2.1 miles. These days the speed limit is 15 mph. The trail has loose rocks with deep bike-eating ruts. Some of the corners are blind and off-camber. As with any ride, it is okay to walk anything you do not feel comfortable riding. At the bottom the trail crosses Cascade Creek several times before ending on a quiet residential street. The loop finishes with a ride through the neighborhood and back through town.

Miles and Directions

0.0 **START** by turning right onto Center Boulevard as you leave the parking lot. This road soon becomes Broadway. After 2 blocks turn left onto Bolinas Road and follow through downtown Fairfax. Turn left onto Porteous Avenue. The road forks almost immediately; bear right, following Porteous to the end. **Option:** Stay on Bolinas Road and ride the narrow and winding paved road to the Pine Mountain trailhead. This cuts off about 2 miles, but watch for cars. Turn right onto the dirt fire road at Pine Mountain trailhead, picking up the directions from Mile 5.8. Parking lot GPS: N 37 59.114, W 22 35.028.

1.1 Arrive at Deer Park parking lot, restroom, and school. Take the dirt path around the left side of the school, across a field, and through a gate to the Deer Park Fire Road.

2.1 Stay left on Deer Park Road at the Boy Scout junction.

2.5 Reach Five Corners junction, and turn right up Shaver Grade.

3.1 Turn right onto paved Sky Oaks Road, watching for cars.

3.5 Turn left onto the fire road through Sky Oaks Meadow. There is no sign here, but it is at the beginning of the parking lot before the ranger station and restrooms. At the end of the meadow (at Mile 3.7), turn right and follow the fire road around the side of the golf course. *Stay off the golf course.* At the end of the fire road, ride through the parking lot of the private Meadow Club and out the entrance to the main road. Do not fill your water bottles at the country club.

4.5 Turn left onto paved Fairfax-Bolinas Road and climb toward the parking lot for Azalea Hill.

5.8 Turn right at the gate to the dirt Pine Mountain Fire Road. The Pine Mountain sign is not visible until you ride through the gate and start up the trail. The trail gets steep and extremely rocky in sections. Keep a heads-up to pick a line through the loose rocks.

6.8 Stay right on Pine Mountain Road at the fork with Oat Hill Road.

7.3 Stay right on San Geronimo Ridge Road at the fork with Pine Mountain Road. **Option:** See Pine Mountain Loop below.

7.7 Turn right onto Repack Fire Road. Do not look for a sign; there isn't one. Officially this is Cascade Canyon Fire Road. After descending 2.1 miles "Finish Line Rock" is at the bottom when you first reach the creek. Cross the bridge to the right and head down Cascade Canyon through Fairfax's Elliot Nature Preserve. There are four stream crossings, which are normally dry. However, in winter they can be challenging and cold. If the creeks are too high, take an alternative route to the left before the first crossing. If it is still posted no bikes, walk your bike. Who is going to complain if you are saving the local amphibian population? The alternative route meets up at the gate exiting the preserve.

10.1 The trail ends through a gate leading onto a paved residential street. Although not signed initially, this is Cascade Drive. Stay on this until Bolinas Road.

11.6 Turn left onto Bolinas Road, returning through downtown Fairfax. Turn right onto Broadway.

12.2 Arrive back at the parking lot.

Pine Mountain Loop Option

The full Pine Mountain Loop option is a popular route, but not unanimously. Some people love this ride; others hate it. Lots of climbing on fire roads is not for everyone. It is a beautiful add-on loop, especially for those who like longer rides and want to earn their ride down Repack. On this side trip the landscape changes from open

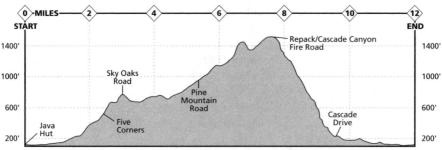

Intervals: Vertical, 400 ft.; Horizontal, 2 mi.

ridge land to lush forests of laurel, oak, mixed conifers, and eventually redwoods at the bottom of the canyon.

Turn left at Mile 7.3 above to do the Pine Mountain Loop. This option will add nearly 10 miles and two hours to the Repack Loop. The fire road drops down near Kent Lake and climbs about 1,000 feet back up again. Near the lake (about 4 miles from the turnoff for this option) and after a long steep descent, the road forks. Make a sharp right turn. Continue on the main fire road, cross some creeks, and climb back out of the hole. At the first crest there is a four-way junction and no signs. Turn right up along the ridge. You are back on San Geronimo Ridge, which is once again steep and rocky. Ride the ridge back up to the turnoff for Repack. On the way you will pass two unsigned forks. The first is to the town of Woodacre, and the second fork

JOE BREEZE'S MEGA RIDE TO MECCA

For the adventurous rider this rigorous over-50-mile option comes with 5,000 feet of total climbing. This will give a great overview of the birthplace of mountain biking. With all the sights along the way, fit riders should allow at least five hours. Verify the mileages for yourself; these numbers rely on Joe's accuracy, which is a safe bet.

Start from San Francisco and ride across the Golden Gate Bridge. Follow along San Francisco Bay, riding Bridgeway Boulevard through Sausalito. At Sausalito Cyclery (Mile 5.5), take the Mill Valley-Sausalito Bike Path to Miller Avenue (Mile 7.0). Ride past Tamalpais High School clock tower and along Miller Avenue to downtown Mill Valley (Mile 8.7). Turn right onto Throckmorton Avenue, then left onto West Blithedale. Take Old Railroad Grade Fire Road (Mile 9.8) to the top of Mount Tamalpais (Mile 16.0). Head west on paved Ridgecrest Boulevard, past Rock Spring on the right and the Pan Toll Road on the left (Mile 19.0). Take in the view of the Pacific Ocean from 2,000 feet. Turn right (heading east) onto dirt Laurel Dell Road (Mile 20.5). Ride around Potrero Meadows. Turn left onto Rock Spring-Lagunitas Fire Road (Mile 22.5). After a steep descent take a sharp left onto Rocky Ridge Road (Mile 24.0). This drops down to Bon Tempe Dam. After crossing the dam turn left onto Bullfrog Road (Mile 26.0) and continue through the gate onto the dirt road. At Sky Oaks Meadow turn left and continue around the golf course and country club. (You are now on the shorter loop described above.) Turn left onto Fairfax-Bolinas Road. Ride to the top of Repack (Mile 30.5) and down, returning to Java Hut in Fairfax.

For the return to San Francisco, continue east on Center Boulevard to San Anselmo. Ride through towns strung along the northern and eastern base of Mount Tamalpais, making your way back to Sausalito Cyclery (Mile 35.0) and to the south end of the Golden Gate Bridge (Mile 50.5). Do not set out on this ride without a good map of the entire area. The best map to bring is the Marin County Bicycle Coalition's *Marin Bicycle Map for Road, Mountain, and Transit Biking*.

is to White Hill and Tamarancho Boy Scout Camp. Stay to the right at both forks. The fork to Repack will appear about 18 miles from the start at Java Hut.

If you want to do the Pine Mountain Loop without Repack, you can start at the trailhead on Bolinas-Fairfax Road. There is parking across the street near Azalea Hill. Starting from there, the Pine Mountain Loop by itself is about 13 miles and takes two to two-and-a-half hours.

Ride Information

Local Events and Attractions

Annual Biketoberfest: Fair Anselmo Plaza, 737 Center Boulevard; sponsored by the Fairfax Chamber of Commerce, P.O. Box 111, Fairfax, CA 94978; (415) 453-5928; www.marin.org/partners (search Fairfax Chamber of Commerce).

Accommodations

Samuel P. Taylor State Park Campground, P.O. Box 251, Lagunitas; (415) 488-9897; www.parks.ca.gov; reservations (800) 444-7275; www.reserveamerica.com.

Restaurants and Java Jolts

Fair Fix Cafe, 33 Broadway, Fairfax; (415) 459-6404.

M&G Drive-In, 2017 Sir Francis Drake Boulevard, Fairfax; (415) 454-0655.

Ross Valley Brewing Company, 765 Center Boulevard, Fairfax; (415) 485-1005; www.rossvalleybrewing.com.

7 China Camp Loop

This is a quick trek into the woods. Enjoy well-maintained singletrack through the hills along San Pablo Bay. Ride toward the ridgeline and follow the contours to China Camp Village. This picturesque spot offers a piece of local history and a beach for picnics, sunbathing, and swimming. Return along the edge of the hills near the shoreline. Beginners can ride the lower trail as an easy out-and-back. Upper trails along the ridge present routes that are more challenging and views of Mount Tamalpais and San Francisco Bay. This is a great introduction to mountain biking.

Start: Entrance to Back Ranch Meadows campground, China Camp State Park, San Rafael.
Distance: 11.4-mile loop.
Approximate riding time: 1.5 to 2 hours.
Difficulty: Moderate; mostly wide and non-technical singletrack; some sharp turns and loose rocks require steady skills; options for beginners and riders that are more advanced.
Trail surface: 93 percent singletrack and 7 percent dirt road.
Terrain: Wooded hillside along the bay; smooth, hard-packed singletrack, some rocks.
Seasons: Year-round; shady ride in summer.
Other trail users: Hikers, joggers, and equestrians.

Canine compatibility: Dogs not permitted.
Land status: China Camp State Park.
Nearest town: San Rafael.
Fees and permits: No fee or permit required to park along North San Pedro Road; day-use fee when parking in the state park campground or picnic areas.
Schedule: Open daily 8:00 A.M. to sunset.
Maps: USGS maps: Petaluma Point, CA; San Quentin, CA; Novato, CA; San Rafael, CA. China Camp State Park brochure and map, available at the entrance kiosk when open.
Trail contact: China Camp State Park, Route 1, Box 244, San Rafael, CA 94901; (415) 456-0766; www.parks.ca.gov.

Finding the trailhead: From San Rafael: From U.S. Highway 101 take the North San Pedro exit east toward the Civic Center. Stay on North San Pedro Road to the park entrance at about 3 miles. There is parking along the road at the entrance to Back Ranch Meadows. There are restrooms at the campground and water at the trailhead.

The Ride

China Camp State Park preserves one of the most undisturbed watersheds along the shores of San Francisco Bay. The ride runs along the north slope of San Pablo Ridge on trails whose names convey their location on the hill. Riding along Bay View Trail gives you glimpses of San Pablo Bay, Carquinez Strait, and the hills of Sonoma and Napa Counties. The return ride along Shoreline Trail brings you to the interface between the hills and the marshland.

The park's name comes from the fishing village that sprang up in the 1800s along the beach at the east tip of the peninsula. More than twenty similar villages once dotted the shores of San Francisco Bay. Chinese immigrants drawn to California's

China Camp Loop

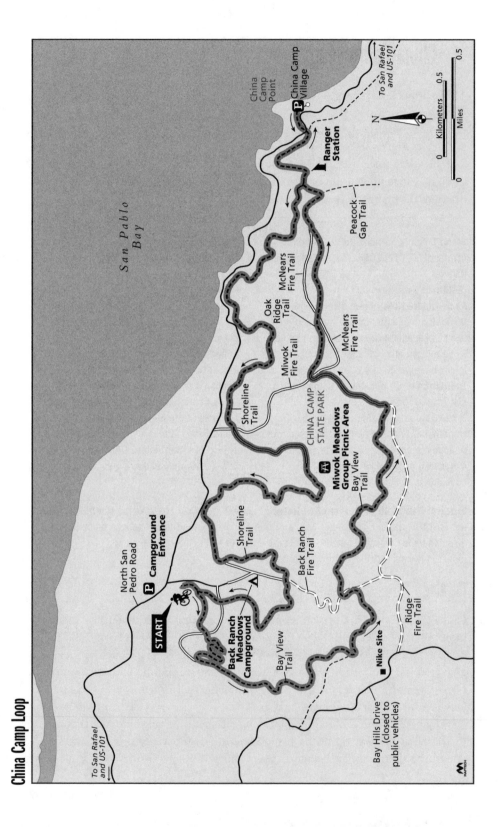

gold rush soon found themselves doing what they did back home—fishing. Harvesting grass shrimp became a profitable niche. An exhibit in one of the remaining buildings at the village explains the history of those shrimp-fishing days. China Camp Village is the halfway point in this loop.

The ride begins at the entrance to Back Ranch Meadows on wide singletrack. You can usually pass another biker head-on if you are careful and lean to the side. Remember, uphill riders have the right-of-way. This is a popular place on weekends and holidays; keep a heads up. If you can get there during the week, it is quiet. Bay View Trail heads west and winds through the woods of oak, bay, madrone, and manzanita. There are three switchbacks to clean on the way. The trail climbs to nearly 600 feet and then heads east along the contour of the hillside. Views of San Pablo Bay and marshland peek through the trees along the way. In winter the red toyon berries make a nice show. Small pockets of redwoods appear along the trail.

The trail widens for a short distance at the junction with the Ridge Trail but soon narrows again to singletrack with a few rubber water bars on the Oak Ridge Trail. The trail crisscrosses the ridge a couple of times before switchbacking down to the Shoreline Trail. At the junction with Shoreline Trail, turn east for an out-and-back ride toward the historic China Camp Village and beach. Enjoy a picnic on the bluff above the bay, or go down to the beach. The snack bar is open in summer. Ironically, the shrimp served are probably not local.

The return ride is along Shoreline Trail all the way back to the start. Along the way you pass through the group picnic area at Miwok Meadows. This is a favorite stop for the WOMBATS' (Women's Mountain Bike & Tea Society) teacup tangos. The Shoreline Trail weaves around behind Back Ranch Meadow campground before rejoining Bay View Trail near the park entrance.

This is one of those places that has something for everyone. Beginners can do an out-and-back along the Shoreline Trail. Intermediate riders can do the full loop. Stronger riders can ride up to the ridge for some white-knuckle downhill or explore some of the trails in the adjoining open space.

China Camp has some of the best weather in the Bay Area. The ridge often protects the park from the summer fog that fans up from the Golden Gate Bridge. The shaded trail keeps it somewhat cool when the sun is blazing elsewhere. The trails are

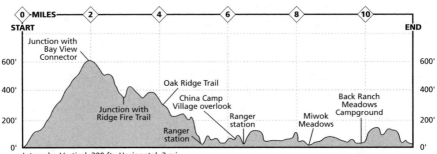

Intervals: Vertical, 200 ft.; Horizontal, 2 mi.

hard packed and can be dusty in summer. In winter some sections can be rather muddy.

Miles and Directions

0.0   **START** at the trailhead to the right of the entrance kiosk to Back Ranch Meadows campground. The wide singletrack begins right at the drinking fountain. Trailhead GPS: N 38 00 31.2, W 122 29 42.2.

0.2   Veer right at the fork, continuing on Bay View Trail. You will complete the loop at this fork, returning from Shoreline Trail on the left.

0.5   Turn right at the junction with Powerline Fire Trail. After 100 feet make a sharp left turn to continue on Bay View Trail.

1.1   Veer left sharply around the fence. The two singletrack trails on the right connect with Powerline Fire Trail.

1.9   Turn left to cross the bridge and continue on Bay View Trail. **Option:** For a more technical and strenuous ride, turn sharply to the right onto the connector trail to Bay Hills Drive. Turn left onto paved Bay Hills Drive and grind to the ridge. At the top are an empty Nike Missile radar site and a panoramic view of San Francisco Bay, the Richmond San Rafael Bridge, and Mount Tamalpais. Continue on paved road past the Nike site and turn left onto dirt Ridge Fire Trail. The trail is very steep and rutted in sections, with loose dirt and eucalyptus debris littering the trail. Ride the ridge until you reach the junction with Bay View Trail at Mile 3.8 below. Continue straight ahead on the wide dirt road.

2.5   Veer left at the junction with Back Ranch Fire Road, continuing on Bay View Trail. About 100 yards down the trail, veer right at the fork to continue on the singletrack. **Shortcut:** Turn left onto Back Ranch Fire Trail, which goes down to the campground.

3.8   Veer left at the junction with Ridge Fire Trail, a wide dirt road. Catch a quick view of the Richmond San Rafael Bridge before heading on.

4.1   Go left at the T intersection with the rutted Miwok Fire Trail. After 30 yards go right onto the singletrack Oak Ridge Trail toward Peacock Gap.

4.3   Stay on Oak Ridge Trail as it crosses McNears Fire Trail and continues south toward Peacock Gap.

4.7   Cross McNears Fire Trail again, continuing on Oak Ridge Trail as it switchbacks away from the ridge.

5.3   Continue straight at the merge of Oak Ridge and Peacock Gap Trails.

5.4   Make a sharp right turn onto Shoreline Trail toward China Camp Village. **Shortcut:** Skip the out-and-back to China Camp Village. Turn left along Shoreline Trail.

5.6   Cross the paved road leading to the ranger station and continue straight on Shoreline Trail.

6.0   Veer left at the fork to China Camp Village.

6.1   Cross the road to pick up a short section of Village Trail.

6.2   Arrive at a parking overlook of China Camp Village. When you are ready to return, backtrack along Village and Shoreline Trails. (If you go down to the beach, stop the odometer readings.)

7.0   Go right on Shoreline Trail. This completes the out-and-back; you are now continuing on the loop.

8.7 Veer left at the unsigned fork. Turn left in 50 yards at the junction with the fire road, still following signs to Shoreline Trail. This takes you to the Miwok Meadows group picnic area.

9.0 Follow the wooden fence to pick up the singletrack on the left near the end of the parking area.

9.5 Veer left at the fork.

9.8 Veer left on Shoreline Trail as it approaches North San Pedro Road.

10.0 Veer left at the first fork toward the campground. The right is a shortcut to the entrance; better not go down there in winter. In 35 yards veer left at a second fork on Shoreline Trail toward Back Ranch Fire Trail. This takes you for a ride around the outskirts of the campground. **Shortcut:** Take a right to return directly to the park entrance.

10.6 Cross the steep and rutted Back Ranch Fire Trail, continuing straight on Shoreline Trail.

10.8 Turn right and cross the bridge. Shoreline Trail continues through the campground. At the end of a gravel parking area, cross Powerline Fire Trail and continue straight on the singletrack.

11.3 Veer right at the merge with Bay View Trail, following the sign to the entrance.

11.4 Arrive back at the park entrance.

Easy Option

A great family ride is an out-and-back along Shoreline Trail. You can go as far as the kids want. The reward of the beach at the end makes a good carrot. Tip: Try to turn back before they have spent all their energy. Worst case if you have two adults: One can ride back to get the car.

WOMBATS
The Women's Mountain Bike & Tea Society (WOMBATS) is the creation of Mountain Bike Hall of Famer and three-time National Champion Jacquie Phelan. From its roots at the base of Mount Tam in 1985, it has grown into an international network of "women who love mud too much." Living the motto "You are never totally out of the woods," members can find compatible riding partners, explore new trails, and encourage the fresh crop of newbies.

The goal of WOMBATS is to bring women of all sizes, ages, and abilities together to have fun on a mountain bike. At teas, clinics, group rides, and training camps, fellow 'bats learn tips for riding, bike repair, maintenance, trail etiquette, and, most of all, safety. Despite the media's picture of a risky extreme sport, dirt riding WOMBAT-style is safe and easy—making accessible the wild pink yonder to novices and instilling a big-sister ethos in the experienced woman.

"Hop on your bike, 'laff at the traff,' and lose the diet," urges Phelan. If there is not a local chapter near you, join WOMBATS individually and consider starting one. Annual dues include merchandise, newsletters, notice of Jacquie's legendary Instant Finesse clinics, and a phone list that is invaluable for traveling women of the dirt.

Women's Mountain Bike & Tea Society headquarters: P.O. Box 757, Fairfax, CA 94978; twenty-four-hour hotline (415) 459–0980; www.wombats.org.

Ride Information

Local Information

San Rafael Chamber of Commerce, 817 Mission Avenue, San Rafael, CA 94901; (415) 454-4163; www.sanrafael.org.

Accommodations

China Camp State Park, Route 1, San Rafael; Back Ranch Meadows walk-in campground; reservations (800) 444-7275; www.reserveamerica.com. Unreserved sites are available on a first-come, first-served basis.

Restaurants and Java Jolts

Taqueria San Jose, 615 Fourth Street, San Rafael; (415) 455-0999.

Bogie's, 48 North San Pedro Road, San Rafael; (415) 492-1530.

In Addition

Recycle Your Bikes—Help a Kid

Trips for Kids is another mountain biking venture born in Marin. This nonprofit organization combines mountain biking with outdoor education for children. While riding up the slopes of Mount Tam in 1986, founder and director Marilyn Price began thinking how great it would be to expose inner-city youth to the outdoors and the physical challenge of riding the dirt. Looking out over San Francisco, she thought about kids surrounded by cement, violence, gangs, and drugs; kids who never get a chance to look back on their city from the hills across the Bay. The seed planted, Trips for Kids incorporated in 1988. It has been growing ever since and is now a nationwide program.

Through the program, volunteer trip leaders take groups of about ten children on trails in the Marin Headlands, China Camp, and other prime spots throughout the Bay Area. Paired with buddies, kids get one-on-one interaction with attentive adults. Children respond to the sights of wildlife and surroundings they may never have seen before—from red-tailed hawks, butterflies, and skunks to rattlesnakes.

This junior expert rider finds fun on a seesaw.

These kids experience both a positive outlet for their youthful energy and physical challenges they would never have otherwise. They feel the mixed pain and euphoria of cresting that first hill then coasting downhill.

Trips for Kids runs a Bicycle Thrift Shop in San Rafael called the Re-Cyclery. This is a place to donate all those outgrown and no-longer-used bikes, parts, and accessories cluttering garages and closets. The Re-Cyclery accepts, refurbishes, and sells just about all bike-related items. Revenue from these sales pays for about 40 percent of the programs cost.

At the Re-Cyclery Workshop, kids learn how to repair, build, and maintain bikes. An Earn-a-Bike program allows youths to volunteer, rebuild bikes, and ride away with a bike of their own.

Annual fund-raising events include the fall Bike Swap and February's Brews, Bikes, and Bucks party, which draws such mountain bike pioneers as Gary Fisher, Joe Breeze, Jacquie Phelan, Scot Nicol, and Otis Guy. The stellar Honorary Board of Directors includes: Peter Coyote, Mickey Hart, Phil Lesh, Huey Lewis, Bonnie Raitt, Carlos Santana, Pete Townshend, Bob Weir, Thomas Weisel, and Robin Williams.

Re-Cyclery Thrift Shop, 610 Fourth Street, San Rafael, CA 94901; (415) 458–2986; www.tripsforkids.org.

8 Olema Valley–Bolinas Ridge Loop

This classic Marin ride has just about everything: oak woodlands, redwood forests, and rolling grass-covered hills. Ride singletrack trails through the wooded Olema Valley, climb a steep and winding road up the western side of Mount Tamalpais, and hammer the roller-coaster ridge home. A changing panoramic view of Bolinas Lagoon, Pine Mountain, the coastal hills of the Point Reyes peninsula, and Tomales Bay follow you most of the way. Although the full loop is strenuous for the distance and climb, you can tailor this ride to your own specifications.

Start: From Olema, at the intersection of Sir Francis Drake Boulevard and California Highway 1, also called the Shoreline Highway.
Distance: 27-mile loop.
Approximate riding time: 3 to 4 hours.
Difficulty: Difficult; strenuous for the distance and long climbs, moderately technical sections with ruts and exposed roots.
Trail surface: 43 percent fire road, 37 percent paved roadway, and 20 percent singletrack.
Terrain: Lush and rugged valley along the San Andreas Fault, then a ride to a ridge (nearly 1,700 feet) on the western side of Mount Tamalpais, passing through redwood forests and cattle pastures.
Seasons: Best in spring, summer, and fall. Olema Valley Trail is unridable in the wet season—horses tear up the trail, meadows in Olema Valley have standing water, and the streams are deep and cold. Although ridable, the lower stretches of Bolinas Ridge can also be muddy and pretty torn up from cattle in the wet season.
Other trail users: Hikers, equestrians, cattle, and vehicles.

Canine compatibility: Dogs not permitted on Olema Valley Trail. Leashed dogs permitted on Bolinas Ridge Trail.
Land status: Point Reyes National Seashore and the Golden Gate National Recreation Area.
Nearest town: Olema.
Fees and permits: No fees or permits required.
Schedule: Open year-round, sunrise to sunset.
Maps: USGS maps: Inverness, CA; San Geronimo, CA; Double Point, CA; Bolinas, CA. Marin County Bicycle Coalition, *Marin Bicycle Map for Road, Mountain, and Transit Biking*, available at most bike shops.
Trail contacts: Point Reyes National Seashore, Bear Valley Visitor Center, Point Reyes, CA 94956; (415) 464-5100; www.nps.gov/pore/.
Marin Municipal Water District, 220 Nellen Avenue, Corte Madera, CA 94925; Sky Oaks Ranger Station, off Bolinas Road at entrance to Lagunitas/Bon Tempe Lake; (415) 945-1195; www.marinwater.org.

Finding the trailhead: From Larkspur: From U.S. Highway 101 exit at Sir Francis Drake Boulevard and head west. Follow Sir Francis Drake Boulevard all the way to its end (20 miles), winding through Greenbrae, San Anselmo, Fairfax, Forest Knolls, and Samuel P. Taylor State Park to a junction with CA 1. There is parking under the eucalyptus trees along eastbound Sir Francis Drake Boulevard. There is no restroom or water.

Velvet hills dominate the eastern view from Bolinas Ridge.

The Ride

The San Andreas Fault runs along CA 1 near the beginning of this ride, forming the Olema Valley. Point Reyes National Seashore is on the west side of the highway and is slowly moving north as part of the Pacific plate. At the same time, the Golden Gate National Recreational Area on the east side of the highway is part of the West American plate, which is moving west. This is where the infamous 1906 San Francisco earthquake originated.

The loop begins with a road ride along the highway. The road is winding and narrow, with little shoulder. Be careful, and ride single file. There have been several bad bicycle accidents along this stretch.

The mountain riding begins at the Five Brooks Trailhead as you head south along the Olema Valley Trail. This is horse territory, so be sure to yield to equestrian traffic. In winter the trail is thrashed. Even in the dry summer and fall, the deep trenches make for some rough going. The climbs along the Olema Valley Trail are some of the steepest of the loop, but they are short. This is a beautiful, cool ride through bay laurel and Douglas fir woodlands with an understory of ferns. The trail eventually narrows to singletrack, with some wider sections of overgrown fire road.

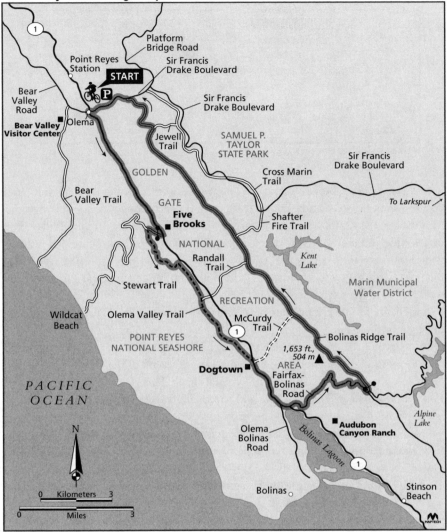

Along the meadows there are lots of blackberry bushes laced with poison oak. Do not look too closely, or you will land in them.

After leaving the Olema Valley Trail, there is a short ride back down CA 1 through sleepy Dogtown (aka Woodville). Lumber mills once flourished here. The turnoff you take from CA 1 to the Fairfax-Bolinas Road is usually unsigned. (Bolinas residents want their quiet coastal town to themselves. Every time Caltrans [California Department of Transportation] puts up a sign, it disappears.)

It is nearly 4 miles of steady climbing to the ridge. When it is not foggy, the ride is still in the shade, passing first through eucalyptus groves. Views of Bolinas Lagoon peek through as the vegetation turns to oak woodlands, then cool, dense redwoods

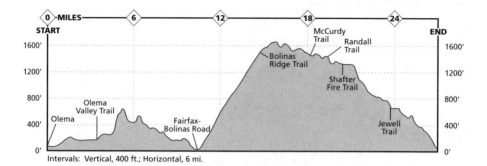

Intervals: Vertical, 400 ft.; Horizontal, 6 mi.

near the top. Again, beware of cars. While it may seem like a quiet road, the blind corners catch drivers—and cyclists—off guard. Resist the urge to ride side by side.

Once at the summit, it is a straight 11-mile ride along the Bolinas Ridge. The trail is wide and undulating, with lots of exposed roots, dips, and rocks. After a storm debris from the trees covers the trail. As the view opens up of Bolinas Lagoon and the ocean, you may notice a low, wire-mesh fence running along the left side of the trail. This is to keep feral pigs from the Audubon Canyon Ranch below. Originally imported for hunting, feral pigs have wreaked havoc on wild plants and animals throughout these hills.

Just beyond the 16-mile point, you reach the highest spot of the ride at nearly 1,700 feet. You'll hardly notice it, since this is not the end of the climbing. Here the forest has given way to chaparral and coastal shrub. The view opens to the east of Pine Mountain, San Francisco Bay, and Mount Tamalpais. To the west you can still see portions of the coast before you drop back down into the second-growth red-wood forest. Shortly past Randall Trail, the forest fades again and the trail opens up to beautiful pastureland. Point Reyes peninsula is on the left. Straight ahead, you follow the view of Tomales Bay all the way to Sir Francis Drake Boulevard.

Temperatures can vary greatly along this loop; be sure to bring layers of clothing. The fog that hugs the coast in summer can mean a drippy, cold ride through the redwoods and chilling winds on the open ridge. However, within days it can be hot in the unshaded sections of the ridge. There is no water along this loop, so bring plenty with you.

This is really two rides linked together: Olema Valley and Bolinas Ridge. Each can be ridden as an out-and-back, but the loop is more interesting than backtracking. There are several options for shorter and easier rides. Whichever way you go, bring a camera.

Miles and Directions

0.0   **START** from the junction of Sir Francis Drake Boulevard and CA 1 in Olema. Head south on the highway. Trailhead GPS: N 38 02.26, W122 47.15.

3.5 Turn right onto the dirt road to the Five Brooks Trailhead. Ride past the stables on left and through the parking lot. This is the only outhouse on the ride.

3.7 Pass through the gate onto the Five Brooks Trailhead.

4.0 Turn left at the fork, following the sign to Olema Valley Trail. The trail soon forks again; again follow the signs to Olema Valley Trail. Ignore the unmarked uphill trail on the right at Mile 5.2.

5.3 Turn left to stay on Olema Valley Trail at the junction with Bolema Trail.

6.5 Turn right to stay on Olema Valley Trail. **Shortcut:** If you are getting anxious to head for Bolinas Ridge, take a left onto Randall Spur Trail. At 6.9 miles turn right onto CA 1, heading south through Dogtown to the Fairfax-Bolinas Road. Pick up the directions below at Mile 10.4.

7.0 Stay on Olema Valley Trail. There are a couple of stream crossings up ahead.

8.8 Veer left on Olema Valley Trail at junction with Teixeira Trail (no bikes allowed).

9.3 Trail ends across from the McCurdy Trail trailhead. Turn right onto CA 1 and head south.

10.4 Turn left onto the Fairfax-Bolinas Road; there is a cattleguard near the entrance. Although unsigned, it is the first road on the left after Dogtown and just past two roads (Olema-Bolinas Road) on the right leading to Bolinas. The Fairfax-Bolinas Road leads up the hill to the ridge.

14.7 Turn left through the gate onto the Bolinas Ridge Trail, entering the Golden Gate National Recreation Area. This is part of the Bay Area Ridge Trail. To the right is a section of the Coastal Trail—*no bikes allowed*.

18.1 Continue straight along the ridge where McCurdy Trail joins on the left. **Option:** This is a great downhill ride, but it's not for beginners. The steep, overgrown fire road drops 1,270 feet in 1.7 miles. The dirt mounded water bars and trenches are bike size. McCurdy Trail drops you back down to CA 1, across the street from the trail back up the Olema Valley Trail. Alternatively, you can turn right onto the highway to the Randall trailhead, where you can grind back up to the ridge.

19.7 Continue straight along the ridge where Randall Trail comes in on the left. **Option:** Turn left down Randall for a steep fire road descent—920 feet in 1.7 miles. This drops you back onto CA 1 across from a trail leading back up Olema Valley.

20.6 Continue on the ridge, ignoring Shafter Fire Trail on the right. The redwoods quickly give way to grassy pastureland. Pass through several gates the rest of way back to Sir Francis Drake. Leave the gates the way you find them. If a gate is closed, unlatch it and pass through; just be sure to close it behind you.

24.4 Veer left to stay on the ridge where Jewell Trail forks to the right.

25.8 Arrive at the lower trailhead for Bolinas Ridge Trail. Next time, you can start here and ride in the other direction. Turn left onto paved Sir Francis Drake Boulevard, a narrow, winding road with no shoulder.

26.9 Finish the loop back in Olema.

Easiest Option

Ride Bolinas Ridge one-way. Find a friend to shuttle you to the upper Bolinas Ridge trailhead at the top of the Fairfax-Bolinas Road. Ride the ridge to Sir Francis Drake Boulevard, where your limo is waiting for you.

Savor the wide ocean view and Bolinas Lagoon from 1,500 feet.

Shorter Loop

Start at the Five Brooks Trailhead. Ride the loop, dropping down from Bolinas Ridge onto McCurdy or Randall Trail. Cross CA 1 and ride back on the Olema Valley Trail. This option cuts out some road riding.

Ride Information

Local Information

Point Reyes National Seashore Web site: community services and lodging in the Point Reyes area; www.nps.gov/pore/visit_services.htm.
Bear Valley Visitor Center, Bear Valley Road, Olema, CA 94950; (415) 464-5100; www.nps.gov/pore/.

Accommodations

Samuel P. Taylor State Park Campground, P.O. Box 251, Lagunitas; (415) 488-9897; www.parks.ca.gov; reservations (800) 444-7275; www.reserveamerica.com.

Hostelling International, HI-Point Reyes, Point Reyes Station; (415) 663-8811; www.norcal hostels.org/reyes.

Restaurants and Java Jolts

Bovine Bakery, 11315 State Route 1, Point Reyes Station; (415) 663-9420.
Cafe Reyes, 11101 State Route 1, Point Reyes Station; (415) 663-9493.
Yellow Door Cafe, 7285 Sir Francis Drake Boulevard, Lagunitas; (415) 488-0311; www.yellowdoorcafe.com.

9 Wildcat Camp Out-and-Back

This is an out-and-back ride to the secluded coastline along the Point Reyes peninsula. The ride is a steady climb over the Inverness Ridge through pleasant mixed coastal woodlands and Douglas fir forests. The climb back from the beach is a grind. This is a cool ride in the hot summer; in fact, it can be quite foggy. Bring a trailer and spend a night at the campground near the beach. Do not expect much traffic out here.

Start: From the Five Brooks Trailhead off California Highway 1, south of Olema.
Distance: 13.2 miles out and back.
Approximate riding time: 2 hours.
Difficulty: Moderate to difficult; nontechnical, but some strenuous climbing for the uninitiated.
Trail surface: Dirt fire road.
Terrain: Steep forested hill and ridge on the way to a pristine beach.
Seasons: Year-round.
Other trail users: Hikers, backpackers, and equestrians.
Canine compatibility: Dogs not permitted.
Land status: Point Reyes National Seashore.
Nearest town: Olema.

Fees and permits: No parking or day-use fee; permit required for camping only.
Schedule: Open 24 hours daily, year-round.
Maps: USGS maps: Inverness, CA; Double Point, CA.
Point Reyes National Seashore Trail Map, available at the Bear Valley Visitor Center and online at www.nps.gov/pore/activ_bike.htm.
Marin County Bicycle Coalition, *Marin Bicycle Map for Road, Mountain, and Transit Biking,* available at most bike shops.
Trail contact: Point Reyes National Seashore, Bear Valley Visitor Center, Bear Valley Road, Olema, CA; (415) 464–5100; www.nps.gov/pore/.

Finding the trailhead: From Larkspur: From U.S. Highway 101 take Sir Francis Drake Boulevard west 20 miles to CA 1 in Olema. Turn left and head south 3.5 miles to the sign for Five Brooks Stable. Turn right onto dirt entry road. Drive past the stables to the trailhead parking lot. There are outhouses at the trailhead and the beach, but no water.

The Ride

President John F. Kennedy established the Point Reyes National Seashore on September 13, 1962. He also said, "Nothing compares to the simple pleasures of a bike." Kennedy sure put it together for this ride.

The 100 square miles of Point Reyes are rich in history, geology, and diversity of plants and animals. All of this is contained in an area of spectacular scenery, particularly along its 80 miles of unspoiled coastline. Only an hour from San Francisco, this is a popular weekend and vacation retreat for more than two million visitors each year. However, you will not see many other people on this trail, one of the lesser traveled trails in the preserve.

The ride begins at the Five Brooks Trailhead and follows the wide Stewart Trail all the way to secluded Wildcat Beach and back. This is a popular trail for equestrians, so be alert. Do not worry; the horse traffic thins out farther up the trail. In the 1950s part of this dirt road was paved for logging. There are still remnants of the pavement just past the summit.

Near the trailhead mixed woodlands of oak and laurel provide plenty of shade. As the trail steadily climbs up and over Inverness Ridge, Douglas fir dominates the forest. The crest of the hill is near Firtop peak, at 1,324 feet. As usual, that is not the last climb; but soon the quick descent begins down to Wildcat Campground. The view opens up past the summit as trees give way to exposed coastal shrub. The campground sits in an open meadow on a bluff near the beach. There is an outhouse here but no potable water.

Walk down and enjoy the beach. This is prime California coastline, and chances are you will have it all to yourself. No bikes are allowed on the beach, so bring a lock if you are walking far. If you ride with hard soles, bring a spare pair of shoes to hike to Alamere Falls, a mile south of Wildcat Camp. Winter and spring are the best times to see the 50-foot cascade over the cliffs. Take the narrow Coastal Trail toward Palmarin; there is a side trail down to the beach before the falls. If you stay on the trail all the way to the falls, you will end up on top of the falls and will not be able to see the wide cascade. The trailhead is between the campground and the beach. Do not try to walk there along the beach; you can get caught on the rocks during high tide.

If you time your ride right, you may even see some whales. The California gray whale migrates south from Alaska to Baja California in mid-January and returns north in mid-March. In late April and early May, mothers and calves come in close to shore. Harbor seals are in the area year-round.

The climb out is steeper than the ride in. There is lots of wildlife in the area. Keep an eye out for bobcat, deer, coyote, raccoon, skunk, and perhaps even a black bear. In 2003 a black bear was seen at Limantour Beach and near the Point Reyes Youth Hostel. This was the first bear seen in the area in more than a hundred years. As you enjoy the final descent near the trailhead, remember to watch for equestrians.

Do not be fooled by hot summer temperatures when you set out on this ride. Although it may be hot inland, it can still be foggy on the coast. Since there is no water at the trailhead or on the ride, bring plenty with you. Bring a camera if you are hiking to the falls.

◀ *For a classic Marinscape, view Bolinas Ridge from Five Brooks.*

Wildcat Camp Out-and-Back

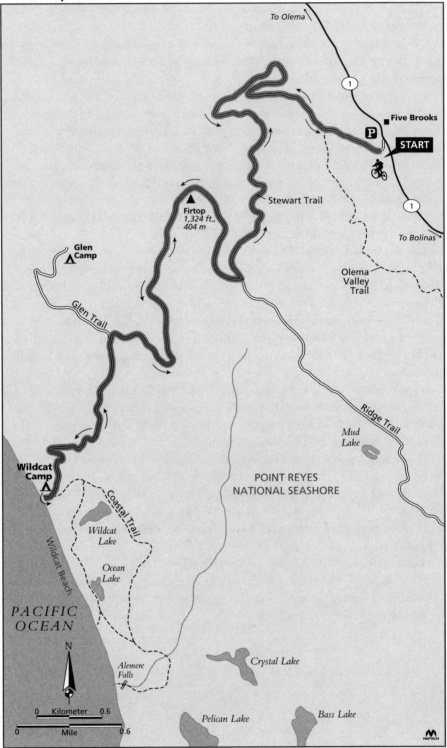

To Olema

Five Brooks

P

START

1

1

To Bolinas

Stewart Trail

Firtop
1,324 ft.,
404 m

Glen
Camp

Glen Trail

Olema
Valley
Trail

Ridge Trail

Mud
Lake

POINT REYES
NATIONAL SEASHORE

Wildcat
Camp

Coastal Trail

Wildcat
Lake

Ocean
Lake

Wildcat Beach

PACIFIC
OCEAN

N

Crystal Lake

Alemere
Falls

Pelican Lake

Bass Lake

0   Kilometer   0.6

0   Mile   0.6

MAPTECH

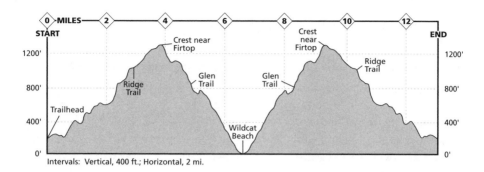

Intervals: Vertical, 400 ft.; Horizontal, 2 mi.

Miles and Directions

0.0 **START** at the Five Brooks Trailhead, riding west on the dirt fire road. Trailhead GPS: N 37 59.51, W 122 45.28.

0.2 Turn right onto the Stewart Trail fire road. This will take you all the way to Wildcat Camp and back. Ignore side trails along the way.

1.2 Veer left, ignoring the singletrack trail coming in from the side.

3.0 Veer right at the junction with the Ridge Trail.

3.8 Arrive at the crest of the hill near Firtop peak.

5.3 Veer left at the junction with Glen Trail. **Option:** Turn right to Glen Camp, another spot to spend the night. This campground is in the trees and more protected from the wind and fog than Wildcat Camp.

6.5 Arrive at Wildcat Camp. Continue straight ahead to the beach.

6.6 The trail ends at the beach. Park your bike and take a walk. When you are ready for a climb, backtrack up Stewart Trail.

7.9 Veer right at the fork to Glen Camp.

10.3 Veer left at the junction with the Ridge Trail.

13.0 Turn left at the junction with Olema Valley Trail

13.2 Arrive back at the trailhead and parking lot.

Ride Information

Local Information

Point Reyes National Seashore Web site: community services and lodging in the Point Reyes area; www.nps.gov/pore/visit_services.htm.
Bear Valley Visitor Center, Bear Valley Road, Olema, CA 94950; (415) 464-5100; www.nps.gov/pore/.

Accommodations

Camping in Point Reyes is by permit only. Permits obtained from the Bear Valley Visitor Center or by calling (415) 663-8054.

Hostelling International, HI-Point Reyes, Point Reyes Station; (415) 663-8811; www.norcal hostels.org/reyes.

Restaurants and Java Jolts

Bovine Bakery, 11315 State Route 1, Point Reyes Station; (415) 663-9420.
Cafe Reyes, 11101 State Route 1, Point Reyes Station; (415) 663-9493.

10 Annadel: Ledson Marsh Loop

This loop offers great singletrack riding through the rolling hills of diverse oak woodlands, grass meadows, chaparral, and forests of Douglas fir and redwood. While there are endless combinations of trails throughout the park, this loop gives an overview of the central and southeastern sections. The size of the park allows you to repeat favorite sections. You will want to go back to explore and piece together your favorite trails. The marsh has some great places to picnic and bird–watch.

Start: From the trailhead for the Warren Richardson Trail, located at the last parking lot on Channel Drive inside Annadel State Park.
Distance: 14.8-mile figure eight.
Approximate riding time: 2 hours.
Difficulty: Moderate; some short, strenuous climbs, rugged descents, and loose rocks.
Trail surface: 68 percent singletrack and 32 percent fire road.
Terrain: Rolling hills packed with diversity—smooth and rocky trails, steep ravines, open meadows, filtered woodlands, and dense forests.
Seasons: Best weather is in spring and fall. Great showing of wildflowers in the spring, hot in the exposed areas during summer; some trails closed in winter.
Other trail users: Hikers, joggers, and equestrians.
Canine compatibility: Dogs not permitted.
Land status: Annadel State Park.
Nearest town: Santa Rosa.
Fees and permits: $4.00 parking fee.
Schedule: Open daily 9:00 A.M. to sunset; check with ranger for seasonal trail closures.
Maps: USGS maps: Santa Rosa, CA; Kentwood, CA.
Annadel State Park map available at the park entrance.
Trail contact: Annadel State Park, 6201 Channel Drive, Santa Rosa, CA 95409; (707) 539-3911; www.parks.ca.gov.

Finding the trailhead: From Santa Rosa: From Interstate 101 take California Highway 12 toward Sonoma. After a mile the freeway ends. Turn left onto Farmers Lane and follow the signs to CA 12. In less than a mile turn right onto Montgomery Drive and travel for nearly 3 miles; be careful to stay right as Montgomery crosses Mission. Turn right onto Channel Drive, following the sign to Annadel State Park. Follow Channel Drive 2 miles to the parking lot at the end. Pick up a map at the ranger station where you pay the entry fee. Restrooms and water are available at the parking lot.

The Ride

Annadel State Park sits on more than 5,000 acres of rolling hills, meadows, and woodlands on the outskirts of eastern Santa Rosa. Here you will find 35 miles of multiuse trail, much of which is legal singletrack for mountain bikers. The trails are marked well, although the 4" x 4" signposts can be a little confusing. Sometimes you may need to check all four sides to make sure you are heading in the right direction. If there is no sign, the trail is probably not legal for bikes.

Dodge boulders along the North Burma Trail.

The geology of the area has molded much of its history. For the early hunting and gathering Native Americans, this land was an important source of obsidian, which they used to make scrapers, knives, arrow points, and spearheads. Despite the Spaniards' shift to farming and ranching, much of the land remained relatively untouched. In the 1880s quarrying operations in these hills provided cobblestones for the first building boom in the Bay Area and later for the rebuilding of San Francisco after the 1906 earthquake. However, the demand for cobblestone dwindled with the advent of the automobile, which lacked full suspension. Early drivers did not care for the bumpy rides. The park derived its unique name from the granddaughter of one of the landowners at the turn of the twentieth century, Annie Hutchinson. This area was referred to as Annie's Dell.

This loop gives an overview of the central and southeastern portions of the park. Combine these trails with those on the Lake Ilsanjo Loop for a longer and more technical ride. The loop begins with a gradual climb up the wide Warren P. Richardson Trail through a mixed forest of Douglas fir, bay, and redwood. (Richardson was a prominent cattle rancher, horseman, and hops grower in Sonoma County.) The forest eventually gives way to mixed oak woodland and open meadows, where wild-

Annadel: Ledson Marsh Loop

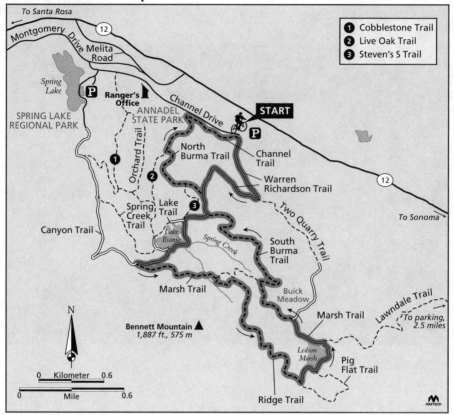

flowers make a big show in spring. From March through June the "mule's ears" are in bloom. These are yellow sunflowers with leaves that look like, do not be surprised, a mule's ear.

Just beyond the eastern outskirts of Lake Ilsanjo and 3 miles of fire road, you begin the coveted singletrack on Marsh Trail. The trail climbs steadily around Bennett Mountain (1,887 feet) through prime oak woodland and bunchgrass. Once in the fir forest, you pick up the park's Ridge Trail for 3 miles of easy, winding singletrack. This brings you to the southeast end of the loop where an occasional glimpse of houses reminds you that civilization is not far away. Quickly forget that thought and ride around Ledson Marsh, which supports more than one hundred species of birds as well as the endangered red-legged frog. Picnic tables are near the marsh and at several spots along the trail.

Back on singletrack, you meander to Buick Meadow and South Burma Trail, where a short climb offers a rewarding descent. Next it is over to North Burma Trail for rockier and more technical singletrack. At the peak there are great views of Lake Ilsanjo before you pass through a high meadow with a slalom course of boulders—big ones. Stay on the main trail, avoiding side trips on unmarked trails. North Burma

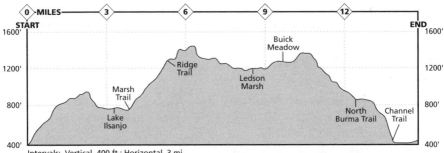

Intervals: Vertical, 400 ft.; Horizontal, 3 mi.

Trail drops down the canyon through dense woods before ending on Channel Drive. For those who never get enough singletrack, stay on Channel Trail as it weaves in and out of the paved road all the way back to the parking lot.

The Park Service continues to build new trails, and some trails close with the season or for repair. Call ahead during winter to check on trail status.

Miles and Directions

0.0   **START** from the parking lot on the Warren Richardson Trail. Ignore Steven's Trail on the right—no bikes allowed on this section. Trailhead GPS: N 38 26.40, W 122 36.569.

0.8   Bear right at the fork, staying on Warren Richardson Trail.

1.5   Continue on Warren Richardson Trail, ignoring Steven's S Trail on the right.

1.9   Continue straight, ignoring North Burma Trail on the right for now. (You catch this trail at the end of the loop.)

2.1   Veer right on Warren Richardson Trail at the junction with South Burma Trail.

2.4   Turn left onto Lake Trail. Stay left on the main road at Mile 2.5.

2.9   Turn left onto Canyon Trail.

3.3   Turn left onto the singletrack Marsh Trail. You are now on a section of the Bay Area Ridge Trail.

4.9   Make a sharp right onto Ridge Trail. Stay on Ridge Trail all the way to Marsh Trail.

8.1   Turn left onto Marsh Trail. (**Option:** Turn right on Ridge Trail, then left onto Pig Flat Trail for an extra 1.2 miles of singletrack.) Stay on Marsh Trail past Pig Flat Trail and Lawndale, where the Bay Area Ridge Trail takes off to the right.

9.3   Turn left onto Marsh Trail at the junction with Two Quarry Trail. **Shortcut:** Turn right and head for Two Quarry Trail and a great descent. This technical singletrack is steep in sections.

10.2   Turn right onto South Burma Trail at Buick Meadow. The summit is about half a mile ahead.

12.2   Turn right onto Warren Richardson Trail for a short backtrack.

12.4   Turn left onto singletrack North Burma Trail. Ignore smaller foot trails coming in from the sides. Also ignore Steven's S Trail coming in from the left near the high point of North Burma Trail.

13.4   Veer right on North Burma Trail at Live Oak Trail.

14.0 Turn right onto the singletrack just before the pavement; this is Channel Trail. This parallels Channel Drive, dropping you onto pavement in a couple of places, but you can pick it up again.

14.8 Arrive back at the parking lot.

Shorter Option

Start and stay on the Warren Richardson Trail until just before Lake Ilsanjo. Turn right onto Steven's S Trail, left onto North Burma Trail, and left onto Live Oak Trail. Turn left onto Rough Go Trail around Lake Ilsanjo, left at Canyon Trail, and right onto Warren Richardson Trail back to parking lot.

Ride Information

Local Information

SonomaNet, parks and recreation in Sonoma County; www.parks.sonoma.net/Annadel.html.

Accommodations

Spring Lake Regional Park, 5390 Montgomery Drive, Santa Rosa; camping information (707) 539-8092; camping reservations (707) 565-2267; www.sonoma-county.org/parks/camping/camp_intro.htm.

Sugarloaf Ridge State Park Campground, 2605 Adobe Canyon Road, Kenwood; (707) 833-5712; www.parks.ca.gov.

Restaurants and Java Jolts

Lepe's Taqueria, 4323 Montgomery Drive, Santa Rosa; (707) 538-8991.

11 Annadel: Lake Ilsanjo Loop

This ride offers great singletrack through pristine oak woodlands and meadows in the rolling hills east of Santa Rosa. Enter through Spring Lake Regional Park and weave through the northwestern part of Annadel State Park. Full suspension is recommended for aptly named trails like Cobblestone and Rough Go. Bay Area fog seldom reaches this park. Even in the shade, summers can be hot here, but you can cool off in Lake Ilsanjo.

Start: From the parking lot near the concession stand at Spring Lake Park.

Distance: 10.0-mile loop.

Approximate riding time: 1.5 hours.

Difficulty: Moderate; short, strenuous climb, loose rocks, and some rugged descents require some technical skills.

Trail surface: 70 percent singletrack, 23 percent dirt roads, and 7 percent paved bike path.

Terrain: Diverse rolling hills; smooth and rocky trails, steep ravines, open meadows, small lake/pond, oak woodlands, and grass-covered hills.

Seasons: Best weather is in spring and fall. Profusion of wildflowers in spring, hot in exposed areas in summer; some trails closed in winter.

Other trail users: Hikers, joggers, equestrians, turkeys, and rabbits.

Canine compatibility: Leashed dogs permitted in Spring Lake Park but not in Annadel State Park.

Land status: Annadel State Park and Sonoma County Spring Lake Regional Park.

Nearest town: Santa Rosa.

Fees and permits: $3.00 parking fee for Spring Lake Regional Park in the off-season; $4.00 when the swimming lagoon is open.

Schedule: Open daily 9:00 A.M. to sunset; check with Annadel State Park for seasonal trail closures.

Maps: USGS maps: Santa Rosa, CA; Kentwood, CA.

Annadel State Park map, usually available at the park entrance.

Trail contacts: Annadel State Park, 6201 Channel Drive, Santa Rosa, CA 95409; (707) 539-3911; www.parks.ca.gov.

Spring Lake Regional Park, Sonoma County Regional Parks Department, 391 Violetti Drive, Santa Rosa, CA 95409; (707) 565-2041; www.sonoma-county.org/parks/pk_slake.htm.

Finding the trailhead: From Santa Rosa: From U.S. Highway 101 take California Highway 12 toward Sonoma. After a mile the freeway ends. Turn left onto Farmers Lane and follow the signs to CA 12. In less than a mile, turn right onto Montgomery Drive for nearly 3 miles; be careful to stay right as Montgomery crosses Mission. Turn right onto Channel Drive. Follow the sign to Spring Lake Park, turning right onto Violetti Road. Enter the park and drive to the parking area near the concession stand. The loop starts on the paved bike path to the right of the concession stand. There are restrooms at the parking lot and throughout the loop. Water is available at the trailhead, but there is no water once you are on the trail.

Lake Ilsanjo—No skinny-dipping!

The Ride

Spring Lake Regional Park is the entry point for this loop through Annadel State Park. Situated on the edge of Santa Rosa, both parks are popular on weekends. This loop zigzags through most of the trails in the northwest end of Annadel. Once you have checked out the trails and terrain, you can go back and design your own from your favorites. Patch this together with the Annadel: Ledson Marsh Loop for a longer, more strenuous ride.

Annadel State Park is truly a testament to the Park Service and mountain bike advocates' ability to work together building and preserving great singletrack. At one time this was a maze of unnamed trails, many of them deteriorating. As in many places, animosity among bikers, hikers, and equestrians was growing. Through the use of diplomacy Annadel has evolved into a multiuse trail system that honors the biker's love of singletrack. This is a hard-won victory; do not blow it. The Park Service is still building new trails and reworking existing ones. Some of the rocky trails today may be smoothed trails tomorrow. Weather and erosion may lead to the closure of some trails to allow for repairs. Call ahead for trail status. Now that trails are well signed, anything *not* signed should be considered closed to bikes.

Annadel: Lake Ilsanjo Loop

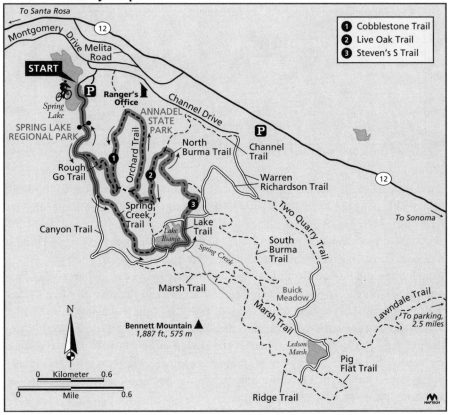

The loop begins on the well-traveled and level Spring Lake Trail, following the creek interface between the residential neighborhood and the grassy, rolling hills. The singletrack starts soon after you enter Annadel State Park. Steep and rocky, Spring Creek Trail takes you through shady woodlands of oak, alder, and occasionally redwood on the way up to Lake Ilsanjo, elevation 750 feet. There is no Spanish meaning for Lake Ilsanjo. It is merely a contraction of the names of previous landowners Ilsa and Joseph Coey. Swimming is allowed in the lake; clothing is *not* optional. This is also a popular fishing hole for black bass (some over nine pounds) and bluegill. Word has it the bass go for the purple plastic worms, while the bluegill like garden worms, grubs, and small crayfish. Licenses are required for all anglers over age sixteen.

A wide dirt road takes you around half the lake, although you will not see it most of the way. Spur trails will take you over to the water's edge. Past the lake, you begin a singletrack trail that weaves through meadow and brush to North Burma Trail. From here there is a good view of the lake and the surrounding valley before a great rocky descent to Live Oak Trail. The trail continues to climb up small canyons,

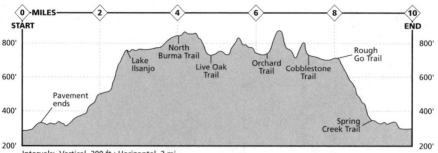

Intervals: Vertical, 200 ft.; Horizontal, 2 mi.

through more meadows, and by several nice picnic spots. With flocks of wild turkeys in the park, it would be surprising if you get out of these hills without seeing any. In spring rabbits are all over the place.

Orchard Trail rambles through the oaks and then a short dense section of Douglas fir forest. Ferns and rare native bunchgrass cover the forest floor. Soon you are on Cobblestone and Rough Go Trails—you will quickly understand where their names came from. Watch for pedal-crunching rocks as you zigzag down the hill. Packed with rocks, this short section offers some of the more technical riding in the park.

All too quickly you drop back onto the wide Spring Creek Trail leading back to the parking lot. Cool off in summer in the lagoon at Spring Lake Park. Riding is year-round, but it can be very hot in summer on some of the open south- and west-facing slopes and ridges. On those days stay in the cooler forests and woodlands—and bring plenty of water with you.

Miles and Directions

0.0 **START** on the bike path near the concession stand at Spring Lake Park and follow the yellow stripe. Trailhead GPS: N 38 27.13, W 122 39.04.

0.3 Just past the dip and culvert, turn left onto another paved bike path. It soon becomes gravel.

0.5 Ride around the gate. You are now riding on the Bay Area Ridge Trail. Ignore incoming trails from the residential area.

1.0 At the junction with Rough Go Trail, veer right onto Spring Creek Trail.

1.2 Continue straight as a trail comes in from the right across the dam. You will soon enter Annadel State Park. (No dogs allowed here.)

1.5 Go left onto the singletrack Spring Creek Trail at the junction with Canyon Trail.

2.7 Turn right across the dam onto the Rough Go Trail. This is a wide dirt road.

2.9 Veer left onto Lake Trail at the junction with Canyon Trail and continue around the lake. Stay on the main fire road, ignoring the side paths. Bear to the right past the outhouse to stay on the main road.

3.4 Cross the intersection with Warren Richardson Trail and take the singletrack Steven's S Trail straight ahead.

3.8	Veer left at the fork. The unnamed trail uphill on the right is a pirate connection to North Burma Trail.
4.1	Turn left onto unsigned North Burma Trail.
4.7	Turn left onto Live Oak Trail.
5.6	Turn right onto Rough Go Trail.
6.0	Turn right onto Orchard Trail.
6.4	Continue to the right on Orchard Trail, ignoring the Orchard Trail Alternate.
6.9	Stay right on Orchard Trail (not loop trail) through the Douglas fir forest. Ignore Orchard Trail Alternate again up ahead. (FYI: The native bunchgrass growing here is rare.)
7.1	Turn left onto Cobblestone Trail. Stay on the main trail through here, ignoring the short side loop on the left after 30 yards.
7.2	Bear right to remain on Cobblestone Trail. The lower reaches of this trail are where it earns its name.
8.0	Turn right onto Rough Go Trail.
8.9	Continue straight, ignoring the unsigned singletrack on the right. You will soon complete the loop. Head straight ahead, back onto Spring Creek Trail.
9.7	Turn right onto the bike path.
10.0	Arrive back at the concession stand and parking lot.

Ride Information

Local Information

SonomaNet, parks and recreation in Sonoma County; www.parks.sonoma.net/Annadel.html.

Accommodations

Spring Lake Regional Park, 5390 Montgomery Drive, Santa Rosa; camping information (707) 539-8092; camping reservations (707) 565-2267; www.sonoma-county.org/ parks/camping/camp_intro.htm.

Sugarloaf Ridge State Park Campground, 2605 Adobe Canyon Road, Kenwood; (707) 833-5712; www.parks.ca.gov.

Restaurants and Java Jolts

Lepe's Taqueria, 4323 Montgomery Drive, Santa Rosa; (707) 538-8991.

12 Skyline Wilderness Loop

This ride boasts narrow and challenging singletrack through oak forests, high grasslands, and rugged chaparral-covered hillsides. There are plenty of technical uphills and downhills, rock gardens, and hairpin turns. The ride begins with a mile of steep climbing to the ridge overlooking the Napa Valley, the North Bay marshes, and surrounding mountains. The trail continues along the ridge until dropping down to Lake Marie. The return ride is on the other side of the canyon, following the contours of the mountain. This park was the venue for the Napa World Cup from 1997 to 1999.

Start: From entrance to Skyline Wilderness Park, Napa.

Length: 7.4-mile loop.

Approximate riding time: 1.5 hours.

Difficulty: Difficult; while it is not *all* difficult, there are plenty of technical, steep, and rocky climbs and descents.

Trail surface: 90 percent singletrack and 10 percent dirt road.

Terrain: Ridgeline along a narrow canyon, small lake, rock gardens, steep hillsides through shaded woodlands, grassy-covered hills, and chaparral slopes.

Seasons: Although this is open year-round, the green hills, wildflowers, and nice weather make spring and early summer the best times. It can be very hot in summer, so start early on warm days.

Other trail users: Hikers and equestrians.

Canine compatibility: Dogs not permitted.

Land status: Private nonprofit park on public land.

Nearest town: Napa.

Fees and permits: $5.00 entrance fee for

cars and $4.00 for ride-in bikes. There is a fine ($200 first offense!) for sneaking into the park without paying, no matter what side trail you take. Rangers patrol the trails and are not known for their leniency. Worse yet, it reflects poorly on us all. We cannot afford to lose any more trails.

Schedule: Generally open 9:00 A.M. to one hour before sunset Monday through Thursday and 8:00 A.M. to one hour before sunset Friday through Sunday. Check the Web site for current hours. The park is open year-round except Christmas Day. Except for the main Lake Marie Road, all biking trails close for at least five days following a heavy rain. Be sure to call ahead in winter to see if trails are open: (707) 252-0481.

Maps: USGS maps: Napa, CA; Mount George, CA.

Park trail maps available at the entrance and online at www.skylinepark.org.

Trail contact: Skyline Wilderness Park, 2201 Imola Avenue, Napa, CA 94559; (707) 252-0481; www.skylinepark.org.

Finding the trailhead: From Vallejo: Take California Highway 29 north to southern Napa (it becomes Soscol Road). Turn right (east) onto Imola Road. Pass the Napa State Hospital on the right. Skyline Wilderness Park is about a mile beyond the hospital on the right.

The Ride

Skyline Wilderness Park was formed in 1979 when Napa State Hospital decided it did not need about 900 acres of its land. A group of concerned citizens got together

Try to clean this slick rock corner—uphill!

and rallied to turn the area into a park. The state of California decided to lease the surplus land to Napa County, which then leased it to the newly formed nonprofit Skyline Park Citizens' Association. Volunteers now operate, maintain, and improve the park, with only a few part-time employees.

The park has two areas: The entry area includes a picnic area, RV park, tent camping area, horse arena, and ranges for archery and disc golf. The rest of the park hosts 16 miles of trails through the wilderness watershed of Marie Creek, and most of that is singletrack. There are plans to upgrade the trail signs throughout the park. Until then, the signs are rather small. Look around for them and carry a map.

The ride begins at the entry kiosk on Lake Marie Road. The wide dirt road takes you through a fenced corridor between Lake Louise and Lake Camille. In less than a mile you are winding up steep singletrack along Lower Skyline Trail through a mixture of grasslands and woodlands of oak, buckeye, and laurels. There is no disgrace if you do not ride all the uphill. Once on the ridge, you are on Skyline Trail and a section of the Bay Area Ridge Trail. The trail opens up to views of Napa Valley, marshlands of North Bay, and, on a clear day, Mount Tamalpais in Marin. At times the trail follows a rock wall built in early ranching days from local volcanic rock. Wildflowers can be stunning in spring and summer, including bright-yellow

Skyline Wilderness Loop

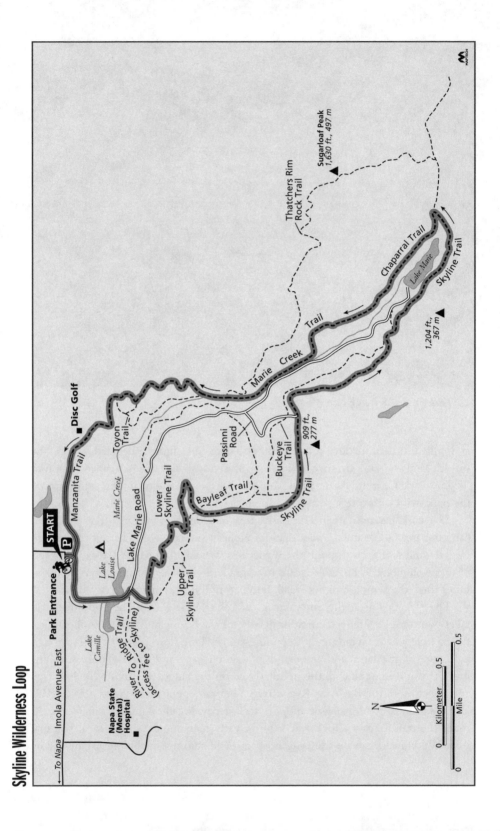

mariposa lilies and light-pink blooms of bitterroot, a delicacy for Native Americans when peeled and cooked. Although there are several steep climbs, they are all short.

Skyline Trail takes you all the way to the southern part of this loop, where the trail eventually drops down toward Lake Marie. Closer to the creek and lake, the woodlands get denser, with an undergrowth of ferns replacing the grasses. Poison oak laces the trail. Along the way you pass the lone chimney of the Sea Captain's House. According to stories, the house was built for the gatekeeper who maintained the dam at Lake Marie. When the state decided the gatekeeper was no longer needed, the house was torn down. The trail continues along contours of the steep hill above Lake Marie. At the end of the lake, there is a stream crossing before you ride back along the sunnier, west-facing side of the canyon.

The returning Chaparral Trail climbs steeply up a rocky hillside overlooking the lake. The trail drops down along Marie Creek for a cool respite in summer, then up again to the rocky, technical Manzanita Trail. Portions of this trail were part of the Napa World Cup cross-country course from 1997 to 1999. Imagine Alison Dunlap (USA) and Miguel Martinez (France) clearing this section. The racecourse was a shorter, multilap circuit.

As the trail levels out near the end, you will find yourself at Hole One of an eighteen-hole disc golf course (that's Frisbee golf). No bikes allowed on the course. Never mind; lock your bike, pull your disc out of your hydration pack, and play a round. Discs are also available at the entrance kiosk.

When you first arrive at the park, pay attention to the closing time displayed at the kiosk. You must be out the front gate by closing. While you might find someone to open the gate to get your car out, you could be charged $20 for the service.

Miles and Directions

(**Note on mileage:** Odometer readings will vary if you carry your bike a lot.)

0.0 **START** to the right of the kiosk at the park entrance on wide, dirt Lake Marie Road. Ride around the picnic area and follow a tiny TO TRAIL sign across the fenced causeway between two small lakes. These ponds are still part of the state hospital grounds. Trailhead GPS: N 38 16.45, W 122 14.58.

0.3 Stay right at the fork, avoiding the entrance to the Napa State Hospital's Camp Coombs on the left.

0.5 Turn right at the junction, following the sign (look carefully to find it) to Skyline Trail. Do not go straight to Lake Marie.

0.6 Turn left onto Lower Skyline Trail, a narrow singletrack. Gear down for some steep grades ahead.

1.6 Reach the end of Lower Skyline Trail. Turn right briefly onto the Bayleaf Trail and then turn left onto Skyline Trail. (If you are thinking you should have come up Skyline Trail, it is worse.) There will be an immediate short, rocky descent. You will follow Skyline Trail, a segment of the Bay Area Ridge Trail along here, all the way to the end of Lake Marie. Ignore all side trails leading down to Bayleaf Trail or Lake Marie.

2.4 Cross over the eroded Passini Road and continue steeply up Skyline Trail. Stay on Skyline Trail, ignoring all side trails such as Buckeye and Lake Marie Trails. After nearly a mile you will pass a brick chimney, all that remains of the gatekeeper's house.

3.8 Cross the creek and ride to a junction. Turn left onto Chaparral Trail, leaving Skyline Trail. **Option:** Ride to the end of Skyline Trail for a short out-and-back. There is currently a gate about a mile up, ending this portion of the Bay Area Ridge Trail. This will eventually open and continue up to the next ridge as part of a regional River to Ridge Trail.

4.4 Turn right at the junction with Marie Creek Trail.

4.5 Continue straight ahead on Marie Creek Trail. Hike your bike up a steep, rocky section to a more ridable rock garden.

4.9 Turn right onto the unsigned Marie Creek Trail and cross the creek twice.

5.4 Bear right onto Manzanita-Toyon Trail. Veer right again in 0.1 mile to continue on Manzanita Trail.

6.0 Turn right onto the unsigned Manzanita Biker Bypass. This is easy to miss. Until the trails are marked better, do not worry if you miss this. You will wind around the hill and eventually join the unmarked bypass at about Mile 6.2. Turn left down the trail. If you find the bypass, it takes you up through an opening in a rock wall and then on a steep descent. You will soon come to an unmarked junction with the hikers-only section; turn right to continue the descent down Manzanita Trail. The distances for both routes are about the same, so the mileage readings should be close. Continue all the way back to the parking lot on Manzanita Trail. You will pass along the edge of the disc golf course along the way.

7.4 Arrive back at the parking lot.

Ride Information

Local Information
Napa Chamber of Commerce, 1556 First Street, Napa, CA 94559; (707) 226–7455; www.napachamber.org.

Accommodations
Skyline Wilderness Park, tent camping and RV park, 2201 Imola Avenue, Napa; (707) 252–0481; www.skylinepark.org.

Restaurants and Java Jolts
South Napa Marketplace is at the junction of Imola Road and Soscol Avenue. There are several places to grab a quick bite here, including Starbucks, Jamba Juice, and In-n-Out Burger.

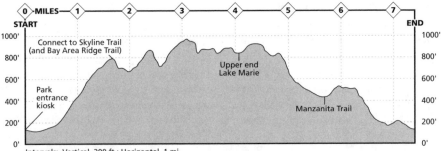

Intervals: Vertical, 200 ft.; Horizontal, 1 mi.

Honorable Mentions

A Muir Woods-Coastal Trail Loop

This is a classic Marin ride with an impressive view of the Pacific Ocean. Ride this as an 8.2-mile loop or as a connector between Mount Tam and Tennessee Valley. Start on the graded Deer Park Fire Road and enjoy a quiet but solid climb along the edge of Muir Woods National Monument. You will be riding among the redwoods near the top. Along the way crisscross the famous Dipsea Trail—path of the long-standing footrace from Mill Valley to Stinson Beach. At about 2.5 miles turn left onto Coastal Trail for a 3-mile downhill run to California Highway 1. Turn left onto the highway and then left again onto Muir Woods Road for a road ride back to the start.

Plans call for some realignment of the Coastal Trail, so check with Mount Tamalpais State Park for trail status (415–388–2070; www.parks.ca.gov). This is a mildly strenuous climb. Time will tell what the Coastal Trail will be like in the future; for now, watch for ruts.

Exit U.S. Highway 101 near Sausalito onto CA 1 to Stinson Beach–Mill Valley. At the crest of the hill, turn right onto the Panoramic Highway. Turn left onto Muir Woods Road. The trailhead for Deer Park Fire Road is on the right about 0.7 mile past the entrance to Muir Woods. Parking is along the road. There is no water or restroom.

B Bear Valley Trail

Bring the family! This is a beautiful and popular ride from the Bear Valley Visitor Center toward the coast. Start from the visitor center on the Bear Valley Trail. The wide dirt road takes you through a lush canyon of pine, oak, and redwoods. Riding is good year-round; the dirt road is well packed in winter and shaded in summer. Be prepared; it can be cold in the summer fog. While this is a good beginner ride, there is a gentle grade to Divide Meadow (1.6 miles) then a downhill cruise. The trail ends for bikes at 3.1 miles, but there is a bike rack. Bring a lock if you want to take a hike. It is 1 mile down to the beach.

Exit U.S. Highway 101 in Larkspur on Sir Francis Drake Boulevard. Head west to Olema. Turn right on California Highway 1 and shortly turn left onto Bear Valley Road. Turn left toward the park headquarters and visitor center. The parking lot is at the end of the road. For information contact Point Reyes National Seashore, National Park Service, Bear Valley Visitor Center, Point Reyes, CA 94956; (415) 464–5100; www.nps.gov/pore.

C Big Rock Trail

Check out the new singletrack in Marin! The Marin County Open Space District built a sweet multiuse singletrack connector from Lucas Valley Road to the Big Rock Ridge Fire Road, part of their Lucas Valley Open Space Preserve.

This is a moderate, mildly technical climb to Big Rock Peak. At 1,887 feet this is the second highest mountain in Marin. The first 2.5 miles is new singletrack and easy to follow. Any side roads are clearly marked PRIVATE PROPERTY. Much of the trail is public easement through private property, and if you venture off the trail, you are trespassing. The ride back is great downhill; watch for ruts on the upper part of the trail.

If you're heading to the top, it is 3.6 miles to the second set of antennae and the best view. From here you can see San Francisco Bay, Mount Tamalpais, and San Francisco. The fire road continues down the ridge and is mighty inviting. If you are a strong rider, go for it. You can extend the ride by heading east along the ridge to Luiz or Queenstone Fire Roads. At either junction you can turn right and make your way down to Lucas Valley Road. Once on the pavement, carefully ride the road back to the trailhead.

To get there exit U.S. Highway 101 at the Smith Ranch Road–Lucas Valley exit, just north of San Rafael. Head west on Lucas Valley Road for just over 5 miles. Big Rock and the trailhead are on the right at the crest of the hill. There is limited parking along the left side of the road. Since there are no U-turns here, continue west less than a quarter of a mile and turn around at the entrance to Lucasfilm on the right. (Yes, as in George Lucas and Skywalker Ranch.)

During hunting season in August and September, Big Rock Trail closes for a few partial days. For information call the district's Lucas Valley Field Office at (415) 499–6405 or log onto www.marinopenspace.org.

The Loma Alta Connection: On the south side of Lucas Valley Road (across the street from Big Rock) is the Loma Alta Fire Road, a public easement through private ranchland. This connector takes you to Loma Alta (1,592 feet) and the Loma Alta Open Space Preserve, and eventually the town of Fairfax. The 20-mile round-trip ride from Fairfax to the top of Big Rock Ridge is a great ride for strong riders.

D Boggs Mountain Demonstration State Forest

Boggs Mountain is over the Napa County border in Lake County. That's a bit of a stretch for the Bay Area, but we'll claim it anyway. Here you will find miles of mild to moderately technical singletrack—the less-traveled kind. Douglas fir, ponderosa pine, sugar pine, oaks, and madrone shade the upper hills. The best times to ride are in spring and fall; it is hot in summer and cold, as in some snow, in winter.

A network of trails meanders through the state forest—up, down, back, and forth, offering all sorts of options. Not all the trails are signed. You can piece together a 13-mile loop encircling the state forest. Favorite trails include Creek, Grizzly, rocky John's, and steep Jethro's (which is more fun to ride down than up). From time to time this is the venue for cross-country races. It is easy to get lost here, so bring a map. There is camping on a first-come, first-served basis.

Take California Highway 29 north through the Napa Valley, past Calistoga to Middletown (about 18 miles north of Calistoga). Turn left (west) onto California Highway 175. Once through the town of Cobb, keep an eye out for the STATE FIRE STATION sign. Turn right here onto Forestry Road. Drive down to the parking lot between the heliport on the right and the forest headquarters on the left. Here you will find an outhouse and the only water in the state forest.

Contact the California Department of Forestry and Fire Protection, Boggs Mountain Demonstration State Forest; (707) 928–4378; www.fire.ca.gov/php/rsrc-mgt_boggsmtn.php. Maps are available online and sometimes at the forest headquarters.

E Oat Hill Mine Road

This overgrown wagon trail is a remnant of mining days; that's cinnabar mining. Wagons hauling supplies to and from town carved ruts in bedrock underlying parts of the trail. This is a rugged and technical out-and-back with plenty of rocks, some basketball-size.

The first half mile is abandoned county road through private property. Conservationists struggled to ward off development and maintain this access to the public land up ahead. The turnaround point is at the pass where the trail levels off, nearly 4.5 miles from the start. The hiking-only Palisades Trail is the cue to turn around. The property owners don't take kindly to trespassers.

Take California Highway 29 north through the Napa Valley and just outside Calistoga. The trail begins on the right about 100 feet north of the junction with the Silverado Trail. There are no signs at the trailhead; just a pipe gate marks the beginning of the trail. For information contact Robert Louis Stevenson State Park (707–942–4575) or Calistoga Bikeshop in Calistoga (707–942–9687).

F Rockville Hills Regional Park

It may not sound like much: 1 square mile of low-lying hill rising from 100 to 550 feet. But this is a mountain biker's playground. Ride through oak woodlands and grasslands, along seasonal creeks, and past still ponds and craggy outcroppings. The trails are on bedrock and hard-packed sand, although the latter is prone to rutting. Mountain bikers enjoy a tenuous existence here, so check on the status of biking before you go. While riding, if you are not sure it is a trail—it's not.

In general the wider trails are the easiest. There are some exciting technical sections, where the park earns its name. Bring a map and a good sense of direction. The park is too small to take any mileage cues, no matter what someone offers you. Lift up your head and follow your nose. If it looks interesting, check it out. There are lots of trails to explore. If you get lost, don't worry; worst case, you may go in circles or end up at the wrong entrance. Be sure to allow enough time so that you are not caught here after dark. You can squeeze in an 8-mile loop in a couple of hours. Check out Upper Tilley Trail (technical), Rock Garden, Outside Loop, Black Oak Trail, Green Valley Trail, and the slick rocks on the northwestern Unknown Trail. Tread lightly here, and watch for trail closures.

From Interstate 80 near Cordelia Junction, take the Suisun Valley Road exit and head north. After passing Solano Community College, turn left onto Rockville Road. The parking lot and trailhead are on the left in 0.8 mile. Contact the Park Ranger, Community Services, City of Fairfield; (707) 428–7614; www.rockvillepark.org.

Note: Even with the honorable mentions, it is difficult to give only a partial listing of trails in the North Bay. There are still more trails out there—more peaks to climb (Barnabe Peak, Sugarloaf Ridge), short jaunts (McInnis Park, Mount Burdell), ridges (Diaz Ridge), and places to explore (Point Reyes National Seashore, Jack London State Park). Of particular note is the Tamarancho Boy Scout Camp Trail, which offers the hands-down best legal singletrack in Marin County. With forty uphill and downhill hairpin turns, this trail is not for beginners. The trailhead is located in Fairfax. The Marin Council, Boy Scouts of America, owner of this trail, currently allows public use on trails only; however, *you must purchase a Friends of Tamarancho pass* to ride there. Without a pass, you are trespassing. Passes are available online at www.boyscouts-marin.org/camps.fot.htm or by calling (415) 454–1081. Some local bike shops also sell passes.

East Bay

The East Bay refers to the combined Contra Costa and Alameda Counties. As you inch through traffic on the East Shore Freeway in Oakland or Interstate 680 in Walnut Creek, it is hard to believe there is any mountain biking nearby. But there is, and it ain't bad. There are two means of escape: the low-lying East Bay Hills and the sentinel Mount Diablo range.

The East Bay Hills rise along the edge of the urban jungle from San Pablo on the north to Pleasanton on the south, the crest of which is open space. The once-dense redwood forest along the Berkeley and Oakland hills has been logged clean, giving way to nonnative grasses and eucalyptus groves. A new generation of redwoods has risen up in some pockets and is a must for anyone exploring this side of the bay.

Then there is Mount Diablo and the fanning foothills below. Miles of challenging trails and top-of-the-world views await the able rider. Miles out, you feel you are truly away from it all.

Much of the East Bay Hills and base of Mount Diablo is cattle country. You will see more cattle here than perhaps anywhere else in the Bay Area. These cattle hold the key to these open space preserves, so make peace with them. While they make trails unridable at times, they have curbed development in an area where there never seems to be enough housing.

From a distance the rolling hills look tame, but don't be fooled. Many of the rides are along rising and falling ridges and through steep ravines. Nearly all the trails in the East Bay are fire roads. There are a few hidden exceptions, and they are legal; check out these featured rides to find them. The most notable exception is the singletrack playground at Joaquin Miller Park. How did the city of Oakland do it? Ride there—and then pay your dues to the Bicycle Trails Council of the East Bay.

Seasons play a big role in riding the East Bay. Spring is the absolute best time. Savor the short-lived verdant grassy hills, crisp views, and wildflowers. You may not be into wildflowers until you ride these hills. They will distract you from even the most die-hard, nose-to-the-terrain training ride. However, catch it quick; things dry out fast in summer, and it gets *hot*. The farther inland you head, as in anything near Mount Diablo, the hotter it gets. If you ride in summer, ride in the early morning or late evening or when the fog has brought in a cool breeze.

In summer head for the redwood groves. They don't grow there without a reason. Redwoods thrive on the coastal fog. The Bay Area's signature fog rolls in from the Golden Gate, hits the Berkeley Hills, and fans out. Tilden, Redwood, and Joaquin Miller Parks are great summer rides.

When the rain sets in, so does the notorious adobe clay. Much of the East Bay becomes unridable. Add our heavy-hoofed friends, and it may take a while to dry out. Take this time to explore other parts of the Bay Area.

"We are cyclists who love long rides in awesome natural settings with technical challenges. To be able to ride over and descend 10,000 feet in one day is a dream come true."

–Paul Nam, ROMP (Responsible Organized Mountain Pedalers) president 2003

13 Tilden Park-Wildcat Canyon Loop

Two loops emanate from Inspiration Point in popular Tilden Park atop the Berkeley Hills. If you go high enough or far enough, you will eventually get away from any crowd. One loop heads south, the other north along the ridge overlooking the expansive San Francisco Bay and surrounding hills. Rolling fire roads cruise through oak and eucalyptus woodlands and along grassy pasturelands. The last part parallels Wildcat Creek through a quiet canyon and climbs back up to Inspiration Point.

Start: From Inspiration Point parking lot, Tilden Regional Park.

Distance: 17.1-mile figure eight.

Approximate riding time: 2 to 3 hours.

Difficulty: Moderate; steady climbs, mostly nontechnical with a short, rugged, and steep decent on Seaview Trail; several sections suitable for beginners and children.

Trail surface: 70 percent dirt fire road and 30 percent paved pathway.

Terrain: Ridgeline along rolling grass-covered hills, patches of eucalyptus trees, shaded creek canyon, and a small lake.

Seasons: Summer and fall are good, but best in spring when the hills are greenest. The Seaview loop is a good winter ride. Wildcat Gorge Trail is closed in winter to protect stream habitat. Avoid Meadow Canyon Trail in the wet season—it is beyond muddy.

Other trail users: Hikers, joggers, equestrians, dogs, cattle, and even cars on a short stretch.

Canine compatibility: Leashed dogs permitted; on Nimitz Trail dogs allowed off leash under voice control.

Land status: East Bay Regional Park District.

Nearest town: Berkeley.

Fees and permits: No fees or permits required.

Schedule: Tilden Park is open daily 8:00 A.M. to 10:00 P.M. or as posted. Wildcat Canyon is open 5:00 A.M. to 10:00 P.M. daily.

Maps: USGS maps: Richmond, CA; Briones, CA.

East Bay Regional Park District maps of Tilden Regional Park and Wildcat Canyon Regional Park, available online and at some trailheads.

Trail contacts: East Bay Regional Park District Headquarters, 2950 Peralta Oaks Court, P.O. Box 5381, Oakland, 94605; (510) 562-PARK. Tilden Regional Park office; (510) 843-2137; www.ebparks.org/parks/tilden.

Wildcat Canyon Regional Park office; (510) 236-1262; www.ebparks.org/parks/wildcat.

Finding the trailhead: From Berkeley: From Interstate 80 (California Highway 17), take the Buchanan Street–Albany exit. Head east, staying on Marin Avenue all the way up to Grizzly Peak Boulevard near the ridge. (Marin is the fastest way to get to the ridge; but if it is too steep for you, follow one of the signs to Tilden Park along the way.) Turn right onto Grizzly Peak, then left onto Shasta Road. Turn right onto Wildcat Canyon Road; and continue about 1.5 miles to Inspiration Point. There are outhouses at the trailhead but no water.

From Orinda: From California Highway 24 take the Orinda exit and head north along Camino Pablo, which becomes San Pablo Dam Road. About 2.2 miles from the freeway, turn left onto Wildcat Canyon Road and follow it about 2.5 miles to the Inspiration Point parking lot on the right.

If the Inspiration Point parking lot is full, park at Quarry Picnic Area and begin the ride from Mile 0.4.

Rolling along the San Pablo Ridge in Tilden, the cyclist is safe from the masses.

The Ride

Tilden Park has been called the jewel of the East Bay Regional Park System. Its 2,077 acres of parkland include miles of trails for cyclists (both road and mountain), hikers, and equestrians. This popular respite above the urban landscape offers picnicking, an eighteen-hole golf course, botanical gardens of California native plants, miniature steam passenger trains, pony rides, an antique merry-go-round, group camping, and swimming and fishing at Lake Anza. However, you will not see most of these things while you are riding. The adjacent 2,428-acre Wildcat Canyon Regional Park is largely undeveloped, featuring a cattle pasture on the ridge and a rich riparian environment along Wildcat Creek.

This figure-eight route starts in Tilden Park and then passes through adjoining Wildcat Canyon Regional Park and Tilden Nature Area on the second loop. The first loop heads southwest to the Quarry Picnic Area for a climb through the hills and up to the ridge. The Seaview Trail runs along the crest of the hill and is a piece of two regional trails: Bay Area Ridge and East Bay Skyline National Recreation Trails. Enjoy panoramic views of the Golden Gate Bridge, San Francisco Bay, surrounding cities, and the tallest mountains—Tamalpais, St. Helena, and Diablo. The descent along Seaview Trail is rocky, with tire-size ruts, making for a somewhat technical ride. Thanks to the rocks, this trail drains in winter, making it one of the few ridable East Bay trails in winter. This is a popular park, so watch for traffic on the downhill. Beginners may want to skip the first loop, with its fairly steep climb and descent.

The second and longer loop begins back at Inspiration Point and heads north along the San Pablo Ridge on Nimitz Way. This wide, paved trail is one of the most popular paths in Tilden, but things will thin out by the time the pavement ends. For the next 5.5 miles, the ride repeats the first loop's expansive view of the bay. At the beginning the trail cuts through dense groves of eucalyptus trees and some low-lying chaparral. This gives way to more grass-covered hills and finally pastureland for cattle. Yes, there are farms in Berkeley. San Pablo Reservoir comes into view on the right. As with most ridges, this is not a constant downhill. There are steep pitches of climbing, but they are always rewarded with quick descents. Away from most other trail users, the wildlife increases. Looking up, you may well see red-tailed hawks, American kestrels, Cooper's hawks, and turkey vultures. At the lower reaches of the ridge, you may even spot a coyote.

TIDBIT: The last major earthquake on the Hayward Fault was 7.0 magnitude in 1868. Considerable damage occurred in the East Bay and San Francisco. At the time people called it the Great San Francisco Earthquake; that was until the big one hit in 1906.

Before the ridge fades into the city of Richmond, you drop into Wildcat Canyon and head up Wildcat Creek Trail to Tilden Park. Although you do not really see the creek, the vegetation changes to a riparian forest of alder, willow, dogwood, and bay laurel. At the beginning of Wildcat Trail, the path will consist of out-of-place and deteriorating pavement. Built for a proposed housing development, the project was abandoned because of unstable soils. You can see the landslides and slumps along the way. The Hayward Fault runs nearby along the canyon, adding to the geologic activity and movement in the area.

Before reaching Tilden Park you ride through Tilden Nature Area, a place for hiking and outdoor education programs. The trees get denser. You are soon riding next to Jewel Lake and on Loop Trail through dense eucalyptus groves. The ride finishes with a steady 1.5-mile climb out of the canyon to Inspiration Point. Although this trail receives lots of sunshine, several springs along the trail keep the upper reaches of Meadows Canyon Trail unridable in winter and early spring. Chains will jam, and it is *work* to clean the adobe clay from your bike.

Tilden Park–Wildcat Canyon Loop

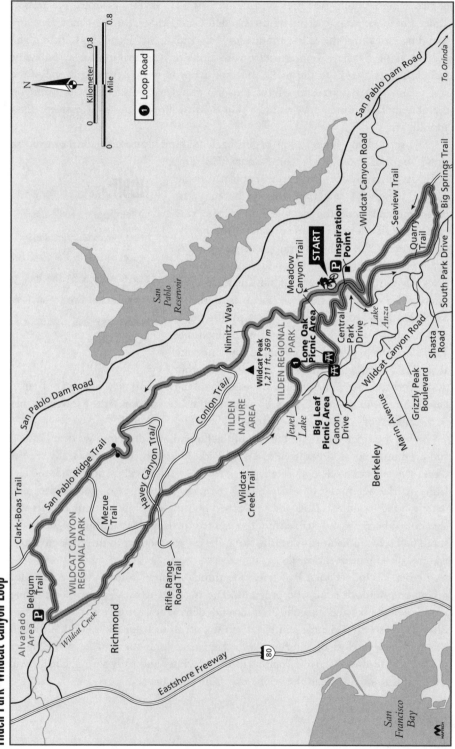

N

0 0.8 Kilometer

0 0.8 Mile

1 Loop Road

San Pablo Dam Road

To Orinda

San Pablo Dam Road

Wildcat Canyon Road

Seaview Trail

START

P Inspiration Point

Meadow Canyon Trail

Nimitz Way

San Pablo Reservoir

Wildcat Peak 1,211 ft, 369 m

Conlon Trail

TILDEN NATURE AREA

TILDEN REGIONAL PARK

1 Lone Oak Picnic Area

Quarry Trail

South Park Drive

Central Park Drive

Lake Anza

Wildcat Canyon Road

Shasta Road

Big Springs Trail

Clark-Boas Trail

San Pablo Ridge Trail

WILDCAT CANYON REGIONAL PARK

Mezue Trail

Havey Canyon Trail

Wildcat Creek Trail

Jewel Lake

Big Leaf Picnic Area

Canon Drive

Grizzly Peak Boulevard

Marin Avenue

Berkeley

Alvarado Area **P**

Belgum Trail

Wildcat Creek

Richmond

Rifle Range Road Trail

Eastshore Freeway

80

San Francisco Bay

MAPTECH

Miles and Directions

0.0 **START** from Inspiration Point parking lot. Turn right onto Wildcat Canyon Road, heading toward Berkeley. Trailhead GPS: N 37 54.115, W 122 14.366.

0.4 Turn left into the Quarry parking lot and picnic area. Ride past the tables and take a right onto Quarry Trail.

0.8 Veer right, staying on Quarry Trail.

1.6 Continue straight through the gate and parking area. Ride up the hill on Big Springs Trail.

2.3 Turn left onto Seaview Trail along the ridge. This is part of the Bay Area Ridge Trail and the Skyline National Recreation Trail. **Option:** Turn right for an out-and-back to Lomas Cantadas–Grizzly Peak Boulevard, around Vollmer Peak (1,905 feet). There is a picnic area and a small-scale steam train you can ride.

3.6 Continue straight on Seaview Trail where Springs Trail comes in on the left. Stay on the main fire road, ignoring unsigned trails on the left. Bikes are allowed only on main fire roads.

4.0 Turn right back onto Wildcat Canyon Road, completing the first loop.

4.2 Arrive back at Inspiration Point. Turn left through the gate and onto paved Nimitz Way. This section is good for beginners and children. The pavement makes for a safe bet in winter.

6.2 You are entering Wildcat Canyon Regional Park.

6.4 Continue straight on Nimitz Way, ignoring Conlon Trail on left. **Shortcut:** Take Conlon Trail down to Wildcat Trail.

8.3 Reach the end of the paved trail. Veer left onto the dirt road, pass through a gate, and continue along the ridge.

8.5 Turn left onto Mezue Trail at the fork near the cattle coral, and then veer right onto San Pablo Ridge Trail.

9.7 Veer left onto Belgum Trail.

9.9 Continue straight on San Pablo Ridge at the intersection with the Clark-Boas Trail.

10.1 Veer left toward the bay at the unmarked fork. (Turning right would continue along the ridge.)

10.7 Continue straight through the gate and onto an unimproved paved road. After 100 yards go left at the first junction, following the sign to the Tilden Nature Area. There will be a break in the pavement, and the road narrows; continue straight along the main road. You are now on Wildcat Creek Trail.

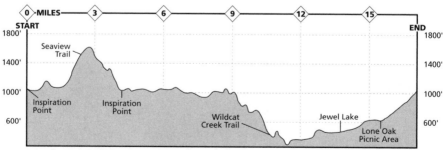

Intervals: Vertical, 400 ft.; Horizontal, 3 mi.

11.5 Follow the road as it veers right and becomes gravel and dirt.

12.5 Continue straight, ignoring the Rifle Range Road Trail on the right. You will enter Tilden Nature Area around Mile 14.

14.5 Turn left just past the beginning of Jewel Lake. Follow the signs to stay on Loop Road. Side trails are marked NO BICYCLES.

15.4 Arrive at an information board, where you may find trail maps. Continue through the gate onto the paved road. Lone Oak Picnic Area will soon appear on the left. Turn left into the picnic area and follow the signs to Meadow Canyon Trail. It starts out as a dual track but soon widens to a fire road. **Winter option:** To complete the loop continue on the paved road past Lone Oak Picnic Area. Turn left onto Central Park Drive. Turn left again to ride Wildcat Canyon Road all the way to Inspiration Point. This is not mountain biking, but it will spare your chain.

17.0 Turn left onto Curran Trail.

17.1 Arrive back at Inspiration Point.

Short, Easy Options

From Inspiration Point: Out-and-back along Nimitz Way.

From the Alvarado Area entrance to Wildcat Canyon, Richmond: Out-and-back along Wildcat Creek Trail.

From the Big Leaf Picnic Area in Tilden Park: Ride Loop Road to Wildcat Creek Trail.

Ride Information

Local Information

East Bay Regional Park District, 2950 Peralta Oaks Court, P.O. Box 5381, Oakland, CA 94605; (510) 562-PARK; www.ebparks.org.

Restaurants and Java Jolts

Fat Apples, 1346 Martin Luther King Junior Way, Berkeley; (510) 644-3230.
Bette's Ocean View Diner, 1807 Fourth Street, Berkeley; (510) 644-3230.

Pyramid Alehouse, Brewery & Restaurant, 901 Gilman Street, Berkeley; (510) 528-9880; www.pyramidbrew.com.

For those who like to wander, head for Shattuck Avenue and Vine Street. This is Berkeley's gourmet ghetto. You will find coffee, lunch, and more.

14 Redwood Park Loop

These wide, well-marked trails through the East Bay hills offer another quick getaway from the urban congestion. Two easy out-and-back rides along the West and East Ridges of Redwood Regional Park are combined into a more challenging loop. After an easy ride along West Ridge, there is a quick descent into the canyon carved by Redwood Creek. You pay for it with a hardy climb back up to the East Ridge. Pass through oak woodlands and redwood forests along the way. Enjoy great views of the open ridgeland and surrounding watersheds.

Start: From Skyline Gate Staging Area to Redwood Regional Park, Oakland.

Distance: 8.4-mile loop.

Approximate riding time: 1 to 1.5 hours.

Difficulty: Moderate; one steep and rocky descent, one strenuous climb; otherwise, relatively easy ride.

Trail surface: Dirt fire road.

Terrain: Rolling ridgeline around a steeply carved canyon; drop down to and grind up from Redwood Creek; woodlands and forest on the west rim; chaparral, oaks, and eucalyptus on the east rim.

Seasons: Year-round, although can be muddy in winter.

Other trail users: Hikers, joggers, equestrians, and dogs.

Canine compatibility: Dogs permitted off leash, except on stream and bridle trails.

Land status: East Bay Regional Park District.

Nearest town: Oakland.

Fees and permits: No fees or permits required at this entrance; $4.00 parking fees at the main entrance at Canyon Meadow Staging Area.

Schedule: Open daily year-round 5:00 A.M. to 10:00 P.M. unless posted otherwise.

Maps: USGS map: Oakland East, CA. East Bay Regional Park District map of Redwood Regional Park, available online and at most trailheads.

Trail contacts: Redwood Regional Park Ranger Station, 7876 Redwood Road, Oakland, CA 94619; (510) 482-6024.
East Bay Regional Park District Headquarters, 2950 Peralta Oaks Court, P.O. Box 5381, Oakland, CA 94605; (510) 562-PARK; www.ebparks.org/parks/redwood.

Finding the trailhead: From Berkeley or San Francisco: Take Interstate 580 to California Highway 24 (toward Walnut Creek) and then head south on California Highway 13 (the Warren Freeway). Take the Joaquin Miller–Lincoln Avenue exit. Turn left, heading toward the hills (east) on Joaquin Miller Road. Just over a mile, turn left at the signal onto Skyline Boulevard. Follow for about 3 miles to the Skyline Gate parking lot of Redwood Regional Park on the right.

The Ride

Not long ago, thick forests of giant redwoods covered the Oakland Hills. Some of these trees were more than 20 feet in diameter, larger than the great redwoods along the Northern California coast. According to logbooks from the 1820s, these trees served as navigational aids to sea captains sailing into San Francisco Bay. From 16

An open space along the East Ridge of Redwood Regional Park breaks up the forest and woodland trails.

miles away sea captains could line their sights on these massive trees and navigate around a perilous rock between Alcatraz Island and San Francisco. One wonders what happened to the ships when these trees disappeared.

Mills in these hills commercially logged every last redwood between 1840 and 1860; even the stumps were removed for firewood. Regrowth redwoods were later logged to rebuild communities after the devastating 1906 earthquake. Once the trees were gone, ranching followed. Some homesteads and orchards were built along the streams. The hills were used for grazing. Today second- and third-growth redwoods make for a refreshing ride along portions of the West Ridge Trail.

While there are several places to start this ride, Skyline Gate Staging Area gives beginners easy out-and-back options along either the East or West Ridge Trail. For those doing the full loop, it also provides a good warm-up before climbing out of the canyon as opposed to starting at the main park entrance at Canyon Meadows Staging Area off Redwood Road.

The wide and well-traveled West Ridge Trail begins through shaded woods of oaks, eucalyptus, and eventually redwoods. The West Ridge Trail is also part of the Bay Area Ridge Trail. Heed the NO BICYCLING signs on the singletrack trails down the canyon. There are big fines if you do not.

Along the way you pass the newly renovated Chabot Space and Science Center. This popular educational facility for the public and schools dates back to 1883. There is a renowned observatory here, along with planetarium and exhibits. It is worth a visit. Near the center there are a couple of places to drop down into nearby Joaquin Miller Park. There you will find gorgeous singletrack through the redwoods before continuing back on West Ridge Trail.

About 2.5 miles down West Ridge Trail used to be one of the best sections of the loop. It once was a wide singletrack with a technical descent over ruts and slabs of rock. It has since been graded; perhaps it will one day return to some of its over-grown beauty. This was a warm-up for the fast, steep, and rutted drop to the bottom of the canyon. There are some blind corners. Watch the speed; there may be uphill traffic, especially on weekends.

At the bottom of the canyon, you wind along Redwood Creek among the redwoods and ferns. Before you cross the bridge, you can take a short side trip on the paved trail up the canyon to where settlers built small homes in the 1920s. Only the foundation of the church and an orchard remain today. The Old Church was originally an exhibit at the 1936 World's Fair on Treasure Island. Donated to the park after the fair, the church was rebuilt at its current site, where it stood until the mid-fifties when vandals destroyed it.

TIDBIT: Redwood Creek carves the main canyon through the park and flows into San Leandro Creek. It was here that the world-famous rainbow trout was first identified as its own species. The trout in the creek today are descendants of that pure strain of native trout. From these origins the rainbow has been introduced to lakes and streams all over the world. Sorry, anglers; fish in this creek are protected and being carefully researched.

Back on the loop, you cross the bridge over Redwood Creek and continue on a paved bike path through the picnic areas before turning up Canyon Trail. This is the climb up to the East Ridge—you knew this was going to happen. Once on the ridge, the view of the surrounding watershed opens up again. Oaks and eventually eucalyptus line the trail. There is a series of short climbs nearly all the way back to the parking lot at Skyline Gate.

Miles and Directions

0.0 **START** from Skyline Gate Staging Area, heading south on the West Ridge Trail. Trailhead GPS: N 37 49.540, W 122 11.072.

1.2 Veer to the left at the junction with the Moon Gate entrance. **Option:** Go right and up an unmarked singletrack to connect with Joaquin Miller Park.

1.5 Cross the paved road at Chabot Space and Science Center to continue on the West Ridge Trail.

1.7 Cross another paved road and continue on West Ridge Trail.

Redwood Park Loop

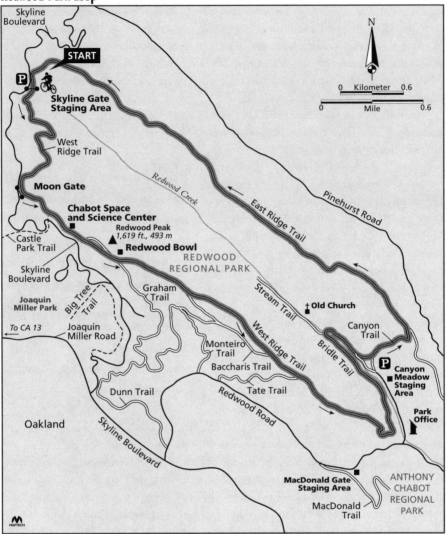

1.8 Reach junction at Redwood Bowl; continue straight on West Ridge Trail.

2.0 Veer left on West Ridge Trail at fork with Graham Trail. **Option:** Turn right onto Graham Trail for a longer, easier side loop through the trees. Turn left onto Dunn Trail, right onto Baccharis Trail, and then right again back onto West Ridge Trail.

2.4 Veer left onto West Ridge Trail at fork with Baccharis Trail.

3.1 Continue straight when the unsigned Baccharis Trail merges from the right. Prepare for a steep and quick descent. Depending on when the trail was last graded, this can be rough. **Shortcut:** Beginners doing an out-and-back on West Ridge Trail should turn around at this point.

4.3 Turn left onto Bridle Trail.

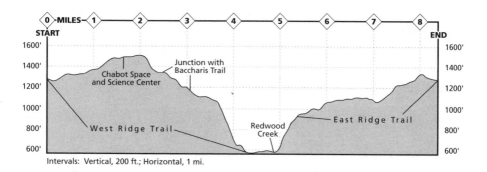

Intervals: Vertical, 200 ft.; Horizontal, 1 mi.

4.8 Turn right onto Stream Trail and then right again over the bridge. Follow the bicycle route signs to Canyon Trail. Pass through Orchard Picnic Area. **Side trip:** Turn left onto Stream Trail before crossing the bridge at the historical marker. This is a short ride up the canyon along Redwood Creek on the wide, paved Stream Trail.

5.1 Turn left onto Canyon Trail and left again past the picnic area. Begin the steep grind up to the ridge.

5.5 Turn left onto East Ridge Trail. Follow this well-marked trail all the way back to Skyline Gate parking lot.

8.4 Finish back at the parking lot.

Ride Information

Local Information

East Bay Regional Park District, 2950 Peralta Oaks Court, P.O. Box 5381, Oakland, CA 94605; (510) 562-PARK; www.ebparks. org/parks/redwood.htm.

Local Events and Attractions

Chabot Space and Science Center, 1000 Skyline Boulevard, Oakland; (510) 336-7300; www.chabotspace.org.

Accommodations

Redwood Regional Park group camping, East Bay Regional Park District reservations (510) 636-1684.

Restaurants and Java Jolts

Flipper's Gourmet Hamburgers, 2060 Mountain Boulevard, Oakland; (510) 339-2082.
Royal Ground Coffee House, 2058 Mountain Boulevard, Oakland; (510) 339-3322.
Fentons Creamery and Restaurant, 4226 Piedmont Avenue, Oakland; (510) 658-7000; www.fentonscreamery.com.

In Addition

Regional Trails

If you explore the Bay Area widely, you will eventually find yourself in a new place on a trail with a recurring and familiar name—the Bay Area Ridge Trail or the Coastal Trail. Granted some trail names are just plain popular and not related, such as wildcat or skyline. However, each of these designated regional trails will be marked with its special signs. Riding on these paths, you feel you are part of a longer journey than you are on for that moment. You are on a journey to be resumed at a later time and place. These trails are joining the ranks of older long-distance masters, such as the Pacific Crest and Appalachian Trails.

Bay Area Ridge Trail

Imagine a 425-mile multiuse trail running along the ridges that encircle San Francisco Bay—a mountain biker's dream. This was also the vision of William Penn Mott Jr. in the 1960s. Today more than half that trail is complete and open to the public. The private, nonprofit Bay Area Ridge Council is diligently working to acquire land, build trails, and maintain this regional trail. In most places the trail connects existing parks and preserved open spaces, often overlapping local, subregional trails. The Bay Area Ridge Trail pops up in nearly a quarter of the featured rides in this guide.

A map of the trail is available on the Web site for the Bay Area Ridge Trail Council: 1007 General Kennedy Avenue, Suite 3, San Francisco, CA 94129; (415) 561–2599; www.ridgetrail.org.

Coastal Trail

Sections of public coastal trails run from Mexico to Canada. It is hoped that one day these trails will connect, forming a continuous path along the Pacific Ocean. However, like the Appalachian Trail, this will take decades to complete. For now each state is doing its part. California kick-started the California Coastal Trail in 1991, and a coalition is currently working on the plan. The California Coastal Conservancy is the lead agency on this daunting project. Portions of the Coastal Trail exist in the North Bay and the peninsula, although not all segments allow mountain bikes. In Marin, San Francisco, and San Mateo Counties, the Coastal Trail and the Bay Area Ridge Trail share the same track; www.californiacoastaltrail.org.

San Francisco Bay Trail

This regional trail will also one day encircle San Francisco and San Pablo Bays; but this path will more closely follow the shoreline. So far, 240 miles of trail are completed. Plans call for 400 miles of recreational corridor for bikers, joggers, hikers, skaters, strollers, anglers, and more. The loop includes multiuse paved paths, dirt trails, bike lanes, sidewalks, and designated bike routes on city streets. It crosses a diverse landscape from urban waterfronts to remote wildlife refuges. Some of these remote areas are great trails for beginners and children.

San Francisco Bay Trails Project is a private nonprofit project administered by the Association of Bay Area Governments, 101 Eighth Street, Oakland, CA 94607; (510) 464–7900; www.baytrail.abag.ca.gov.

15 Joaquin Miller Park

This is the best singletrack in the East Bay. Ride through dense redwood groves in Oakland's Joaquin Miller Park. Although the park is less than a square mile, there are enough trails to wind around for several miles and a couple of hours. There are too many short trails and options to spell out mileage directions for a specific route. Bring the map, and have fun exploring. Trails range from easy, smooth fire trails to technical singletracks with roots, rocks, and drops. Connect these trails with loops in Redwood Regional Park or Lake Chabot for a longer ride.

Start: From the parking lot at the entrance to Joaquin Miller Park, 3590 Sanborn Drive, Oakland.

Length: Some loops can add up to 7 to 10 miles.

Approximate riding time: 30 minutes to 2 hours (as long as you want).

Difficulty: The dirt roads along the contour offer easy rides for beginners. Much of the singletrack requires intermediate to advanced technical skills. Some of the climbs are strenuous, albeit short.

Trail surface: Dirt singletrack and dirt roads.

Terrain: Dense redwood canyon, sometimes steep.

Seasons: Year-round. Cool riding when it is hot everywhere else; some trails are closed in winter.

Other trail users: Hikers, joggers, equestrians, and sometimes groups of children on field trips (usually on fire roads).

Canine compatibility: Leashed dogs permitted.

Land status: Oakland City Park.

Nearest town: Oakland.

Fees and permits: No fees or permits required.

Schedule: Open year-round from dawn until dusk. (This is still Oakland; you do not want to be out here at night.) Big Trees and Upper Palos Colorados Trails are closed from November 15 to April 15.

Maps: USGS map: Oakland East, CA. City of Oakland, Joaquin Miller Park trail map, available at the ranger station—if you are lucky.

Trail contact: Joaquin Miller Park Ranger Station, 3590 Sanborn Drive, Oakland, CA 94602; trail conditions (510) 482-7857; ranger station (510) 482-7888; www.oaklandnet.com/parks/facilities/parks_joaquin_miller.asp.

Finding the trailhead: From San Francisco or Berkeley: Take Interstate 580 to California Highway 24 (toward Walnut Creek) and then head south on California Highway 13 (the Warren Freeway). Take the Joaquin Miller-Lincoln Avenue exit. Turn left, and head toward the hills (east) on Joaquin Miller Road. Turn left into the main park entrance on Sanborn Drive. Parking is on the left, and the trails begin directly on the right.

Take a break among the redwoods on the Sinawik Loop. ▶

Joaquin Miller Park

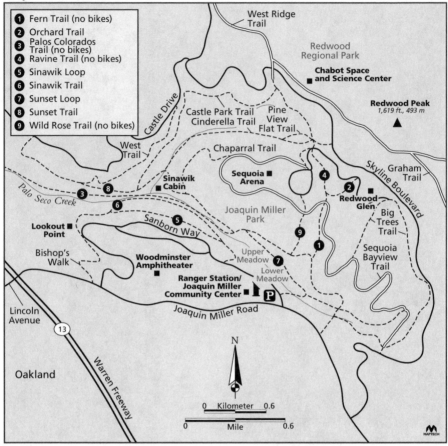

Legend:
1. Fern Trail (no bikes)
2. Orchard Trail
3. Palos Colorados Trail (no bikes)
4. Ravine Trail (no bikes)
5. Sinawik Loop
6. Sinawik Trail
7. Sunset Loop
8. Sunset Trail
9. Wild Rose Trail (no bikes)

West Ridge Trail

Redwood Regional Park

Chabot Space and Science Center

Redwood Peak
1,619 ft., 493 m

Castle Drive

Castle Park Trail
Cinderella Trail

Pine View Flat Trail

West Trail

Chaparral Trail

Skyline Boulevard

Graham Trail

Sinawik Cabin

Sequoia Arena

Redwood Glen

Palo Seco Creek

Big Trees Trail

Sanborn Way

Joaquin Miller Park

Sequoia Bayview Trail

Lookout Point

Bishop's Walk

Woodminster Amphitheater

Upper Meadow

Lower Meadow

Ranger Station/ Joaquin Miller Community Center

Lincoln Avenue

13

Oakland

Warren Freeway

Joaquin Miller Road

N

0   Kilometer   0.6
0   Mile   0.6

MAPTECH

The Ride

This is not your typical urban park. Joaquin Miller Park is 425 acres of lush forest owned and operated by the city of Oakland. Once on the trail, it is hard to believe you are in a city of 2.4 million people. The park is sandwiched between the dense urban landscape on the west and Redwood Regional Park on the east. This may well be the only urban redwood forest in existence. Most of the park's native coast redwoods (*Sequoia sempervirens*) are second or third growth. While the redwoods are the most prominent, other native trees and shrubs include manzanita, madrone, huckleberry, bay laurel, Pacific ninebark, golden chinquapin oak, and coast live oak. The dense cover makes for a cool ride in summer; although the frequent East Bay fog keeps the summer temperatures down anyway.

The park gets its name from the legendary "Poet of the Sierras" and avid arborist Joaquin Miller (1841–1913). Miller bought seventy barren acres in the hills above the City of Oaks in 1886. Here he built his home and planted thousands of trees.

His home, the Abbey, is still standing and has become a historical landmark, along with monuments he built in honor of fellow poets Robert and Elizabeth Barrett Browning, explorer John Fremont, and Moses. These are scattered in the west end of the park along Sanborn Drive. After Miller's death the city of Oakland purchased most of his estate. In 1928 the Save the Redwood League purchased surrounding land to ward off intense development pressures and donated it to the city.

For those who live near acres of open space with no legal access to singletrack trails, it is impressive that this little park has managed to accommodate mountain bikers where others have failed. This is truly a testament to the Bicycle Trails Council of the East Bay (BTCEB). Maintaining bike access in the park is an ongoing effort. Consider joining the council and volunteering to help with trail maintenance projects. At the very least use your best trail manners; stay on designated trails and be courteous to all users. Continued access to these trails depends on it. The BTCEB coordinates a bike patrol program with the Oakland police. Its goal is to educate, aid, and inform trail users of the rules.

Trying to follow mileage directions through this park would drive you crazy— you would have to stop every few minutes to check directions. The trails are well marked, so bring a map and explore. The park is small enough that if you get lost, oh, well; it will be an adventure. You won't go too far before you hit a paved road. Just be sure to stay off trails prohibited to bikes, which include any unofficial trail.

No bikes are allowed on Wild Rose Trail, Fern Ravine Trail, and Palos Colorados Trail between Sinawik Cabin and Joaquin Miller Court (downstream from the cabin). In addition, Big Trees and Upper Palos Colorados Trails are closed to bikes in winter (typically November 15 to April 15). Keep an eye out for signs on seasonal trail closures.

There are several places to start, but the easiest parking is at the main entrance near the Joaquin Miller Community Center. The best singletrack trails are Big Trees Trail, Cinderella Trail, and Sinawik Trail and Loop. The latter is a beautifully lush ride through the redwoods along Palo Seco Creek. The most technical downhill is on the lower end of Castle Park Trail. Watch for logs, roots, and rocks.

Miles and Directions

Suggested Route

Start at the main park entrance and head counterclockwise to the perimeter portion of Big Trees Trail. Follow the paved road past the Sequoia Staging Area and up to the top of Castle Park Trail. Enjoy the technical ride down Castle Park Trail. At the bottom turn left onto Sunset Trail and ride back toward the park entrance. Combine this with an inner loop: Continue counterclockwise on Sunset Trail and Loop, veering left on the uphill. At Sequoia Bayview Trail turn left and traverse the hillside. Once past the Sequoia Staging Area, turn left down Cinderella Trail. At the bottom turn left onto Sunset Trail, and then quickly drop to the Sinawik Trail. Ride down one side of Palo Seco Creek and up the other side on Sinawik Loop. Return back on Sunset Trail.

Options

Combine a loop or two in Joaquin Miller Park with the Redwood Park Loop. Suggested loop: Enter Joaquin Miller Park from the West Ridge Trail, crossing Skyline Boulevard above the Chabot Space and Science Center and above the Castle Park Trailhead. Take a perimeter route to Big Trees Trail; connect with the southern end of Sunset Trail near Skyline Boulevard. Ride down to Sinawik Trail and Loop along the creek. Return up Sunset Trail to Sequoia Bayview Trail. Pass the Sequoia Horse Arena and Staging Area; cross Skyline Boulevard to connect back to West Ridge Trail.

Ride Information

Local Information

City of Oakland, Office of Parks and Recreation, 1520 Lakeside Drive, Oakland, CA 94612; general information and reservations (510) 238-3187; security (510) 482-7888; www.oaklandnet.com/parks/facilities/parks_joaquin_miller.asp.

City of Oakland Visitor Information, City Hall, One Frank H. Ogawa Plaza, Oakland, CA 94612; (510) 444-2489; www.oakland net.com.

Local Events and Attractions

Chabot Space and Science Center, 1000 Skyline Boulevard, Oakland; (510) 336-7300; www.chabotspace.org.

Woodminster Theater: Summer Musicals: summer series of outdoor American musicals, 3300 Joaquin Miller Park; (510) 531-9597; www.woodminster.com/.

Restaurants and Java Jolts

Flipper's Gourmet Hamburgers, 2060 Mountain Boulevard, Oakland; (510) 339-2082.

Royal Ground Coffee House, 2058 Mountain Boulevard, Oakland; (510) 339-3322.

Fentons Creamery and Restaurant, 4226 Piedmont Avenue, Oakland; (510) 658-7000; www.fentonscreamery.com.

16 Lake Chabot Loop

This is a pleasant ride around Lake Chabot and the upper reaches of Grass Valley Creek. The final climb to the ridge offers a classic view of the bay before a swift descent back to the lake. While the picnic area and marina are busy on weekends, you will escape the crowd as you ride up the canyon and into the hills. Ability will dictate how far you go. This is a good place for children and beginners. Strong riders can connect with Redwood Park Loop for some distance and climbs that are more strenuous.

Start: From Lake Chabot Marina, Castro Valley.
Distance: 13.7-mile loop.
Approximate riding time: 1.5 to 2 hours.
Difficulty: Moderate; some challenging hills; nontechnical except for one steep descent that is not advisable for beginners.
Trail surface: 75 percent dirt road and 25 percent paved path.
Terrain: Popular fishing lake, gentle canyon with shade along the creek, grassy pastureland, chaparral and eucalyptus groves along the canyon to the ridge.
Seasons: Year-round but best in spring and fall. Can be hot in summer; trails along Grass Valley Creek are muddy in winter.
Other trail users: Hikers, anglers, strollers, equestrians, and cattle.
Canine compatibility: Leashed dogs permitted on trail but not allowed in lake.

Land status: East Bay Regional Park District.
Nearest town: Castro Valley.
Fees and permits: $4.00 fee for parking and $1.00 fee for dogs at the marina entrance; plenty of street parking outside the entrance.
Schedule: Open daily 7:00 A.M. to 10:00 P.M.
Maps: USGS maps: Hayward, Oakland East; Las Trampas Ridge, CA.
East Bay Regional Park District map, Anthony Chabot and Lake Chabot Regional Parks, available online and at the entrance.
Trail contact: Anthony Chabot and Lake Chabot Regional Park Ranger Station, Castro Valley; (510) 639-4751.
East Bay Regional Park District Headquarters, 2950 Peralta Oaks Court, P.O. Box 5381, Oakland, CA 94605; (510) 562-PARK; www.ebparks.org/parks/anchabot.htm.

Finding the trailhead: Marina entrance from San Leandro: Exit Interstate 580 at Fairmont Drive. Go east (uphill) on Fairmont Drive, which becomes Lake Chabot Road. The marina entrance is on the left at the bottom of the hill, about 2 miles from the freeway. Drive or ride past the marina entry kiosk into the parking lot. The ride (and odometer readings!) begins at the information board near the first service gate on the right. There are restrooms and water at marina. There is no other water once you are on the trail.

    Grass Valley Road entrance from Oakland: This quiet entrance misses the congestion of the marina. For riders wishing to bypass the paved section, this is a great place to start, especially if you want to head north toward Redwood Regional Park. Take the Golf Links exit from I-580. Head east up the hill on Golf Links Road past the entrance to the Oakland Zoo. Just past 1.5 miles, veer left onto Grass Valley Road. The parking lot is on the right where the road bends to the left becoming Skyline Boulevard. To get to the trailhead from the parking area, go around the service gate and turn left to access Goldenrod Trail. There is no restroom here. A drinking fountain is located near a picnic table on Goldenrod Trail. Trailhead GPS: N 37 45.16, W122 07.02.

    There are several additional places to access this loop. Check the park's Web site for a map of other entry points.

The upper end of Lake Chabot.

The Ride

Like much of the East Bay hills, this area once supplied Native Americans with plenty of acorns and other staples for their diet. Imagine a gentle valley without the lake. The early settlers later developed the northern portion of this ride into ranches. The southern portion was divvied up as part of the Spanish and Mexican land grants. Cattle grazed much of the land, as they still do today.

The park and lake name comes from Anthony Chabot, a hydraulic engineer and philanthropist who built the earth-fill dam that created Lake Chabot in 1875. At the time, this became a primary water supply for the East Bay. The surrounding land gradually became preserved watershed. By 1928 ownership evolved into the East Bay Municipal Utility District, which now leases the land to the park district. Today Lake Chabot is a reserve water supply. While there is no swimming allowed in the lake, there is plenty of boating and fishing. Word has it the lake is well stocked with trout, catfish, bass, bluegill, and crappie. Stop into the snack and bait shop at the marina to find out what's biting.

This bike loop begins at the popular Lake Chabot Marina and Picnic Area. The easiest way around the lake is clockwise. The deciding question is: Do you want to ride *up* Live Oaks Trail or *down* it? The 3-plus miles of paved path along the lake can be crowded on weekends. This part of the ride is great for kids, especially those who like to fish.

Just past the dam, the trail becomes dirt and remains a well-maintained fire road throughout the park. The oaks around the lake provide welcome shade in summer. As the trail leaves the lake, it passes through low chaparral. The disquieting gunshots you may hear echoing in the distance are from the Marksmanship Range across the lake. This is operated by the Chabot Gun Club.

Just beyond the Grass Valley Road entry point, the trail drops near Grass Valley Creek for a cooler ride up the canyon. At the turnaround point you cross over the creek and join a section of the Bay Area Ridge Trail and Skyline National Recreation Trail. Those seeking a longer and more strenuous ride can continue up Mac-Donald Trail. This connects to Redwood Regional Park. Otherwise, this loop takes you back through cattle pastures along the other side of Grass Valley Creek. The seriously pockmarked trail can be a muddy mess in winter or a hard-tail discomfort when it dries.

At the Stone Bridge the trail leaves the creek and gently climbs toward the ridge. You will pass through a eucalyptus forest that was planted in 1910 by the People's Water Company of Oakland. These trees spread rapidly, taking over the native landscape. While this loop sticks to the main fire road, you will pass several side trails begging to be explored. If you venture far, bring a map. There are stories of people getting lost as the sun sets.

Once on the ridge, the trees give way to grassland and an impressive view of more East Bay hills and part of San Francisco Bay. Leaving the Bay Area Ridge Trail, this loop quickly drops back down to Lake Chabot. Before returning to the paved path around the lake, you cross a bridge barely wide enough for your handlebars. There is a hike-a-bike at the end up some steep stairs. From there it is an easy cruise back to the marina, dogging increasing traffic along the way. The biggest obstacles on this ride will be the traffic along the lake.

Miles and Directions

0.0 START from the marina parking lot. Just past the entry kiosk, there is a service gate on the right with an information board and map. Odometer readings begin here. This is next to a small bridge you will cross at the end of the ride. Begin the ride by heading left on West Shore Trail. Ride through the picnic area and past the marina to ride clockwise around the lake. Stay on the main paved path until just past the dam. Ignore any side trails along the way. Trailhead GPS: N37 42.578, W122 06.085.

1.7 Halfway up the hill past the dam, turn right onto the dirt Bass Cove Trail. The sign is small and easy to miss. (If you come to the outhouse, you have gone too far.) Almost immediately, you will cross a small paved path to an overlook; continue straight. Ignore unmarked side trails while you parallel the lake.

Lake Chabot Loop

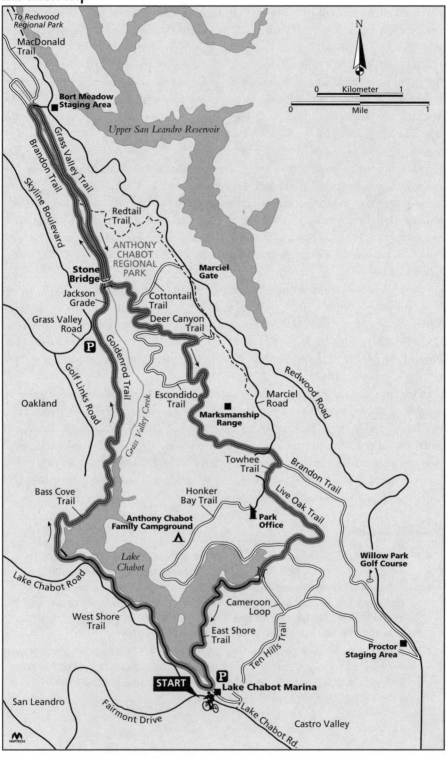

To Redwood Regional Park

MacDonald Trail

Bort Meadow Staging Area

Upper San Leandro Reservoir

N

Kilometer
0   1

Mile
0   1

Grass Valley Trail

Brandon Trail

Skyline Boulevard

Redtail Trail

ANTHONY CHABOT REGIONAL PARK

Marciel Gate

Stone Bridge

Jackson Grade

Cottontail Trail

Grass Valley Road

Deer Canyon Trail

Grass Valley Road

P

Goldenrod Trail

Golf Links Road

Oakland

Grass Valley Creek

Escondido Trail

Marciel Road

Redwood Road

Marksmanship Range

Towhee Trail

Brandon Trail

Bass Cove Trail

Honker Bay Trail

Live Oak Trail

Anthony Chabot Family Campground

Park Office

Willow Park Golf Course

Lake Chabot

Lake Chabot Road

West Shore Trail

Cameroon Loop

East Shore Trail

Ten Hills Trail

Proctor Staging Area

START

P

Lake Chabot Marina

San Leandro

Fairmont Drive

Lake Chabot Rd.

Castro Valley

MAPTECH

2.8   Continue straight onto Goldenrod Trail where Bass Cove Trail turns right and becomes restricted to bikes. Stay on Goldenrod Trail, ignoring all other side trails. There is a very short section of pavement along here.

4.1   A couple of trails on the left lead to the Grass Valley Road parking lot. Continue straight ahead. There is a drinking fountain near the lone picnic table.

4.2   Veer right and downhill on the main trail, ignoring the dirt trail going uphill along Skyline Boulevard.

4.3   Turn right down Jackson Grade.

4.6   Continue straight ahead on Brandon Trail at the Stone Bridge. **Shortcut:** If you want to cut off a couple of miles, turn right. Cross the bridge and head uphill on Brandon Trail.

5.9   Turn right and cross the gravel path over the creek culvert. Past the creek, make a sharp right onto Grass Valley Trail. Follow this trail back to the Stone Bridge. **Option:** A popular alternative off the Grass Valley Trail is to climb up Redtail Trail at Mile 6.9. Follow Redtail Trail until it connects with Brandon Trail at Marciel Road. **Option to Connect with Redwood Regional Park:** For a longer and more strenuous ride, follow the signs at the beginning of Grass Valley Trail uphill to MacDonald Trail. This is the connector trail to Redwood Regional Park. It is about 2.7 miles to MacDonald Staging Area on Redwood Road. From there turn right and ride the road to the Redwood Gate entrance to Redwood Regional Park.

7.4   At the Stone Bridge take a left turn up Brandon Trail. This loop follows the main Brandon Trail for nearly 4 miles and skips some trails along the way. If you have a map and the time, check out Cottontail, Escondido, and Loggers Loop Trails.

10.5   Cross the paved Marciel Road that leads to the campground and park office. Continue straight ahead on Brandon Trail.

10.7   At the bench make a sharp right turn down the unsigned Towhee Trail fire road. A narrower Towhee Trail is signed going uphill here and is off-limits to bikes.

11.0   Turn left onto Live Oak Trail for a steep descent. **Side trip:** Continue straight onto the paved road and cruise through the campground. There is drinking fountain near the entry kiosk.

11.8   Turn left onto Cameron Loop Trail. You will cross a narrow bridge and hike your bike up about twenty steps. Turn right at the top of the steps onto East Shore Trail.

12.1   At the fork continue straight on East Shore Trail. Pass through the gate and onto the paved path once again. When you get to the picnic area, continue straight on the path until you cross the bridge to the information board and the parking lot where you began.

13.7   Arrive back at the parking lot.

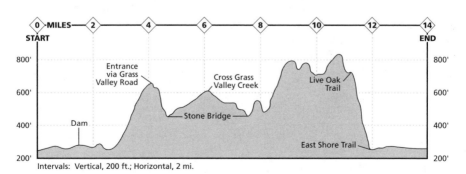

Intervals: Vertical, 200 ft.; Horizontal, 2 mi.

Sailing down Towhee Trail.

Ride Information

Local Information

East Bay Regional Park District, 2950 Peralta Oaks Court, P.O. Box 5381, Oakland, CA 94605; (510) 562-PARK; www.ebparks.org/parks/.
San Leandro Chamber of Commerce, 262 Davis Street, San Leandro, CA 94577; (510) 351-1481; www.sanleandrochamber.com.

Local Events and Attractions

Lake Chabot Marina, boat rentals and fishing; Lake Chabot Drive Road, Castro Valley; (510) 582-2198; www.ebparks.org/dropdown/boating.htm#CHABOT.

Accommodations

Anthony Chabot Campground, 9999 Redwood Road, Castro Valley; reservations (510) 562-2267.

Restaurants and Java Jolts

La Imperial (super burrito!), 948 C Street, Hayward; (510) 537-6227.
Everybody's Bagel, 1099 MacArthur Boulevard, San Leandro; (510) 430-8700.

17 Briones Loop

A ridge runs through the steep, grass-covered hills and wooded canyons of Briones Regional Park. This loop offers a peripheral view of both sides of the ridge. Wide dirt roads take you up one side of the park, down the other, and back up again. There are some killer climbs, but they are rather short-lived. The payoff is long downhill runs. This is a good place to build strength. There are plenty more trails to come back and explore once you get the lay of the land.

Start: From the trailhead to Abrigo Valley Trail near the Bear Creek Staging Area.

Distance: 13.3-mile loop.

Approximate riding time: 2 to 2.5 hours.

Difficulty: Difficult; challenging climbs; moderately technical on the steep inclines—up and down—otherwise nontechnical dirt roads.

Trail surface: Wide dirt road, occasionally fading to dual track.

Terrain: Hilly and steep pastureland, mixed woodlands in the canyons.

Seasons: Wildflowers make this best in spring; fall is nice and summer is hot. Avoid when there's any possibility of mud; things dry slowly out here.

Other trail users: Hikers, equestrians, and cattle.

Canine compatibility: Leashed dogs permitted. Unleashed dogs permitted in undeveloped areas provided they're under control at all times.

Land status: East Bay Regional Park District.

Nearest town: Orinda/Lafayette.

Fees and permits: $4.00 fee for parking and $1.00 fee for dogs at entrance, when kiosk attended.

Schedule: Open daily 8:00 A.M. to sunset.

Maps: USGS maps: Briones, CA; Walnut Creek, CA.

East Bay Regional Park District map of Briones Regional Park, available online and usually at the park entrance.

Trail contacts: Briones Regional Park Ranger Station, 5363 Alhambra Valley Road, Martinez, CA 94553; (925) 370-3020.

East Bay Regional Park District Headquarters, 2950 Peralta Oaks Court, P.O. Box 5381, Oakland, CA 94605; (510) 562-PARK; www.ebparks.org/parks/briones.htm.

Finding the trailhead: From Orinda: From California Highway 24 take the Orinda exit and head north along Camino Pablo; this becomes San Pablo Dam Road. About 2.2 miles from the freeway, turn right onto Bear Creek Road. Continue 6.8 miles and turn right into the Briones Regional Park–Bear Creek Staging Area entrance. Just past the entry kiosk, turn left into the Oak Grove parking area, where there are restrooms and water. The Abrigo Valley Trail begins immediately on the right at the service gate.

The Ride

During the 1800s Briones Regional Park was a collection of land grant farms and ranches. The park's name comes from Felipe Briones, the original Spanish land grant owner in the area. He built his home near today's Bear Creek entrance, cultivated

Rolling through a pasture...

the land, and raised cattle. On the other side of the hill, in the Alhambra Valley, farmers planted orchards and vineyards in the 1850s and 1860s. Some of the old fruit
trees are still there. In 1906 People's Water Company began purchasing watershed
land for the rapidly growing East Bay communities. The land became an open-space
park in 1957. Today the park encompasses nearly 6,000 acres. Cattle still graze on
these grasslands during winter and spring.

This is one of the lesser traveled parks in the East Bay Regional Park system. On
a bike you can quickly get up to the ridge and away from it all. Most of the time
the busy world below is out of sight and easily forgotten. Nearly all the bike trails
are wide dirt roads, occasionally fading to dual track. The cattle leave their mark in
winter and spring—deep hoof tracks and thrashed trail.

Briones Regional Park has been the site of several state championship races.
Since the race route changed each time, there is no single racecourse to offer. This
reflects the network of trails and many different ways to experience this park. This
loop encircles much of the park and offers pieces from each race. Whichever way
you go, this is a good place to build strength and endurance.

The ride begins up the Abrigo Valley Trail, passing through canyons of oak and
laurel. The climb to the grass-covered ridge is steady. In spring, wildflowers make a
show throughout the hills. Near the top, views open up of Mount Tamalpais to the

west and the Carquinez Strait to the north. In the middle of Suisun Bay sits a flotilla of old warships—the Navy's Mothball Fleet. The view of Mount Diablo to the southeast is one that will be revisited more closely as you ride out of the Alhambra Valley.

From the ridge it is a fun drop to the backside through mixed woodlands of oak, toyon, and pine; all reflected in the trail names. Keep an eye out for roaming cattle—you do not want to startle one on a blind corner. The ride calms down along Orchard Trail to the Alhambra Creek Staging Area and park entrance. From there it is another climb back to the ridge. Views of Mount Diablo follow you up the hill. Most of the climb is in the shade of the canyon woodlands. The climb is not constant; there are respites of downhill and areas where you simply following the contours of the hillside. There are also some killer climbs—Ass Kicker 1 and 2. Okay, there could be better names, but bikers call it as it is.

TIDBIT: The military calls this the MARAD Reserve Fleet; others refer to it as the Mothball Fleet. From the top of Briones Ridge, it looks like a fleet of warships lined up in a bathtub. If the need arises, 20 to 120 days are all it should take to activate these ships. In the 1950s there were more than 500 tankers, cargo ships, landing vessels, tugs, and barges lined up down there. Now there are fewer than a hundred.

Once on the ridge you can catch your breath under the shade of the oaks before the payoff: the roller-coaster ride down Crescent Ridge and Yerba Buena Trails. Again, check your speed and keep an eye out for other trail users.

For a shorter option that cuts the climbing in half (missing AK 1 and 2), just skip the northeastern side of the park: Stay on Briones Crest Trail (skipping the downhill onto Lagoon Trail) and follow it all the way around to Crescent Ridge Trail, picking up the last part of the featured ride.

For those seeking an epic ride, connect with the Briones–to–Mount Diablo Trail. You can ride all the way to Shell Ridge and Mount Diablo for a real death march.

Miles and Directions

0.0 **START** from the trailhead to Abrigo Valley Trail at the Oak Grove parking lot near the entrance kiosk. Trailhead GPS: N 37 55 38.4, W 122 09 29.2.

0.9 Veer left on Abrigo Valley Trail at the fork with Mott Peak Trail.

1.9 Turn right onto the Briones Crest Trail.

2.1 Turn left onto Lagoon Trail. The trail is covered in grass and loses the feel of a fire road. Here you can enjoy a nice view of the bay and the Mothball Fleet. **Option:** For a shorter loop and half the climbing, continue straight on Briones Crest Trail all the way to Crescent Ridge Trail. Turn right onto Crescent Ridge Trail, picking up directions from the longer loop at Mile 10.3.

2.5 Veer right at the unsigned fork.

3.3 Turn left onto Toyon Canyon Trail.

Briones Loop

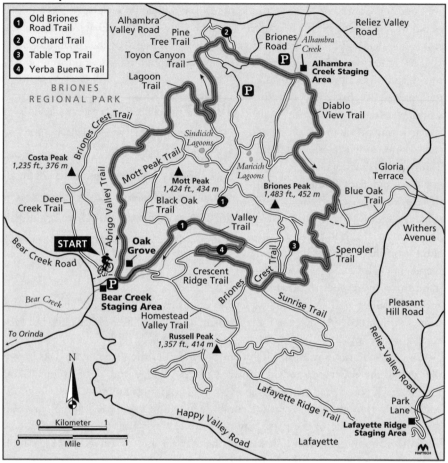

Map legend:
1. Old Briones Road Trail
2. Orchard Trail
3. Table Top Trail
4. Yerba Buena Trail

BRIONES REGIONAL PARK

Alhambra Valley Road
Pine Tree Trail
Toyon Canyon Trail
Lagoon Trail
Briones Road
Alhambra Creek
Reliez Valley Road
Alhambra Creek Staging Area
Diablo View Trail

Briones Crest Trail
Costa Peak 1,235 ft., 376 m
Deer Creek Trail
Abrigo Valley Trail
Mott Peak Trail
Sindicich Lagoons
Maricich Lagoons
Mott Peak 1,424 ft., 434 m
Black Oak Trail
Valley Trail
Briones Peak 1,483 ft., 452 m
Gloria Terrace
Blue Oak Trail
Withers Avenue

START
Bear Creek Road
Oak Grove
Bear Creek
Bear Creek Staging Area
Homestead Valley Trail
Crescent Ridge Trail
Briones Crest Trail
Sunrise Trail
Spengler Trail
Pleasant Hill Road

To Orinda
Russell Peak 1,357 ft., 414 m
Lafayette Ridge Trail
Happy Valley Road
Reliez Valley Road
Park Lane
Lafayette Ridge Staging Area
Lafayette

N

0 Kilometer 1
0 Mile 1

4.3 Turn left onto Pine Tree Trail.

4.4 Turn right onto Orchard Trail near the pond and picnic table. You will pass through a gate at mile 4.7.

4.8 Veer right on the main fire road where a road merges from the left.

5.0 Cross the paved Briones Road, continuing on Orchard Trail. The paved road leads to another parking lot and entrance to the park. **Shortcut:** Turn right onto the pavement and ride up to the parking lot. Pick up Old Briones Road Trail, following it over the hill and back to the start. The ride back to the start from here is about 3.5 miles.

5.6 Turn left onto the packed gravel road. There is a picnic area and outhouse here. Up ahead is the Alhambra Creek Staging Area, an alternative parking lot and entrance to the park. There is water here to top off your hydration pack for the ride back. Continue uphill past the parking area on Diablo View Trail. Ignore all side trails along the way, staying on Diablo View Trail until Spengler Trail.

5.9 Veer left to stay on Diablo View Trail (unsigned here), leaving the gravel fire road.

6.7 Turn left at the T intersection onto Spengler Trail. Stay on Spengler until Mile 8.2 when it ends at Table Top Trail. There are several dead-end side trails over the next 3 miles. The Park Service recently marked these. The new markers and the following odometer readings will help keep you on course.

7.1 Veer right to stay on Spengler Trail.

7.4 Veer right, and right again, where Blue Oak Trail comes in from the left.

7.6 Veer left; the right takes you to a dead end.

7.9 Continue straight *up* Spengler Trail for Ass Kicker 1. There is a tempting legal singletrack on the left, but that takes you out of the park.

8.2 Turn left at the T intersection with Table Top Trail, continuing on Spengler Trail. **Option:** Turn right up Table Top Trail for a steady 0.4-mile grind to Briones Crest Trail. The reward is a great panoramic view on the ridgetop. Continue down the other side of the ridge on Table Top Trail. At the end, turn right to Briones Crest Trail. Pick up directions below at Mile 9.9.

8.7 Veer right where the trail forks to a gate down to the left. Spengler Trail is grassy here and less worn. The trail weaves through a cool canyon with madrone, laurel, and a few ferns. Up ahead is Ass Kicker 2. Several slick rocks bring some interest to the trail.

9.5 Turn right to climb uphill at the unsigned junction.

9.8 Turn left at the T intersection with Table Top Trail. Go through the gate up ahead.

9.9 Continue straight as the trail becomes Briones Crest Trail.

10.1 Veer right at the junction with Sunrise Trail to continue on Briones Crest Trail. The sign may still refer to Sunrise Trail as NO NAME TRAIL. Do not be confused; you are not taking the trail anyway.

10.3 Turn right onto Crescent Ridge Trail, passing through a gate. This is a great downhill roller coaster.

11.0 Turn right onto Yerba Buena Trail and ride through the meadow.

11.6 Turn left onto Valley Trail.

12.1 Turn left onto wider Old Briones Road Trail, following this all the way back to the parking lot. Ignore Homestead Valley Trail on the left along the way. Old Briones Road Trail becomes paved. Veer right past the first parking lot on the left.

13.3 Arrive back at the parking lot where you began.

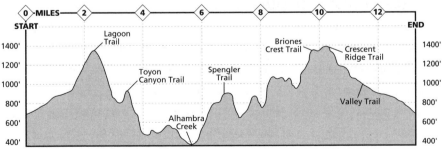

Intervals: Vertical, 200 ft.; Horizontal, 2 mi.

Savor the oak-studded hillsides.

Ride Information

Local Information

East Bay Regional Park District, 2950 Peralta Oaks Court, P.O. Box 5381, Oakland, CA 94605; (510) 562-PARK; www.ebparks.org/parks/briones.htm.

Restaurants and Java Jolts

Bo's Barbecue & Catering, 3422 Mount Diablo Boulevard, Lafayette; (925) 934-4738. **Starbucks,** 1 Camino Sobrante #9, Orinda; (925) 253-0447.

BRIONES-TO-MOUNT DIABLO TRAIL This 9.2-mile multiuse trail begins (or ends) at the Lafayette Ridge Staging Area at the southeast corner of Briones Regional Park. On the way to Mount Diablo State Park, it connects to several regional trails and serves as a community bikeway for Walnut Creek. This paved and unpaved path is a key link for epic bike rides between the open-space preserves. From Briones Regional Park the trail passes over Acalanes Ridge in the Walnut Creek Open Space and into Larkey Park in Walnut Creek. From there it shares right-of-way with the Contra Costa Canal Trail, passes Heather Farms Park, and heads into Shell Ridge Open Space. The trail continues into Diablo Foothills Regional Park and up into Mount Diablo State Park at Pine Ridge. The trail is open 5:00 A.M. to 10:00 P.M. unless posted otherwise.

18 Black Diamond Mines Loop

You do not need to go far to taste the Wild West. Warm up with a gradual climb over the grassy hillside above the old abandoned Black Diamond Mine. Enjoy 2 miles of roller-coaster downhill before cruising up the floor of the lazy canyon. Pass remnants of early mines and ranching along the way. Near the end face a steep (but not so long) climb back to the ridge. Bring a flashlight and a sense of adventure for exploring an old mine tunnel. Those seeking a longer and more challenging ride can add an adjoining loop.

Start: From the trailhead and parking lot at the end of Somersville Road.
Distance: 6.6-mile loop.
Approximate riding time: 1 hour.
Difficulty: Moderate; nontechnical, although some steep descents and one strenuous climb.
Trail surface: Dirt road.
Terrain: Grass-covered hills, roller-coaster ridge, steep canyon out of a gentle valley.
Seasons: Best in spring and fall. Hot and dry in summer; muddy, as in unridable, in winter.
Other trail users: Hikers, equestrians, and cattle.
Canine compatibility: Leashed dogs permitted; unleashed dogs okay in the open areas.
Land status: East Bay Regional Park District.

Nearest town: Antioch.
Fees and permits: $4.00 parking and $1.00 dog fee when kiosk attended, usually only on weekends.
Schedule: Open daily 8:00 A.M. to dusk.
Maps: USGS maps: Antioch South, CA; Clayton, CA.
East Bay Regional Park District map, available at the park and online.
Trail contacts: Black Diamond Mines Regional Preserve Park Office, 5175 Somersville Road, Antioch, CA 94509; (925) 757-2620.
East Bay Regional Park District Headquarters, 2950 Peralta Oaks Court, P.O. Box 5381, Oakland, CA 94605; (510) 562-PARK; www.ebparks.org/parks/black.

Finding the trailhead: From Oakland: Take Interstate 80 north to California Highway 4 and head east. (Or take California Highway 24 east to Interstate 680 north. Take California Highway 242 to CA 4 east.) Follow CA 4 to the Somersville Road South exit in Antioch. Turn right (south) and follow Somersville Road (away from the river) to the end. The first parking lot is just past the entry kiosk to the Black Diamond Mine Preserve. The park office and an interpretive center are here. If you are chomping at the bit to get on your bike, you can park here and ride Railroad Bed Trail up to the next parking lot. Otherwise, drive nearly a mile to the last parking lot and trailhead. Water and an outhouse are at the parking lot.

The Ride

As you drive up the canyon to the Black Diamond Mine Preserve, you enter a pastoral world and step back in time. This is an area with rich and intense history. For thousands of years this area was the backcountry for Miwok Indians. But, like in much of California, this way of life disappeared with the arrival of the Spanish, Mexican, and

The Black Diamond Mines Loop feels like a backdrop for a Western movie.

American settlers in 1772. Cattle ranching and nonnative grasses took over. Change came again when black diamond (coal) was discovered in these hills.

As you ride these quiet trails today, it is hard to imagine five coal-mining towns in the Black Diamond area. Not even a ghost town remains. From the 1850s to the early 1900s, this was California's largest coal-mining region. Four million tons of coal were dug out and hauled away. Up to 900 miners from all over the world worked hundreds of miles of underground tunnels. The coal mines eventually closed down as sources of better-grade ore were found.

From the 1920s to the late 1940s, sand mining took over near the deserted town-sites of Somersville and Nortonville. More than 1.8 million tons of sand was mined for glassmaking and the casting of steel. When sand mining died out in the 1940s, cattle ranching returned.

This is a great intermediate ride that can be expanded for stronger riders. All bike trails in the preserve are smooth, hard-packed dirt roads. The basic loop is easy to follow; trails are well signed.

The ride begins on a warm-up climb to the ridge. The best part of the ride follows—2 miles of enjoyable roller coaster. You then ride up a gentle canyon, where there are lots of options for exploring on your own. Bring a flashlight and check out Prospect Tunnel along the way. All side trips off Stewartville Trail are out-and-backs.

No bikes are allowed on the connector trails that would make side loops. This is the case for the Star Mine Trail and both the Lower and Upper Oil Canyon Trails. When you reach the end of the canyon, you face The Wall—450 feet of climbing in 0.7 mile. For intermediate bikers welcome to the world of mountain biking. Once you reach the ridge, it is an easy cruise back to the parking lot.

As always, this ride can be reversed. But think twice. Going counterclockwise, you can enjoy riding down The Wall, but it is over too soon. Then, what would be a longer roller-coaster ride down Ridge Trail is now a long climb out.

Before heading home, kick around and explore this fascinating place. Ride up toward the Greathouse Visitor Center. On a hot day you can sit here and catch the nice cool air coming up from the old mine. You will see mounds of mine tailings and an odd collection of trees brought in by the miners. Bikes can ride up the Chaparral Loop Trail as far as the Hazel-Atlas Mine Portal, where tours are offered. If you take one of the tours, your bike can be safely locked inside the tunnel. To ensure a spot on the tour, call ahead for reservations. Both the visitor center and mine tours are open seasonally on weekends.

Take another side trip and ride up Nortonville Trail to the Rose Hill Cemetery. While the towns are gone, the cemetery remains—the Protestant one anyway. Walking through the Rose Hill Cemetery tells the silent stories of epidemics, mining disasters, and death during childbirth.

Stronger riders can add on the more challenging Nortonville–Black Diamond Loop. For those seeking to connect with other East Bay rides, there is the Mount Diablo–to–Black Diamond Regional Trail. This connects near the Bruce Lee Trail and Donner Canyon Trail Road on the north side of Mount Diablo in Clayton.

Miles and Directions

0.0 **START** from the information board and historical marker at the end of the parking lot. This is the only potable water on the trail, so make sure to fill up. In less than 0.1 mile, turn left onto Stewartville Trail. Trailhead GPS: N 37 57 29.9, W 121 51 47.6.

0.2 Pass through the gate and continue straight up the valley at the junction with Railroad Bed Trail on the left.

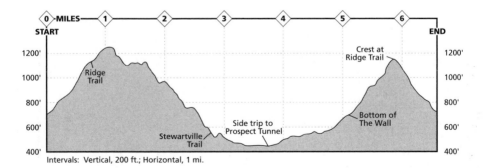

Intervals: Vertical, 200 ft.; Horizontal, 1 mi.

Black Diamond Mines Loop

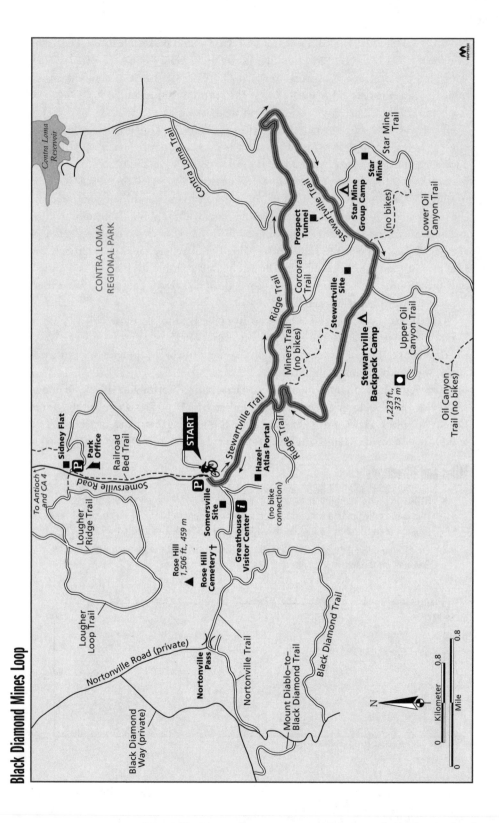

As you ride by, imagine coal miners burrowing under these hills.

0.7 Pass through the gate and go left at the fork onto Ridge Trail. You will complete the loop at this spot coming in from the right. Stay on Ridge Trail to the end at Stewartville Trail, ignoring side trails.

1.4 Continue straight on Ridge Trail. **Option:** Turn right down Corcoran Mine Trail. This steep descent cuts about 2 miles off the full loop.

2.1 Continue straight on Ridge Trail. **Option:** Turn left onto Contra Loma Trail and ride a little over 2 miles to Contra Loma Reservoir for a swim. Make sure you have a park map with you to find your way there and back.

2.8 Turn right onto Stewartville Trail.

3.7 Continue straight up the valley on Stewartville Trail at this four-way junction with Star Mine Trail on the left and Prospect Tunnel on the right. **Recommended side trip:** Turn right to Prospect Tunnel. Stay right on the singletrack that takes you up a side canyon. This is a great little out-and-back, although it's only 0.3 mile round-trip. With a flashlight you can walk about 400 feet into the tunnel. Keep your helmet on, the ceiling's low.

3.9 Continue straight where Corcoran Mine Trail takes off on the right. Follow Stewartville Trail up the valley and climb The Wall back up the ridge to complete the loop. Pass turnoffs to Lower and Upper Oil Canyon Trails. **Side trip:** Take a left at the fork to Upper Oil Canyon Trail at Mile 4.2. This is a 2.5-mile round-trip ride to an overlook at 1,223 feet.

5.8 Turn left at the crest of the ridge, still on Stewartville Trail. This completes the loop. Head back the way you came, turning right at the bottom of Stewartville Trail to return to the parking lot. **Side trip:** Turn left at the bottom of Stewartville Trail to explore the old mine tailings, visitor center, and Rose Hill Cemetery and to tour the Hazel-Atlas Mine. If you are up for another loop, try the Nortonville–Black Diamond Option.

6.6 Arrive back at the parking lot.

Nortonville–Black Diamond Loop Option

From the parking lot and trailhead, head straight up the main trail to a major mining area. (Do not turn left onto Stewartville Trail.) Turn right onto Nortonville Trail and climb up past Rose Hill Cemetery. Continue up to the ridge and junction with Black Diamond Trail. Take the right fork to stay on Nortonville Trail. (You will return to this point via Black Diamond Trail to complete the loop.) From here it is a quick descent. Go through the gate at the bottom and onto the Black Diamond Trail. When the trail hits the paved road, turn left and climb steeply up to the locked gate. Turn left onto the dirt Black Diamond Trail. Ride back to Nortonville Trail. Turn right and return through the old mining area back to the parking lot. This is a nearly 6-mile loop.

Ride Information

Local Information
East Bay Regional Park District, 2950 Peralta Oaks Court, P.O. Box 5381, Oakland, CA 94605; (510) 562-PARK; www.ebparks.org/parks/.
Antioch Chamber of Commerce, 324 G Street, Antioch, CA 94509; (924) 757-1800; www.antiochchamber.com.

Local Events and Attractions
Greathouse Visitor Center and Hazel-Atlas Mine Tours: Both open Saturday and Sunday 10:00 A.M. to 4:30 P.M. March through November; information (925) 757-2620; reservations (925) 676-0192; www.ebparks.org/new.htm#MINE.

Black Diamond Regional Concerts: Saturday night in summer, 7:00 to 9:00 P.M.; www.ebparks.org/parks/black.htm.

Accommodations
Black Diamond Mine Regional Preserve camping, Stewartville Backpack Camp and Star Mine Group Camp; reservations (510) 636-1684.

Restaurants and Java Jolts
Schooners Grille & Brewery, 4250 Lone Tree Way, Antioch; (925) 776-1800; www.schoonersbrewery.com.
In-n-Out Burger (fast-food junkies), 4550 Delta Gateway Boulevard, Pittsburg; (800) 786-1000.

19 Mount Diablo: Mitchell Canyon-Summit Loop

This ride is for those who like to climb and love great views. (If you just like down-hill, get a friend to drop you off at the top.) This is a breathtaking loop up, around, and down Mount Diablo, the highest peak in the Bay Area. A short paved section in the middle takes you to the summit at 3,849 feet. On a clear day you can see Yosemite's Half Dome. A technical singletrack hugs the mountain before a white-knuckle descent back through cattle country.

Start: From Mitchell Canyon Ranger Station and trailhead.
Distance: 14.8-mile loop.
Approximate riding time: 2.5 to 3.5 hours.
Difficulty: Difficult; strenuous and technical. The climbing is relentless; roots and rocks on the singletrack, loose and steep descent.
Trail surface: 72 percent dirt fire road, 21 percent paved road, and 7 percent single-track.
Terrain: A big, steep mountain: Start at 620 feet and climb to the summit at 3,849 feet.
Seasons: Best in spring and fall; avoid the heat of summer. Lower Mitchell Canyon Road, Donner Canyon Road, and Bruce Lee Trail are a muddy mess in winter. Snow is an occasional winter novelty on the peak.
Other trail users: Hikers, equestrians, cattle, and vehicles.

Canine compatibility: Dogs not permitted.
Land status: Diablo State Park.
Nearest town: Clayton.
Fees and permits: $3.00 parking fee.
Schedule: Open daily 8:00 A.M. to sunset.
Maps: USGS map: Clayton, CA.
Mount Diablo Interpretive Association, *Trail Map of Mount Diablo State Park*, available at local REI stores and online at www.mdia.org/mdiastore.htm.
Trail contacts: Mount Diablo State Park: Headquarters, 96 Mitchell Canyon Road, Clayton, CA 94517; (925) 837-2525. Junction Ranger Station at North Gate and South Gate Roads, Mount Diablo; (925) 837-6129; www.parks.ca.gov and www.mdia.org/spinfo.htm.

Finding the trailhead: From Walnut Creek: Exit Interstate 680 on Ygnacio Valley Road and head east. Stay on Ygnacio Valley Road through Walnut Creek and into Clayton, about 7.5 miles. Turn right onto Clayton Road for about a mile. Turn right onto Mitchell Canyon Road. The park entrance, parking lot, and trailhead are at the end of the road.

The Ride

Is it time to pay back those friends who drag you on endless climbs? Hand them this ride. The paved Summit Road is a popular road ride up Mount Diablo. But fewer folks are willing to mountain bike to the top—more than once. Attacking the summit more than once a year puts you in the category of serious trainer.

The ride begins up the cool, shaded canyon carved by Mitchell Creek. As you climb, the oak woodlands give way to grass, chaparral, and isolated stands of pine. In

Mount Diablo: Mitchell Canyon–Summit Loop

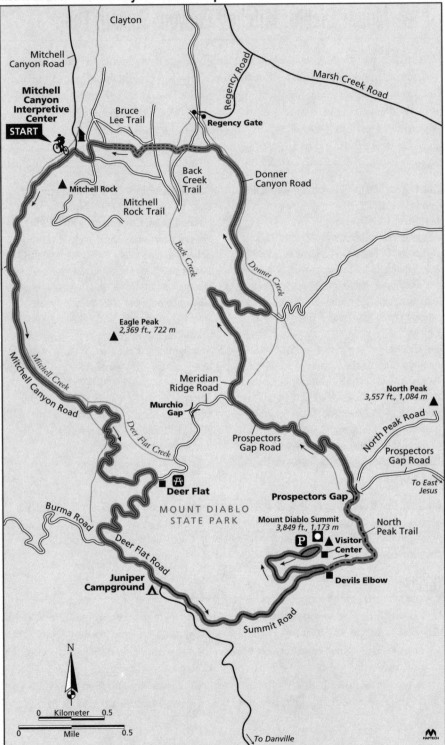

spring the wildflowers provide a nice distraction to the climb. Do not look at your odometer, set your eyes on each new rise in the trail. There is no sugar-coating this climb, but the views are worth it.

If you stop, turn, and look around on the way up, you can see the Carquinez Strait and the Napa Hills beyond. As you approach Juniper Campground, you may be able to see the Golden Gate Bridge, Mount Tamalpais, and even the Farallon Islands sitting in the Pacific Ocean on a particularly clear day. At the top the view extends to the San Joaquin and Sacramento River Delta, with the Central Valley and the Sierra Mountains beyond. With a good eye, or some change for the telescopes, you can see Yosemite's Half Dome. Unfortunately there is often haze, particularly in summer. The clearest days are often the day after a winter storm.

If you need to be the only one on top of a mountain, this may not be the peak for you. While the dirt trails on this loop are rather quiet, there is a parking lot and the historic stone Summit Building and Visitor Center at the top. To set foot on the actual peak, you need to step inside the museum. (It can be a welcome spot out of the wind.) The sandstone blocks for the museum were quarried from the mountain. Look for marine fossils embedded in the stones, evidence of the mountain's rise from the ocean floor millions of years ago.

The ride down is part of the payoff. Once off the pavement, the singletrack North Peak Trail offers challenging rocks, ruts, stumps, sharp turns, steep drop-offs, and loose dirt. In spring this is one of the best places to see wildflowers. The single-track ends at Prospectors Gap, where you cross back over to the other side (western drainage) of the mountain. A wrong turn on this mountain can lead to some painful backtracking. The remaining descent is very steep, with rutted sections and more loose gravel. Stay back behind the seat. If you find your tires skidding, feather your front brake. Once on Meridian ("Median" on some maps) Ridge and Donner Canyon Roads, the cattle chew up (figuratively speaking) sections of the trail. The ride levels out the last couple of miles through grass pastureland. The view back up to the summit is the classic Mount Diablo landscape.

Mount Diablo State Park is a national landmark that's rich in flora, fauna, and history. Both the Summit Museum and the Mitchell Canyon Interpretive Center offer a wealth of information and resources. This mountain was a sacred place for California Indians. Miwoks and others considered this mountain the creation spot for their people and made pilgrimages to the top for special ceremonies. So, pilgrim, go out and enjoy the view.

Temperatures can vary dramatically from the canyon floor to the summit. Clouds and fog can quickly shroud the mountain. Bring several layers of clothing for this ride, particularly dry undergarments and windbreakers. Your clothes will most likely be soaked by the time you get to the top. A change into dry clothing can be welcome on the windy summit, as well as making for a more comfortable descent.

Miles and Directions

0.0 **START** from the parking lot and gated trailhead for Mitchell Canyon Road. Follow the signs to Deer Flat Road. Note the trail coming in on the left as you start; you will return on this trail at the end. Trailhead GPS: N 37 55.123, W 121 56.302.

1.0 Veer left toward Deer Flat Road at the fork to the park boundary on the right. The climb begins at Mile 2.0. There is a picnic area with a great view just before the turnoff to Murchio Gap.

3.7 Turn right onto Deer Flat Road toward Juniper Campground. **Shortcut:** Turn left onto Meridian Ridge Road toward Murchio Gap. Turn left at the junction with Prospector Gap Road. Pick up the next direction below at Mile 12.3. There is still a short climb this way, but this cuts off about 1,500 feet of climbing and the technical singletrack along North Peak Trail.

4.8 Veer left on Deer Flat Road at the intersection with Burma Road.

5.3 Veer left on the paved road through Juniper Campground. There are restrooms and water here. Follow the white pavement arrows out of the campground.

5.5 Turn left onto Summit Road.

6.7 Continue left on Summit Road at Devils Elbow. There is tempting dirt on Summit Trail, but it is posted off-limits to bikes on the top end. Do not despair; it is not all ridable uphill anyway. **Option:** Skip the up-and-back to the summit and go straight onto the North Peak Trail, picking up the directions at Mile 8.6 below.

7.6 Arrive at the summit. Check out the Summit Museum and, hopefully, the view. Return down the road to Devils Elbow. (Depending on how much riding around you do at the top, the odometer readings may be off for the way down.)

8.6 Arrive back at Devils Elbow. Turn left onto the dirt, picking up the singletrack North Peak Trail.

9.6 Turn *left* through Prospectors Gap onto Prospectors Gap Road (toward Murchio Gap) at the four-way intersection. (This is a confusing junction. Straight will take you *up* to North Peak. A right turn on Prospectors Gap Road will take you to a locked gate at the *bottom* and a lo-o-o-o-ong ride and hike back up.) You pass a perennial puddle as you go through the gap. Veer right past the puddle, staying on Prospectors Gap Road and ignoring Bald Ridge Trail to the left.

10.9 Turn right onto Meridian Ridge Road. Coming from this direction, the sign is hidden.

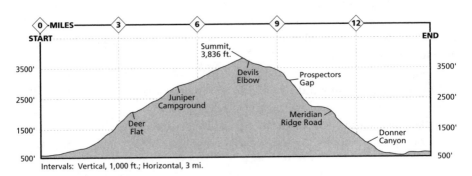

Intervals: Vertical, 1,000 ft.; Horizontal, 3 mi.

12.3 Turn left onto Donner Canyon Road toward Regency Gate. You will pass the trail to the Donner Cabin site at Mile 12.9.

13.6 Turn left to the Bruce Lee Trail. Continue straight on the Bruce Lee Trail toward Mitchell Canyon Staging Area as trails come in from both sides through the grassy fields. From here on, maps may differ on what trail you are on. For some this is Murchio Road; others call it Corral Road. The trail signs may never mention either. Heads-up and pedal west. You will eventually make your way back to where you started.

14.0 Continue straight on Mitchell Trail at the crossroads. Ignore the right turn to the Mitchell Canyon Staging Area. As of this writing, grass-restoration efforts have eliminated the direct access that way.

14.5 Turn left at T junction to Mitchell Rock Trail. You will see the parking lot below.

14.6 Turn right toward Mitchell Canyon Road. Turn right again once you reach the road.

14.8 Arrive back at the parking lot.

Ride Information

Local Information

Mount Diablo Interpretive Association, P.O. Box 346, Walnut Creek, CA 94596; (925) 927-7222; www.mdia.org; specific biking information: www.mdia.org/biking.htm. **Weather on the mountain:** (925) 838-9225.

Local Events and Attractions

Mitchell Canyon Interpretive Center, 96 Mitchell Canyon Road, Clayton; www.mdia.org. **Chronicle Pavilion at Concord Amphitheatre,** 200 Kirker Pass Road, Concord; (925) 363-5701; www.chroniclepavilion.com.

Accommodations

Mount Diablo State Park camping; (800) 444-7275; click online reservations from www.parks.ca.gov/ or www.reserveamerica. com/jsp/commonpage.jsp?goto=/usa/ca/ mtdi/newindex.html.

Restaurants and Java Jolts

Ed's Mudville Grill, 6200 Center Street, Clayton; (925) 673-0333; www.edsmudville grill.com.

20 Shell Ridge Loop

This is a great intermediate ride on the lower ridges of Mount Diablo. Wide dirt roads take you on an undulating ride over grass-covered hills. Get close with the cattle along the way. Practice creek crossings—ten times. Take this ride as far as you like. Strong riders can try the longer option and check out the new singletrack connector to Rock City at 1,600 feet. Time of year is critical on this ride; the mud will swallow your bike in winter, and the heat will consume you in summer.

Start: From the entrance to Shell Ridge Recreation Area at the end of Marshall Road, next to Indian Valley School, Walnut Creek.

Distance: 10.8-mile out-and-back loop, with 17.8-mile loop option.

Approximate riding time: 1.5 hours.

Difficulty: Moderate; short spurts of climbing. The first half of the ride is nontechnical. Beginners can ride as far as they want. There is a steep descent on slick rock and tricky stream crossings on the second half of the ride. The longer Rock City–Wall Point option is difficult.

Trail surface: Wide dirt roads; longer option offers 3 miles of singletrack.

Terrain: Grass-covered rolling hills; wooded short, steep ravines; shaded canyon with rocky creek crossings.

Seasons: Best in spring and fall. Wait for the trails to dry out and the creeks to subside in spring; unridable in winter and triple-digit hot in summer. Ride early in the morning if you must ride during summer.

Other trail users: Hikers, equestrians, and cattle.

Canine compatibility: Unleashed dogs under positive voice and sight command permitted in Shell Ridge Recreation Area and Diablo Foothills Regional Park. Dogs not permitted on the trails in Diablo State Park.

Land status: City of Walnut Creek Open Space, Diablo Foothills Regional Park, Diablo State Park, and public trail easement through private property.

Nearest town: Walnut Creek.

Fees and permits: No fees or permits required.

Schedule: Open daily year-round. Shell Ridge Recreation Area open daylight hours only; Diablo State Park open 8:00 A.M. to sunset. Diablo State Park may close during the hot and dry season if the fire danger is very high. Call for conditions and closures: (925) 837-0904.

Maps: USGS maps: Walnut Creek, CA; Diablo, CA; Clayton, CA.
City of Walnut Creek, Shell Ridge Open Space map, available online at www.ci.walnut-creek.ca.us/openspace/shell_ridge.htm.
Mount Diablo Interpretive Association, *Trail Map of Mount Diablo State Park,* available at local REI stores and online at www.mdia.org/orderfm.htm.
East Bay Regional Park District, Diablo Foothills Regional Park map, available online at www.ebparks.org/parks/diablo.htm.

Trail contacts: City of Walnut Creek Open Space and Trails Division, Borges Ranch Ranger Station, 1035 Castle Rock Road, Walnut Creek, CA 94598; (925) 942-0225; www.ci.walnut-creek.ca.us/openspace/shell_ridge.htm.
East Bay Regional Park District Headquarters, 2950 Peralta Oaks Court, P.O. Box 5381, Oakland, CA 94605; (510) 562-PARK; www.ebparks.org/parks/diablo.htm.
Mount Diablo State Park: Headquarters, 96 Mitchell Canyon Road, Clayton, CA 94517; (925) 837-2525.

Junction Ranger Station at North Gate and
South Gate Roads, Mount Diablo; (925)

837-6129; www.parks.ca.gov and
www.mdia.org/spinfo.htm.

Finding the trailhead: From Walnut Creek: Exit Interstate 680 on Ygnacio Valley Road and
head east. After a mile turn right onto Homestead Avenue. Take the first left onto Marshall Drive.
Continue for about a mile to the end at Indian Valley School. There is no water or restroom.

The Ride

Mount Diablo is the highest point in the Bay Area and the Coastal Range. There are
few other places in the world where you can see as far as you can from atop Mount
Diablo—amazing since it is only 3,849 feet high. The surrounding rolling hills allow
you to see more than 400 miles of unobstructed view. It is these rolling hills, and
some of them roll rather steeply, that make for great mountain biking. A park this
grand attracts loads of visitors; but it is big enough and there are plenty of trails; you
can usually find some solitude (except when you need to pee).

Starting at the edge of town, this ride takes you as far as you want. Beginners can
do an out-and-back along the Briones–Mount Diablo Trail. Older children in the
right mood can ride to Borges Ranch historic site. Intermediates can do the full
loop and then some. Strong riders can hammer all the way to the top of the mountain. There is a new singletrack connecting this ride to Rock City for a signature
roller-coaster ride down Wall Point Road.

Beginning on the low-lying Shell Ridge, this ride tours the western side of the
mountain. You follow the undulating Briones–Mount Diablo Trail through oak-
studded grasslands. This well-marked road connects with a series of side trails from
the surrounding neighborhoods. Passing through several gates reminds you of all the
different agencies and private landowners holding title to this mountain. Preserving
the open space on Mount Diablo has been a collaborative effort, with large credit
going to the nonprofit group Save Mount Diablo.

There is little shade for the first half of the loop. This is cattle country, and you
may well find yourself face to face with a few. Be patient; they will move out of your
way. It is not wise to startle cattle. Unfortunately, when you mix cattle with this clay
soil in the winter, you get unridable mud. As it dries, the pockmarked trails are
annoyingly bumpy. With use, the trails smooth out. You want to catch this ride as
soon as it becomes ridable in spring to enjoy the fields of wildflowers. Watering
holes for the cattle are scattered along the way. Except for riders taking the longer
loop, there are no watering holes for bikers, so bring plenty with you.

Once you leave the ridge, you drop into Pine Canyon and follow the creek
through shaded riparian woodlands of oak, willow, sycamore, cottonwood, and poison oak. A series of ten creek crossings livens up the ride, especially if the creek is
flowing. Even in early fall, there is still water and mud in some of the crossings—the
rocks are always there. If you do this ride when there is water, be sure to clean your
bike when you finish. The mud is abrasive and will grind out your drive train.

Before leaving Pine Creek you pass Castle Rock on the right. This is a large sandstone outcropping over the canyon and popular rock climbing area. These formations pop up in veins throughout the mountain and are a preview of what you would see on the extended loop to Rock City. The short and moderate ride out of the canyon is mostly shaded. Once up on the ridge, it is a smooth backtrack to the start.

Miles and Directions

0.0   **START** at the entrance to Shell Ridge Recreation Area at the end of Marshall Drive. Take the right fork near the information board. You are on the Briones–Mount Diablo Trail, which you will follow for the next 4.7 miles. Trailhead GPS: N 37 52.219, W 122 27.212.

0.1   Stay to the right at the fork next to the school fence. The left trail is a nice connector, but technically there are no bikes allowed. The city of Walnut Creek prohibits bikes on trails less than 8 feet wide, unless otherwise posted. Ignore any such side trails along the way.

0.2   Turn left to stay on Briones–Mount Diablo Trail at the junction with Fossil Hill Trail.

0.3   Stay right as the connector trail comes in on the left.

0.4   Veer left to miss Fossil Hill Trail.

1.0   Veer right to stay on Briones–Mount Diablo Trail at the fork with Ginder Gap Loop Trail.

1.1   Continue straight at the singletrack shortcut on the right.

1.2   Turn right. Ignore the singletrack shortcut when it merges from the right up ahead.

1.3   Stay left on Briones–Mount Diablo Trail at the junction with Joaquin Ranch Road.

1.9   Veer left on Briones–Mount Diablo Trail at the junction with Sugarloaf–Shell Ridge Trail.

2.3   Continue straight at the intersection with Borges Ranch Trail. You will first pass it on the right and then pass it on the left. Go through the gate and continue on Briones–Mount Diablo Trail. Look down the small valley on the left for a glimpse of the historic Borges Ranch. The trail is dual track until the next gate. (FYI: There are restrooms and water at the ranch.)

2.5   Pass through the gate into East Bay Regional Park District land—Diablo Foothills Regional Park. Take the right fork to continue on Briones–Mount Diablo Trail. You will return from the left on the Shell Ridge Loop Trail.

2.9   Veer left at the Stonegate Trail.

3.7   Veer left at the Hanging Valley Trail.

3.9   Pass through the gate into Diablo State Park.

4.1   Veer left at the unsigned fork.

4.3   Stay left at the tempting unsigned shortcut on the right. Continue on the main dirt road past the singletrack trails on both sides up ahead.

4.7   This is the end of the Briones–Mount Diablo Trail. Turn left onto Wall Point Road toward the Summit Trail. **Longer Loop Option (only for the hardy):** Continue straight on Wall Point Road to Macedo Ranch for a ride to Rock City via the new singletrack Green Valley Trail. It will take some careful navigating to follow the singletrack around backyards and over

◄ Ride in the shadow of Castle Rock.

Shell Ridge Loop

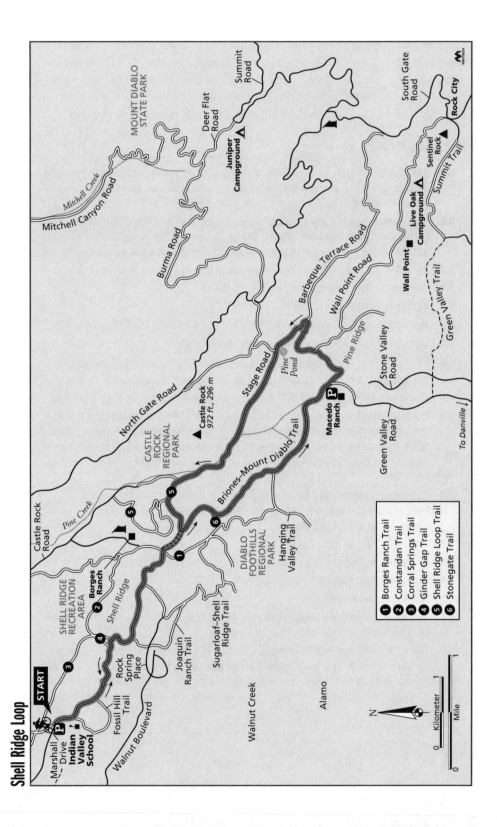

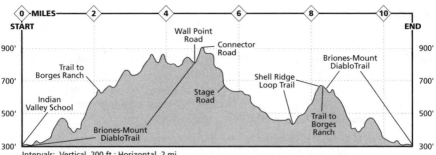

Intervals: Vertical, 200 ft.; Horizontal, 2 mi.

pastureland, eventually ending up on Summit Trail. Climb up to Rock City and take the paved South Gate Road up to the inconspicuous trailhead of Wall Point Road. Enjoy the downhill run along the ridge. At the bottom, turn right on the connector trail to Stage Road. You will be at Mile 5.2 below. This option adds 7 miles and 1,500 feet of climbing. Allow 2.5 to 3.5 hours for the full 17.8-mile loop. Green Valley Trail is unridable in the winter.

5.2 Veer left on the Connector Trail to Stage Road. Heads up for some steep, slick sandstone slabs (say *that* five times) for a road. Wall Point Road continues up the ridge on the right. This is where the optional loop to Rock City comes in.

5.7 Turn left onto Stage Road and make the first of ten crossings on Pine Creek. **Option:** Go right on Stage Road to Barbeque Terrace Road. Power your way up to Summit Road. Turn right and connect with Wall Point Road for a steep downhill run.

6.1 Veer left staying on Stage Road to Diablo Foothills. Pine Pond is hiding in the thicket of cattails on the left. **Option:** Make a right turn up Burma Trail. This popular but strenuous connector to the summit will take you to Deer Flat Road and Juniper Campground.

7.8 Turn left onto Shell Ridge Loop Trail.

8.0 Just past the picnic table, veer left, heading back up to Briones–Mount Diablo Trail.

8.3 Turn right, completing the loop. Pass back through the gate on Briones–Mount Diablo Trail.

8.5 Pass through the gate and cross the Borges Ranch Trail. Retrace your tracks, following the Briones–Mount Diablo Trail back to the start.

9.7 Turn left at the junction with Ginder Gap Trail.

10.8 Arrive back at the end of Marshall Drive.

Ride Information

Local Information

Mount Diablo Interpretive Association, P.O. Box 346, Walnut Creek, CA 94596; (925) 927-7222; www.mdia.org; specific biking information: www.mdia.org/biking.htm. **Weather on the mountain:** (925) 838-9225.

Local Events and Attractions

Historical Borges Ranch, 1035 Castle Rock Road, Walnut Creek; (925) 943-5860; www.ci.walnutcreek.ca.us/openspace/osborges.htm. **Castle Rock Park,** 1200 Castle Rock Road, Walnut Creek; (510) 562-PARK or (925) 462-1400; www.ebparks.org/parks/castle.htm and www.picnicpeople.com.

Accommodations

Mount Diablo State Park camping; (800) 444-7275. Click online reservations from www.parks.ca.gov/ or www.reserveamerica.com/jsp/commonpage.jsp?goto=/usa/ca/mtdi/newindex.html.

Restaurants and Java Jolts

A Sweet Affair Bakery and Cafe, 1815-F Ygnacio Valley Road, Walnut Creek; (925) 944-1910. **Pioneer's Gourmet Hamburgers,** 1815-D Ygnacio Valley Road, Walnut Creek; (925) 938-0778.

TARANTULAS ON THE TRAIL In fall keep an eye out for these big (as in up to 5 inches big) hairy spiders. This is their mating season and they are out cruising. Let's hope the season is good; the males usually die a few months after mating. Meanwhile, the female may go on to live twenty-five years, still producing eggs.

It is best to leave the spiders alone; they have a rightful place outdoors. Their venom is nontoxic to humans (unless you are allergic to it), but their bite is comparable to a bee sting. What might be more irritating is the itching and skin rash from their hair—which they release when *provoked.* This would only happen if you encroach upon their space. If you come into contact, tape will help remove these hairs from your skin. Treat a bite with soap and water.

The word *tarantula* means dance. The old belief was that their bite would cause a person to dance around and twitch. A good scare can do that.

21 Morgan Territory Loop

This ride offers a good introduction to mountain biking. That does not mean flat; it means gently rolling hills and short climbs. Before you arrive at the trailhead, a narrow winding road to Morgan Territory Regional Preserve takes you to the more remote eastern side of Mount Diablo. Here you can enjoy great views of the summit and the Central Valley without the crowd (or any serious climbing). This is a pleasant ride on a wide dirt road along a grassy, oak-studded ridge.

Start: From the staging area for Morgan Territory Regional Preserve, at the trailhead for Volvon Trail.

Distance: 6.2-mile loop.

Approximate riding time: 1 hour.

Difficulty: Easy; nontechnical, wide, and smooth trail along a gently rolling ridge.

Trail surface: Dirt road.

Terrain: Ridge along grass-covered hills with oak woodlands; backdrop view of Mount Diablo.

Seasons: Best in spring and fall. Hot in summer, muddy in winter.

Other trail users: Hikers, equestrians, and cattle.

Canine compatibility: Leashed dogs permitted in the parking and picnic areas. Unleashed dogs allowed in the open space under voice control at all times.

Land status: East Bay Regional Park District.

Nearest town: Livermore.

Fees and permits: No fees or permits required.

Schedule: Open daily 8:00 A.M. to dusk.

Maps: USGS map: Tassajara, CA. East Bay Regional Park District map, Morgan Territory Regional Preserve, available at the trailhead and online at www.ebparks.org/parks/morgan.htm. Mount Diablo Interpretive Association, *Trail Map of Mount Diablo State Park*, available at local REI stores and online at www.mdia.org/orderfm.htm.

Trail contact: East Bay Regional Park District Headquarters, 2950 Peralta Oaks Court, P.O. Box 5381, Oakland, CA 94605; (510) 562-PARK; park office in Antioch (925) 757-2620; www.ebparks.org/parks/morgan.htm.

Finding the trailhead: From Livermore: Exit Interstate 580 onto North Livermore Avenue and turn north. About 4 miles from the freeway, North Livermore Avenue curves sharply to the left (west) and becomes Manning Road. Very soon, turn right onto Morgan Territory Road. Follow another 6 miles up the narrow (sometimes one-lane) and winding road.

The Ride

These foothills were once home to the Volvon Indians, one of five nations in the Diablo area that spoke the local Miwok language. Isolated on the eastern flanks of Mount Diablo, the Volvon were some of the last Native Americans to succumb to the Spanish missionaries by 1806. To the Volvon Mount Diablo was *Tuyshtak* and considered the birthplace of the world. This is where the First People lived—supernatural beings named for animals that reflected their inherent strength. First People,

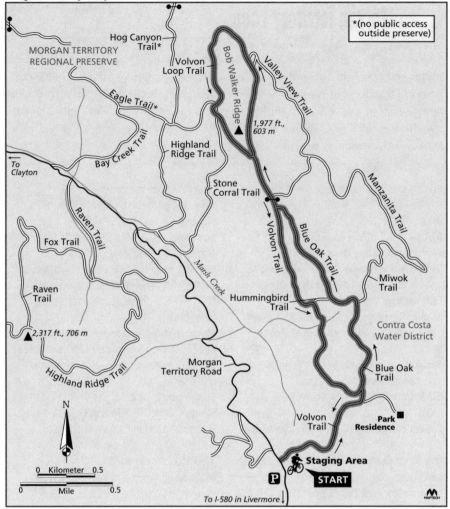

*(no public access outside preserve)

MORGAN TERRITORY
REGIONAL PRESERVE

Hog Canyon
Trail*

Volvon
Loop Trail

Bob Walker Ridge

Valley View Trail

Eagle Trail*

Bay Creek Trail

Highland
Ridge Trail

1,977 ft.,
603 m

To
Clayton

Stone
Corral Trail

Manzanita Trail

Raven Trail

Volvon Trail

Blue Oak Trail

Fox Trail

Marsh Creek

Miwok
Trail

Raven
Trail

2,317 ft., 706 m

Hummingbird
Trail

Contra Costa
Water District

Morgan
Territory Road

Blue Oak
Trail

Highland Ridge Trail

N

Volvon
Trail

Park
Residence

0   Kilometer   0.5

Staging Area
START

0   Mile   0.5

P

To I-580 in Livermore

MAPTECH

such as Coyote, Eagle, and Prairie Falcon, created the Native Americans and gave them a plentiful and beautiful world. Many of the trail names in the preserve commemorate the influence of these early residents.

A beautiful world indeed describes the Morgan Territory Regional Preserve today. This is the quiet, less developed side of the mountain. Rolling hills offer panoramic views of looming Mount Diablo to the west and the Central Valley on the east. The spring brings a spectacular display of wildflowers, including the Diablo sunflower, which grows only on the foothills of Mount Diablo.

The preserve gets its name from the man who first started a ranch here in 1857. Jeremiah Morgan was a real pioneer who arrived in a covered wagon at the beginning of the gold rush. Later, after exploring the land on a hunting expedition, he returned to set up a ranch with his family. Cattle still roam parts of the preserve, leaving their mark on the trails. Watering holes are scattered about.

In a region where most rides entail some steep climbs, this is a more comfortable ride along a gentle ridge. Beginners can get the feel of riding on dirt through remote hills, while enjoying the view. There is just enough uphill to get a taste of downhill. The highest point is about 2,090 feet and the lowest 1,750 feet, not a big difference by mountain biking standards.

There are plenty of side trails to challenge strong beginners and intermediate riders. As soon as you leave the ridge, these trails dip into canyons with short climbs back up. A popular detour is on Valley View Trail. This has a cool downhill, but be careful who tries it. Although this is a short scramble back up, it may be more than some beginners would smile about. Kids have been known to throw bikes off the trail when faced with this climb.

Stronger riders will have fun exploring the western side of the preserve, riding Highland Ridge to Finley Road. You can reach Highland Ridge Trail from the Volvon Loop Trail via Stone Corral or Eagle Trail. You can also connect to other parts of the mountain on the regional Diablo Trail. This is a relatively new link connecting the diverse collection of landowners on the mountain. Bring the full map of the mountain before venturing too far. There are pockets of private land and dead-end gates you do not want to face when you are tired and lost.

The legal bike trails are well-signed, wide dirt road. While this is a remote open space, the rangers still patrol it all. The route is simply an out-and-back on Volvon Trail with a side trip on Blue Oak Trail. However, there are lots of intersecting trails that make the directions sound more complicated than they are. If you can read a map well, you can disregard the detailed directions.

Miles and Directions

0.0 **START** from the trailhead to Volvon Trail. Head east. Trailhead GPS: N 37 49.07, W 121 47.44.

0.3 Continue straight on Volvon Trail as a gravel road merges from the right.

0.6 Turn left to stay on Volvon Trail. Straight ahead goes to the park residence.

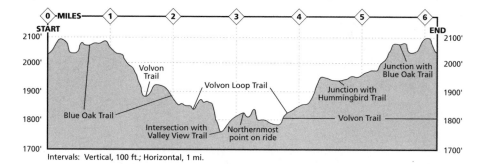

Intervals: Vertical, 100 ft.; Horizontal, 1 mi.

0.7 Turn right at the fork onto Blue Oak Trail.

1.2 Veer left to stay on Blue Oak Trail at the fork with Miwok Trail.

1.4 Veer right to stay on Blue Oak Trail at the fork with Hummingbird Trail.

2.0 Turn right onto Volvon Trail.

2.1 Pass through the gate and continue straight on Volvon Trail. **Option:** Turn right and take the Valley View Trail. Prepare for a steep descent and a matching climb out. Follow trail signs to stay on Valley View Trail, picking up Volvon Loop Trail in 1.2 miles. Enjoy great views of the Central Valley along the way.

2.3 Take the right fork where the Volvon Loop Trail begins.

2.7 Bear left on Volvon Loop Trail at forks with Valley View Trail. You will soon round the hill and start heading south.

3.5 Turn left on Volvon Loop Trail at the junction with Eagle Trail. Stay left again at the junction with Stone Corral Trail.

3.9 Turn right onto Volvon Trail completing the first loop.

4.1 Return through the gate where Valley View Trail comes in from the left.

4.2 Stay right on Volvon Trail where Blue Oak Trail comes in from left.

4.8 Stay right on Volvon Trail at the fork with Hummingbird Trail. Ignore tempting side trails that are off-limits to bikes.

5.5 Make a sharp right to stay on Volvon Trail at the fork with Blue Oak Trail. This completes the second loop; you are now backtracking to the parking lot. In 100 yards turn right at the fork with the gravel road.

5.9 Veer right at the fork.

6.2 Arrive back at the parking lot.

Ride Information

Local Information

East Bay Regional Park District, 2950 Peralta Oaks Court, P.O. Box 5381, Oakland, CA 94605; (510) 562-PARK; www.ebparks. org/parks/.

Tri-Valley Convention and Visitors Bureau, 260 Main Street, Pleasanton, CA 94566; (888) 874-9253 or (925) 846-8910; www.trivalley cvb.com.

Local Events and Attractions

Mount Diablo Interpretive Association, P.O. Box 346, Walnut Creek, CA 94597; (925) 927-7222; www.mdia.org.

22 Pleasanton Ridge Loop

A steady climb takes you up grassy slopes and along the oak-studded ridge west of Pleasanton. The climb is worth the classic views of surrounding mountains and valleys. The trail passes through picturesque oak woodlands before dropping into Kilkare Canyon for a ride along Sinbad Creek. The reward come at the end with an out-and-back along the singletrack Sinbad Creek Trail. There are options for longer rides with several remote loops at the upper end of the park.

Start: From Pleasanton Ridge Regional Park entrance, Oak Tree Staging Area on Foothill Boulevard southwest of Pleasanton.
Distance: 15.5-mile loop.
Approximate riding time: 2.5 to 3 hours.
Difficulty: Difficult; nontechnical dirt roads, challenging climbs, and sweet singletrack with some sharp turns.
Trail surface: 82 percent dirt fire road and 18 percent singletrack.
Terrain: Wide fire roads along grass-covered ridge, deep wooded canyons, and meandering creek; brilliant singletrack weaves through the lower hills in a small valley.
Seasons: Best in spring and fall. Some trails are unridable in the wet season when cattle are in the park, particularly the beginning of Oak Tree Trail. The park prefers bikers to stay off the muddy trails to avoid rutting. The ridge can be hot in summer. The park may be closed due to extreme fire danger in summer and early fall. Call (510) 544-2222 for park closure information.
Other trail users: Hikers, equestrians, cattle, and sheep.

Canine compatibility: Leashed dogs permitted. Dogs may be off leash in the open spaces, if under control, but you must have a leash with you. Leash those pit bulls at all times in Augustin Bernal Park.
Land status: East Bay Regional Park District and city of Pleasanton.
Nearest town: Pleasanton.
Fees and permits: No fees or permits required.
Schedule: Open 5:00 A.M. to 10:00 P.M. daily, unless otherwise posted.
Maps: USGS maps: Dublin, CA; Niles, CA. East Bay Regional Park District, Pleasanton Ridge Regional Park map, available at the trailhead and online at www.ebparks.org/parks/pleasrig.htm.
Trail contacts: East Bay Regional Park District Headquarters, 2950 Peralta Oaks Court, P.O. Box 5381, Oakland, CA 94605; (510) 562-PARK; park ranger (925) 862-2963; www.ebparks.org/parks/pleasrig.htm. City of Pleasanton, Community Services Division, Pleasanton; (925) 931-5340; www.ci.pleasanton.ca.us/rec_sportscomm.html.

Finding the trailhead: From Pleasanton: Take Interstate 680 south and exit at Castlewood Drive. Turn right at the end of the off-ramp and make a quick right onto Castlewood Drive. Turn left onto Foothill Road. You will be heading south toward the town of Sunol. Turn right into the Foothill Staging Area about 2 miles from Castlewood Drive.

 Note for Pleasanton residents: Residents can access Augustin Bernal Park and the middle of this loop from Golden Eagle Estates, a gated community at 8200 Golden Eagle Way off Foothill Road. Access permits are available from the City of Pleasanton, Community Service Division.

Share the trail—the cows were here first!

The Ride

Pleasanton Ridge offers a quick escape into more than 4,000 acres of open space in the hills west of the Livermore and Pleasanton Valley. To preserve the pastoral nature of the hills, this park has successfully warded off fierce development pressures. Telltale signs of these battles are the concrete headstones marking water lines that traverse portions of the parks.

This ride is not a simple loop. It is really an out-and-back with some alternate trails home. As with many other wilderness and open space parks, there are more trails to explore. The park continues to expand, so watch for changes and ride sensibly. The park is trying to accommodate mountain biking.

There is no warm-up for this ride. It begins with a steady climb up to the ridge and continues to climb, often in steep, short spurts, along the ridge. The fire road takes you over the grassy oak-studded hillsides with wide-open views of Mount Diablo to the distant north, Livermore Valley to the east, and more hills along the Sunol Ridge to the west. To the south you can see Sunol Valley, with Mission Peak Regional Park and Sunol Regional Wildness beyond. The freeway noise from below can be a bit annoying, but it disappears after a few miles.

Pleasanton Ridge Loop

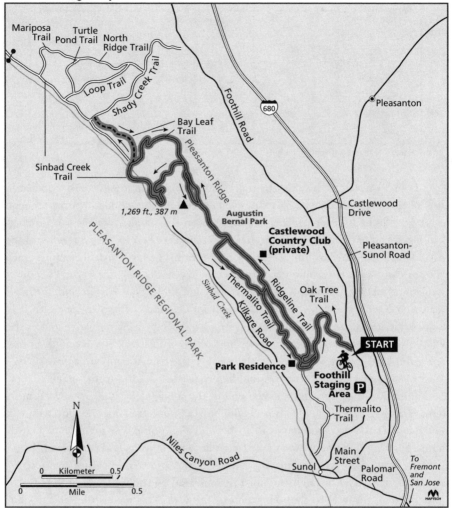

This is clearly cattle country. Cattle graze in the first portion of the park from mid-December until June, depending on the yield of grass. Unfortunately, after a good rain Oak Tree Trail and parts of Ridgeline Trail can become unridable. Thermalito Trail is maintained with gravel for the park residents and is a better bet in the wet season.

At one point Ridgeline Trail passes through a healthy olive grove. This and other orchards in the park were planted between 1890 and the 1920s, although there are no records of who planted them. The trees are reminders of a history of orchards farther south along the ridge above the town of Sunol. The Thermal Fruit Company cultivated apricots, cherries, prunes, and almonds to produce nuts and dried fruit during the early 1900s.

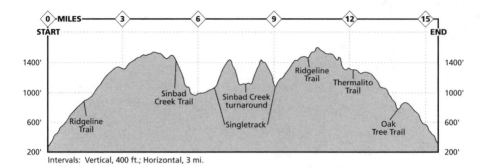

Intervals: Vertical, 400 ft.; Horizontal, 3 mi.

About 3 miles into the ride, the trail winds through picturesque oak woodlands. It is an easy cruise before quickly dropping down into the wooded Kilkare Canyon carved by Sinbad Creek. During the wet season the creek crossings can be challenging. The real cache is the singletrack trail that takes you to the far reaches of the park. This is the only technical section of the ride, but it's worth the effort. Steep hairpin climbs are rewarding descents on the way back, and vice versa. This sweet singletrack takes you through oak woodlands and more grass pastureland, this time for sheep. Sheep graze in the upper canyon for a month or two in spring to help reduce the fire hazards and maintain a diverse habitat, especially for native grasses and wildflowers. Be forewarned; the upper end of the singletrack is thick with poison oak—the kind that reaches out on the narrow trail. Souls trapped in poison oak–sensitive skin may want to turn around before the last descent to the creek.

While this loop turns back at the end of the singletrack, there are several more remote trails to explore. Unfortunately the North Ridge Trail does not connect with Ridgeline Trail. Any climbing you do beyond this point will not take you back home. Save enough energy for the last big climb back up to Ridgeline Trail.

Take note, there have been some name changes and trail openings at the upper end of the park. The once closed Sinbad Creek Trail on the west side of the creek is now open all the way to the upper end of the park. This means the last out-and-back on the singletrack section of the Bay Leaf Trail can be turned into a loop; but with so little singletrack, why waste it?

Miles and Directions

0.0 **START** from the trailhead on Oak Tree Trail. Ignore Sycamore Trail about 0.6 mile up on the right. Trailhead GPS: N 37 36.532, W 121 52.564.

1.2 Turn right, pass through the gate, and turn right again onto Ridgeline Trail. Stay on Ridgeline Trail for several miles; ignore Olive Grove and Thermalito Trails coming in from the left.

2.7 Stay right on Ridgeline Trail. (On the return you will take Thermalito Trail at this point.)

3.1 Pass through the gate and head downhill on Ridgeline Trail. Bear right at the first sharp turn, then left at the next sharp turn. You will soon enter the city of Pleasanton's Augustin Bernal Park. The trail levels out and narrows.

4.0 Continue through the gate and turn right onto Ridgeline Trail.

4.5 Turn right to continue on Ridgeline Trail. **Shortcut:** Turn left and head back, after a half-mile you will pick up directions from Mile 10.9 below.

4.6 Turn left down Sinbad Creek Trail. Cross the creek at the bottom; turn right after the creek to follow Sinbad Creek Trail upstream on the level fire road.

6.2 Turn right to cross the creek again and head uphill. **Easier option:** Continue up Sinbad Creek Trail. This will take you to the upper end of the park, bypassing the singletrack.

6.3 Turn left onto singletrack Bay Leaf Trail.

7.7 Reach the end of the singletrack. Turn left down to the creek for a break before turning around and returning on the singletrack. **Options:** There are several loops to explore farther up the canyon. You can turn right up Shady Creek Trail to North Ridge Trail. From there you can come down Loop, Turtle Pond, or Mariposa Trail. Each of those leads back to the singletrack Bay Leaf Trail. You can also opt for the easier return on Sinbad Creek Trail. If you bypass the singletrack, take the wide Bay Leaf Trail up to Ridgeline Trail. Although this is a steady climb, it is easier than climbing out of the canyon on Sinbad Creek Trail.

9.1 Turn left up Bay Leaf Trail.

9.9 Turn right onto Ridgeline Trail. Stay to the left on Ridgeline Trail where Sinbad Creek Trail comes in on the right.

10.4 Stay to the right on upper Ridgeline Trail.

10.9 Pass through the gate and continue on Ridgeline Trail. Veer right, bypassing Valley View Trail on the left into Augustin Bernal Park.

11.4 Turn right onto Thermalito Trail and stay on it until Oak Tree Trail. Ignore side trails leading back up to Ridgeline Trail and the olive grove.

13.9 Turn left onto the gravel Oak Tree Trail. You will pass the lattice remains of an old fruit-drying shed on the right. Veer right when passing the park residence.

14.3 Continue straight across the Ridgeline Trail. Pass through the gate and turn left, returning on Oak Tree Trail.

15.5 Arrive back at the parking lot.

Ride Information

Local Information

East Bay Regional Park District, 2950 Peralta Oaks Court, P.O. Box 5381, Oakland, CA 94605; (510) 562-PARK; www.ebparks.org/parks/.
Pleasanton Chamber of Commerce, 777 Peters Avenues, Pleasanton, CA 94588; (925) 846-5858; www.pleasanton.org.
Town of Sunol; www.sunol.net.

Local Events and Attractions

Niles Canyon Railway, Main Street and Kilkare Road, Sunol; (925) 862-0963; www.ncyr.org.

Honorable Mentions

G Sand Hill Ranch II

Sand Hill Ranch is a private venture and a legal option for some insane bumps and jumps. This bicycle terrain park sits on nearly seven acres south of Brentwood in the foothills between Mount Diablo and the delta. This is a training ground for the big races, and you will find man-made courses for four-across biker cross, dual slalom, and trials, along with some downhill training sections. Test your skills on tabletops, berms, doubles, rock gardens, logs, drops, and an assortment of obstacles. Jump over a car, with your friends sitting inside with the camera. There is a $10 per day fee to ride here. The park is open Saturday and Sunday 10:00 A.M. to 5:00 P.M. year-round and Wednesday 2:00 to 7:00 P.M. from April to October, weather and dirt permitting. The schedule changes when there are races. Call the hotline before heading there: (925) 240–6247; www.sandhillracing.com.

From Concord go east on California Highway 4 through Antioch and Oakley to Brentwood. Turn right onto Oak Street and cross the railroad track. Turn left (south) onto Walnut Boulevard for about 4 miles, veering right at the split with Vasco Road. At the stop sign turn left onto Camino Diablo Road. Sand Hill Ranch II is about 0.5 mile down the road on the right at 50 Camino Diablo Road.

H Coyote Hills Regional Park

Grassy hills stand out among the surrounding wetlands and shoreline along San Francisco Bay. The fairly flat and paved Bay View Trail encircles these hills for a great 3.5-mile family ride. The gravel and pavement make this a safe bet in winter. Trails east of the visitor center take you around the wetland for some great bird-watching and a visit to the Ohlone Indian archaeological site. Dirt paths up and over the hill offer an initiation into mountain biking. Keep it short, or hit every trail for a substantial workout. You can even ride south on the gravel Apay Way, cross California Highway 84, and visit the San Francisco Wildlife Refuge and Visitor Center.

Coyote Hills is at the west end of Patterson Ranch Road–Commerce Drive in Fremont. From Interstate 880 in Newark, take CA 84 west. Exit at Paseo Padre Parkway and drive north. Turn left onto Patterson Ranch Road to the park entrance; there is a parking fee. For more information contact the East Bay Regional Park District, Coyote Hills Regional Park; (510) 795–9385; www.ebparks.org.

I Mission Peak Regional Preserve

This is a fine local conditioning ride with a spectacular view of Mount Diablo, San Francisco Bay, and the surrounding peaks. With 2,000 feet of climbing, there is no sugarcoating this ride; visualize the downhill return. It is mostly graded fire road, but it gets rough and rocky in spots, depending on when they lay the gravel. This fully exposed peak is wicked hot in summer and often windy, which explains its popularity for hang gliding. Try this ride in spring when the hills are green and covered in wildflowers. Those seeking a longer ride (up to 15 miles worth) can head south on the Bay Area Ridge Trail to Ed R. Levin County Park; (408) 262–6980; www.parkhere.org.

There are two main starting points in Freemont:

1. The Stanford Avenue entrance is the steepest way to the top, offering a 6-mile round-trip up-and-back. Going northbound on Interstate 680 to Freemont, take the first Mission Boulevard exit and head east. Turn right onto Stanford Avenue. The trailhead is at the end of the road. There are two ways to the top: Peak Meadow Trail is smoother dirt, but bumpy. The Hidden Valley Trail is gravelly.

2. For a more moderate ride with a hint of shade, start from Ohlone College. Take the second Mission Boulevard exit (California Highway 238) and head south past Mission San Jose. Turn left onto Anza Pine Road into Ohlone College; make your way to the east end of the campus to the Peak Trail. There is a parking fee when classes are in session.

The preserve is open until 10:00 P.M., making this a good spot for night riding. For more information contact the East Bay Regional Park District; (925) 862–2218; www.ebparks.org.

J Sunol Regional Wilderness

Sunol Regional Wilderness offers rugged hills, steep climbs, and fine views in cattle country. Ride this in spring, when the grass-covered hills are green and laced with wildflowers. Skip the summertime if you are heading to the peaks; there is no shade. Winter brings sticky gumbo clay. All the trails are wide dirt roads, with cow pies the only real obstacles.

The Camp Ohlone Road to "Little Yosemite" is suitable for beginners. Hayfield Road offers a moderate climb. The loop up Cerro Este Road to Cave Rocks is strenuous but worthwhile; do it counterclockwise. There is not much traffic, except for cattle. The out-and-back to Vista Grande Overlook is also strenuous but beautiful. Maguire Peaks Loop is off the beaten path for most park users, but unfortunately, the cattle really chew up the trail out there. Camping, water, and restrooms are located at the park entrance.

From Pleasanton take Interstate 680 south to Sunol and exit on Calaveras Road/California Highway 84. Turn left onto Calaveras Road and follow for 4 miles. Turn left onto Geary Road, which takes you directly to the park.

For more information contact the East Bay Regional Park District Ranger Station at (925) 862–2244; www.ebparks.org. Trails may close for high fire danger and severe storm damage; call (510) 544–2222 for updates.

South Bay

For the purpose of this guide, South Bay refers to Santa Cruz County and most of Santa Clara County. While South Bay typically refers to the whole of these two counties, trails and terrain have no respect for political boundaries. In this guide a part of Santa Clara is lumped with the Peninsula section. (This is just a point of clarification for those who are sticklers for detail. Don't come after us on that one.)

What matters is that South Bay offers some of the most challenging and remote riding in the Bay Area, including some of the absolute best singletrack. The Hayward and San Andreas Faults have done their job well down here! Rugged mountains flank both the east and west sides of South Bay.

To the east side is Henry W. Coe State Park, the largest state park in California. You may have to travel a bit to reach this wilderness, but that remoteness coupled with the rugged terrain keeps the crowds away. For mountain bikers the journey is worth it for the miles of singletrack, killer climbs, expansive views, and solitude. You can ride hours and rarely see another soul. Carefully pick the time of year to visit. Spring and fall are hands down the best times of year. This is the drier east side of the Santa Clara Valley, and it gets hot in summer. It is ridable in winter, if you choose your route carefully. Most streams are impassable in winter.

By contrast, the west side of South Bay is ridable year-round. The Santa Cruz Mountains run along the coast, offering more challenging singletrack in steep mountains. Coastal fog and dense forests of redwood and Douglas fir make for an inviting pilgrimage in summer. Big Basin State Park feels like the heart of the surviving redwoods. Here you can ride over the mountain to the ocean and back. Not all the rides in South Bay are difficult. There are some great family rides along ocean bluffs, through the redwoods, and along lush creeks.

Responsible Organized Mountain Pedalers (ROMP), Mountain Bikers of Santa Cruz, and groups of faithful volunteers have successfully lobbied and maintained some amazing trails through these mountains. Henry W. Coe State Park, Wilder Ranch State Park, and Soquel Demonstration Forest are so bike-friendly, you wonder what the big deal is. You can ride for days on singletrack, all legal, and not feel like a criminal.

"Realize the damage we do to the world is damage we do to ourselves."

—Paul Nam, ROMP (Responsible Organized Mountain Pedalers) president 2003

23 Joseph D. Grant Ranch Loop

Dirt roads take you through the rolling foothills of an old ranch. Ride the range to the ridge, while the congestion of the Santa Clara Valley remains miles below. The rewards are panoramic views and stellar downhill runs. Never mind that it takes you hours to get to the top and minutes to get down. A network of trails offer options for those averse to too much climbing.

Start: From Joseph D. Grant County Park parking lot.

Distance: 16.8-mile figure eight.

Approximate riding time: 3 hours.

Difficulty rating: Difficult; mostly dirt road, but enough steep, loose, and rutted descents to keep your head up; climbs require stamina or determination.

Trail surface: 92 percent dirt road and 8 percent singletrack.

Terrain: Wide dirt road through rolling hills of pastureland and oak woodlands; steep climbs to ridgetop views of the Santa Clara Valley.

Seasons: Ridable year-round, but best in spring with the wildflower show. Can be hot in summer, but the coastal breeze usually keeps it comfortable. Trails drain well in winter, although the cattle can really churn it up.

Other trail users: Hikers, equestrians, and cattle.

Canine compatibility: Dogs not permitted.

Land status: Santa Clara County Park.

Nearest town: San Jose.

Fees and permits: $4.00 parking fee.

Schedule: Open daily 8:00 A.M. to sunset.

Maps: USGS maps: Lick Observatory, CA; Mt. Day, CA.

Santa Clara County map of Joseph D. Grant Park, usually available at the park entrance and trailhead.

Trail contact: Santa Clara County Parks & Recreation Department, 298 Garden Hill Drive, Los Gatos, CA 95032; park office (408) 274-6121; www.parkhere.org (search Joseph D. Grant Park).

Finding the trailhead: From San Jose: Take U.S. Highway 101 or Interstate 680 to Alum Rock Avenue. Exit and head east for nearly 2 miles. Turn right onto Mount Hamilton Road (California Highway 130) and follow for about 8 miles to the main entrance to Joseph D. Grant Park. This is a narrow, winding road and a twenty-minute drive from the freeway. Pay the vehicle fee at the kiosk or "iron ranger," then drive straight ahead toward the Ranch House. Turn left at the last junction and park near the Rose Garden and sign to Hotel Trail. There are restrooms and water at the parking lot.

The Ride

Joseph D. Grant Park has been a challenging venue for several cross-country and downhill races. Gone with the races is the jarring hoof-impacted "singletrack" through the cattle pasture. Few will miss that. The trails remaining today are packed and well-graded dirt roads—for the most part. Their condition reflects the county's budget.

From Mariposa Point you can spot Lick Observatory atop a distant hill.

Joseph D. Grant was a wealthy businessman who owned the land that now bears his name. While he lived in mansions in San Francisco, Burlingame, and Pebble Beach, this was his retreat. He elaborately remodeled the old ranch house but, like the previous owners, continued to pasture cattle and horses. He came here for sport and pleasure, often accompanied by the rich and influential, the likes of Herbert Hoover. The Grant family owned pieces of this land for nearly a hundred years. When J. D.'s daughter died, the land was set aside for public trust. Joseph D. Grant Park opened to the public in 1978.

Covering 9,522 acres, this is the largest park operated by Santa Clara County. The rolling hills are deceiving. With the Calaveras Fault running through these hills, there are some real roller-coaster sections. The feel of the old ranch still exists in the park. You will ride through the old corral before heading up to check out the upper range. Cattle still graze in portions of the park; you will see their evidence along the trails.

The ride starts near the Ranch House complex on a gentle grade up the canyon carved by San Felipe Creek. These smooth lower dirt roads are great for children and beginners to explore. This is a quiet and pastoral ride, except for the odd sounds of wild pigs echoing through the valley.

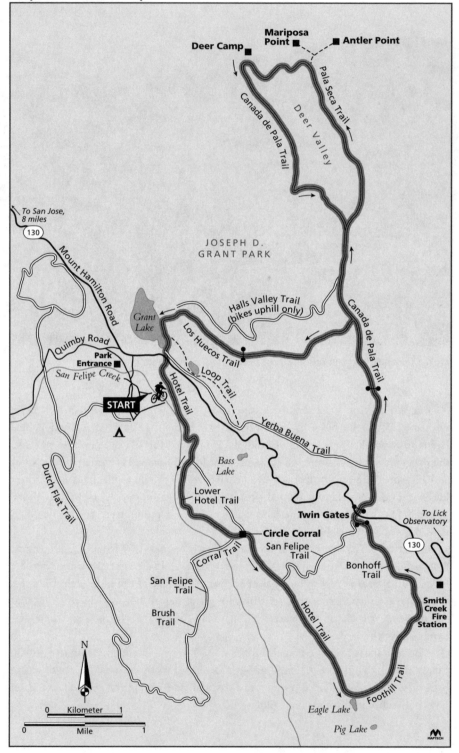

Deer Camp

Mariposa Point

Antler Point

Pala Seca Trail

Deer Valley

Canada de Pala Trail

To San Jose, 8 miles

130

Mount Hamilton Road

JOSEPH D. GRANT PARK

Halls Valley Trail (bikes uphill only)

Canada de Pala Trail

Quimby Road

Grant Lake

Los Huecos Trail

Park Entrance

San Felipe Creek

Loop Trail

START

Hotel Trail

Yerba Buena Trail

Bass Lake

Dutch Flat Trail

Lower Hotel Trail

Twin Gates

To Lick Observatory

Circle Corral

San Felipe Trail

130

Corral Trail

Bonhoff Trail

San Felipe Trail

Hotel Trail

Smith Creek Fire Station

Brush Trail

N

Foothill Trail

Eagle Lake

0 Kilometer 1

0 Mile 1

Pig Lake

MAPTECH

After a couple of warm-up miles, the rolling hills become steep. The series of climbs is broken with short, level sections. The pastureland gradually gives way to oak woodlands mixed with laurel, buckeye, and manzanita. Short, steep descents break up the grind, but overall you are gaining elevation. Eventually weaving through a forest of scraggly digger pine, you begin to feel you are away from it all. Just then, Lick Observatory comes into view. Where do the telescopes point during the day?

After crossing Mount Hamilton Road, you continue the climb along the grass-covered ridge. It can be windy up here. Views of the Santa Clara Valley are below. In spring, wildflowers surround you. Working your way across the ridge to Antler Point, you will do what mountain bikers do: Reach the highest spot. Few people get this far, so the singletrack (yes!) paths to the two overlooks may be overgrown. Benches mark the spots—grand spots. After all the effort, hope for a clear day. Leaving Antler Point, you pass by an old cabin that is being restored to its 1920s self. This was once a deer camp, a place to stay overnight while out on the hunt.

The real payoff comes at the top of Los Huecos Trail. Check the speed here and, as the altered sign says, WATCH YOUR PEE. If you liked it enough, next time skip the 12-mile warm-up; do a shorter loop up Halls Valley Trail and run down Los Huecos Trail. Repeat this as often as you can climb it.

Riding the ridges of Joseph D. Grant is for strong riders. It can be a death march for the uninitiated. The network of trails offers ways to cut back the amount of climbing. Omit the upper loop and enjoy a 10-mile single loop instead.

Miles and Directions

0.0 **START** from the sign to Hotel Trail near the Rose Garden, proceeding through the first gate. Go straight on the dirt path where the trail forks. (The paved path will loop back to the parking lot from where you just came.) You will soon come to another gate. Turn right here onto Hotel Trail. Trailhead GPS: N37 20 13.1, W 121 42 51.6.

0.7 Veer right onto Lower Hotel Trail.

1.7 Turn left to stay on Lower Hotel Trail at the junction with Corral Trail. You will soon come to Circle Corral. Ride straight through the corral and turn right onto Hotel Trail (at Mile 1.8). You will soon climb the first in a series of steep hills.

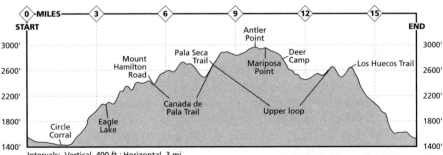

Intervals: Vertical, 400 ft.; Horizontal, 3 mi.

2.3 Continue straight on Hotel Trail at the intersection with the San Felipe Trail.

3.4 Arrive at Eagle Lake (actually, a pond). Stay to the left at the gate and drop down onto Foothill Trail. The trail narrows at one point and goes down the middle of the rocky creekbed. Prepare for a series of steep ascents.

4.5 Turn left at the junction onto Bonhoff Trail. That first steep grind is not the last, but it is the longest.

5.4 Turn right onto the short singletrack to cross Mount Hamilton Road. Head into the Twin Gates parking lot, and take the dirt road on the left near the outhouse. This is Canada de Pala Trail. You will pass under some serious power lines. The intergalactic humming may be a little unnerving.

5.9 Continue straight on Canada de Pala Trail at the junction with Yerba Buena Trail. **Shortcut:** You can check out parts of the Sizzle Classic downhill course by opting down Yerba Buena Trail. For some singletrack pick up the Loop Trail on the right about 1.3 miles down. At the bottom cut back over to Yerba Buena Trail. Take the short path to Ranch House and cross Mount Hamilton Road. You are back on Hotel Trail, which will take you to the parking lot.

7.2 Continue straight where Los Huecos Trail comes in on the left. **Shortcut:** Skip the upper loop. Turn left and head down Los Huecos Trail. At the bottom pick up directions at Mile 15.6 below.

7.6 Ignore Halls Valley Trail coming up on the left. No bikes are allowed down this trail. It is an option for a shorter ride up next time. (Maybe you do not want to hear that now.)

8.1 Turn right at the fork onto Pala Seca Trail.

9.4 Turn right onto the narrow Antler Point Trail.

9.6 The narrow singletrack splits to become a footpath. There is not much traffic up here so you may have to tromp around a bit to find the trail. Take the right path to Antler Point. The trail stops at a bench overlooking the deep gorge of Arroyo Hondo. When you return take the other fork to Mariposa Point (although there may be no sign). There is also a bench here for a sweeping view (if it is clear) of the Santa Clara Valley. Backtrack to the dirt road.

10.7 Turn right, returning to the dirt road.

11.4 Pass Pala Seca Deer Camp. Follow Canada de Pala Trail through the peaceful valley and newly evolved meadow.

12.6 Bear left to stay on Canada de Pala where Washburn Trail comes in from the right.

13.1 Turn right on Canada de Pala, completing the upper loop.

14.0 Turn right down Los Huecos Trail. Watch for monster-size trenches if the trail has not been graded.

15.6 At the bottom turn left onto Halls Valley Trail toward Grant Lake.

16.0 Turn left at the lake.

16.2 Turn left onto Yerba Buena Trail just before the parking lot. Follow the signs to the Ranch House.

16.3 Turn right onto a short path through an opening in the fence. Cross Mount Hamilton Road, go through the gate, and head right on Hotel Trail.

16.7 Turn right at the gate back to the parking lot, completing the loop.

16.8 Arrive back at the parking lot.

Option to Try the Sizzle Classic Cross-Country Course

This route follows most of the former race course. Start from the parking lot near the campground and head south on San Felipe Trail. Turn right onto Dairy Trail and switchback up to Dutch Flat Trail. At the end of Dutch Flat Trail, turn right onto Brush Trail, left onto San Felipe Trail, and then right onto Corral Trail. Turn left onto Hotel Trail back to the parking lot. Portions of the race were truly through the cattle pasture and not on bona fide trails. They are gone, but you will not miss these sections. The climbing still makes this a hardy ride. If you watch the speed on the downhill, it is not too technical. This is a moderate 8-mile loop entirely on dirt road, taking 1.5 to 2 hours.

Ride Information

Local Events and Attractions

University of California Observatories—Lick Observatory, University of California, Santa Cruz; (831) 459-2513; www.ucolcik.org.

Accommodations

Halls Valley Campground, Joseph D. Grant Park, Santa Clara County Park and Recreation Department, 298 Garden Hill Drive, Los Gatos; reservations (408) 355-2201; www.parkhere.org.

Restaurants and Java Jolts

Rafiki's Coffee Hut, 3101 Alum Rock Avenue, San Jose; (408) 259-4000.

La Barca de Oro (great burritos), 3141 Alum Rock Avenue, San Jose; (408) 926-4403.

White Rock Cafe, 3116 Alum Rock Avenue, San Jose; (408) 729-4843.

LICK OBSERVATORY The distant white domes atop Mount Hamilton are the Lick Observatory. A trust from eccentric millionaire James Lick funded the building of the original telescope in 1888. The dying wish of the "generous miser" was to build the greatest telescope in the world. Thanks to this wish, the University of California operates this state-of-the-art facility and conducts leading-edge research in astronomy. Except for a few holidays, the observatory is open daily to the public. To reach the observatory continue up winding Mount Hamilton Road. Mount Hamilton WebCam sends updated images every few minutes from the summit of Mount Hamilton (4,200 feet). For current weather conditions and a view from the top, check out their Web site: www.ucolick.org.

24 Henry W. Coe Park: Middle Ridge Loop

Welcome to miles of legal singletrack in a state park! This ride is a good introduction to Henry W. Coe State Park. If you like it, there is more to come back for. A meandering singletrack takes you up to Frog Lake. From there it is a steady climb up to Middle Ridge, with a view of the deeply carved canyon below. Ride the ridge through oak woodlands, giant manzanita, scattered ponderosa pines, and grassy meadows before a long technical descent to the canyon floor. It is payback time on the long climb out the steep dirt road.

Start: From the visitor center, Coe Ranch Headquarters.

Distance: 10.8-mile loop.

Approximate riding time: 2.5 hours.

Difficulty rating: Difficult; a rigorous workout, with some strenuous climbs, especially the long grind out of the valley. Strong technical skills will make the steep and rocky singletrack more enjoyable.

Trail surface: 54 percent single track, 44 percent dirt road, and 2 percent paved road.

Terrain: Rugged mountain wilderness, grass-covered hills, oak woodlands, meadows, steeply carved canyons, uneven ridgeline, and stream crossings.

Seasons: Best in spring and fall. Coe can be wicked hot in summer, although when it is foggy on the coast, the breeze makes it bearable. High water in the streams may prevent passage in winter and early spring.

Other trail users: Hikers, backpackers, equestrians, and an occasional vehicle.

Canine compatibility: Dogs not permitted.

Land status: Henry W. Coe State Park.

Nearest town: Morgan Hill.

Fees and permits: $5.00 parking fee on weekends.

Schedule: Open 24 hours daily. Singletrack trails close for 48 hours after rainfall over half an inch. Check with park rangers for status of trails. Check to make sure Middle Fork Coyote Creek is passable before you set out in winter and early spring.

Maps: USGS maps: Mt. Sizer, CA.
State Park map: *Henry W. Coe State Park California, Trail and Camping Map* (2002), available for purchase at the visitor center.
Henry W. Coe State Park, *The Bike Map* flyer for trails in the northern section of the park, Coe HQ edition, available free at visitor center.

Trail contact: Henry W. Coe State Park, P.O. Box 846, Morgan Hill, CA 95038; (408) 779-2728; www.parks.ca.gov.

Finding the trailhead: From San Jose: Take U.S. Highway 101 south to Morgan Hill. Take the East Dunn Avenue exit and follow the signs east to Henry W. Coe State Park. It is 13 miles of narrow, winding road. There are two parking lots, which can fill up on weekends and holidays. If the upper lot is full, a nice half-mile singletrack connects the lower lot to the visitor center. When both lots are full, they turn folks away. There is no other parking along the road leading up to the park. The ride starts at the visitor center at the park headquarters, where there are restrooms and water.

Cut through the grass along Middle Ridge Trail on this great singletrack.

The Ride

You may have lived in the Bay Area a long time and never heard of Henry W. Coe State Park. Tucked away in the southeast bay, there are miles of legal singletrack to explore. Only a handful of singletrack is off-limits to bikes. Check at the visitor center to be clear which trails are closed, but they are well marked. Despite the wilderness feel out here, do not ride off the legal trails. Stay off anything not posted as a trail or on the current map.

The remote location and ruggedness keep the crowds away. This is the largest state park in Northern California, with more than 86,000 acres of wild open spaces. Henry Willard Coe began purchasing the land along Pine Ridge in the 1880s from homesteaders. His family raised cattle on the land, but the ranching out here was rough. His daughter, Sada Coe, donated the land to Santa Clara County in 1953 to preserve it as parkland. Five years later the land became part of the state park system. Through the years the park has continued to acquire more ranches. There is still some private property out there, explaining the rare rancher's truck you may encounter on the dirt roads. However, do not expect a lift out.

The real riding in Henry Coe Park is on the singletrack. The fire roads, like Hobbs and Poverty Flat Roads, are merely connectors. Unfortunately they usually

Henry W. Coe Park: Middle Ridge Loop

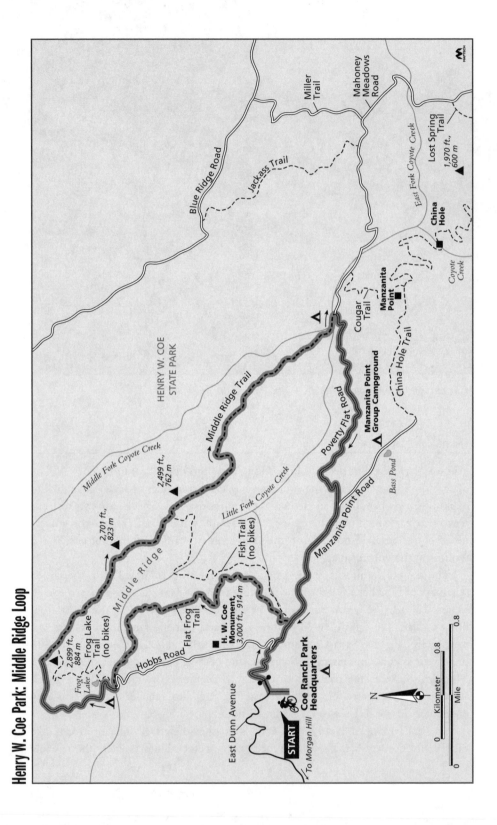

involve a climb. The ride really begins on Flat Frog Trail. "Flat" qualifies the trail; it is unlikely you will encounter any roadkill. This is a pleasant meander along the contours of the hill through oak woodlands, making this one of the easier rides near the park headquarters. From the singletrack you climb up the dirt road to Middle Ridge Trail—the heart of this loop. This singletrack meanders along the ridge through oak, evergreen, and huge manzanita woodlands. Sections cut through meadows of *tall* grass, with their signature display of wildflowers in spring. There are a few short, steep climbs along the first mile, but it is generally a smooth ride. The last half of the trail drops down to the canyon floor; the descent is technical—steep, loose dirt, rocky, and twisty. Beware of poison oak.

The ridge trail drops you onto Middle Fork Coyote Creek. This can be a fun crossing and a great place for a break before the long climb out. There are also several nice campsites along the creek. What follows is the ride out, and it is not pleasant. The first 2 miles have some particularly steep pitches. If you have the stamina, the longer climb out via the China Hole option is more pleasant.

The mileage readings start from the visitor center at Coe Park Headquarters. Check in here for an update on trail conditions, to pick up a park map, and to let them know where you are heading. If you ride this in winter or spring, find out how high the water is in Middle Fork Coyote Creek. You do not want to have to turn around and retrace your tracks because you cannot cross the river. There are no bridges out there.

There are maps, water, and restrooms at the visitor center but no food. The water there is the only potable water in the park. Bring lots of water—a hundred-ounce hydration pack and a couple of water bottles. This is beautiful country for bike camping; reservations are first-come, first-served. Bring a water filter. If you are sensitive to poison oak, bring some preexposure lotion.

Miles and Directions

0.0   **START** from the visitor center at the park headquarters. Turn left (heading north) up paved East Dunn Avenue. After 200 feet turn right up paved Manzanita Point Road. Trailhead GPS: N 37 11 12.3, W 121 32 48.5.

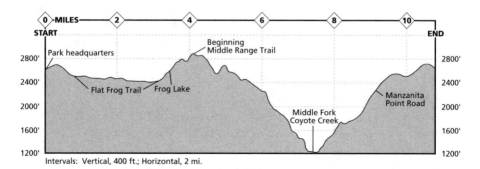

0.1 Pass through the gate. The pavement quickly ends.

0.5 Veer right on Manzanita Point Road at the fork with Hobbs Road. Do not be fooled by the mileage on the road sign: Although Hobbs Road is a more direct way to Frog Lake, it is not nearly as nice.

0.8 Turn left at the beginning of three singletrack trails. Take the far left branch onto Flat Frog Trail. Caution signs along the way will tell you to walk your bike down some wooden steps. You be the judge.

3.0 Turn right onto wide Hobbs Road; cross the creek, and climb.

3.2 Continue straight on Hobbs Road at Frog Lake. There are some campsites here and an outhouse. **Side trip:** Walk or ride down to the pond. The road is steep and rutted but short. This is a pleasant spot, but it's not too inviting for a swim. No bikes are allowed on the singletrack Frog Lake Trail up to Middle Ridge.

4.0 Turn right onto Middle Ridge Trail. (**Side trip:** Before you make the turn, check out the overlook up ahead off Hobbs Road. This is a great view of Blue Ridge and the deeply carved canyon below.) Continue on Middle Ridge Trail all the way to the creek below. Ignore Frog Lake Trail at Mile 4.1 and Fish Trail at Mile 5.4. No bikes are allowed on these trails.

7.5 Cross Middle Fork Coyote Creek. Depending on the season, this is a good place to cool off and wash off the poison oak. After crossing the creek ride past some campsites; ford the creek once more before pushing your bike up to the dirt road.

7.6 Turn right onto Poverty Flat Road for the steep climb out. There is shade along the steepest stretches; nonetheless, it is still hot in summer. **Option:** Turn left onto Poverty Flat Road. After 0.3 mile turn right up the singletrack Cougar Trail to Manzanita Point. This is a steep 0.8 mile. Once at Manzanita Point, turn right onto the China Hole Trail. Turn right onto Manzanita Point Road, following it back to the visitor center. This option adds 1.3 miles to the total loop.

9.2 Turn right onto Manzanita Point Road. The worst climbing is behind you. Stay on Manzanita Point Road back to park headquarters.

10.0 This completes the loop. Continue straight on the main road at the junction with Flat Frog Trail.

10.3 Veer left at the junction with Hobbs Road.

10.8 Arrive back at the visitor center.

Easiest Option

The 6.4-mile out-and-back to Frog Lake is a wonderful singletrack ride, without too much climbing. (There is one unpleasant but short climb from the singletrack up to the lake.) The rivulet dips in the trail may be bothersome to a complete newbie. Since it is a narrow trail along the contours of the hills, it is not advisable for anyone who cannot ride a straight line.

Long and More Strenuous Options

Back way to China Hole: At Mile 7.6 above turn left onto Poverty Flat Road. After 1.5 miles turn right onto Mahoney Meadows Road. After another mile turn right onto the singletrack Lost Spring Trail. At the end of this 0.9-mile trail, turn right onto singletrack China Hole Trail. Follow to Manzanita Point Group Campground, about 5 miles from Poverty Flat. Turn right onto Manzanita Point Road and follow it back to park headquarters. This adds 7 miles and 1,600 feet of climbing, but it is a lot more interesting ride than the grind out Poverty Flat Road.

Blue Ridge Loop: At Mile 7.6 above turn left onto Poverty Flat Road. After 1.5 miles turn left at the fork to Miller Trail. Stay on the main dirt road. After a mile turn left onto Blue Ridge Road. After 0.9 mile turn left onto Jackass Trail singletrack. At the bottom of the singletrack, turn right back onto Poverty Flat Road. Continue back to park headquarters, turning right at Manzanita Point Road. This loop adds about 6 miles and 2,000 feet of climbing (and descent!).

Ride Information

Local Information

The Pine Ridge Association, P.O. Box 846, Morgan Hill, CA 95038; (408) 779-2728; www.coepark.org.

Morgan Hill Chamber of Commerce, 17450 Monterey Road, Suite B, Morgan Hill, CA 95037; (408) 779-9444; www.morganhill.org.

Local Events and Attractions

Annual Events at Coe Park: Mother's Day Breakfast, Fall Tarantula Fest and Barbecue, Backcountry Weekend (April); Morgan Hill; (408) 779-2728; www.coepark.org.

Accommodations

Henry W. Coe State Park camping: For car-accessed campground contact (800) 444-7275 or www.reserveamerica.com. For group camping and bike camping/backpacking, call park headquarters at (408) 779-2728. Camping is on a first-come, first-served basis. There is usually space available, except on weekends in spring and on holidays.

Holiday Inn Express, 17035 Condit Road, Morgan Hill; (408) 776-7676; www.hiexpress-morganhill.com.

Restaurants and Java Jolts

Dusty Trail Barbeque, 16490 Monterey Road, Morgan Hill; (408) 776-9072.

Starbucks, 17015 Walnut Grove, Morgan Hill; (408) 465-2107.

Group Rides

Coe mountain-biking Web site: www.coecore.homestead.com.

25 Henry W. Coe Park: China Hole Out-and-Back

This is one of the few intermediate rides in Henry W. Coe State Park and requires some stamina. There is no bailing on the ride out. A smooth dirt road takes you down to and back from Manzanita Point group campground. From the campground a singletrack trail switchbacks 1,100 feet down to Coyote Creek. At the right time of year, this is good splash. The ride out on the singletrack is not bad; the ride out on the dirt road seems longer.

Start: From the visitor center, Coe Ranch Headquarters.
Distance: 10.0 miles out and back.
Approximate riding time: 1.5 to 2 hours.
Difficulty rating: Moderate; graded dirt road, well-built singletrack with some switchbacks, mostly hard-packed surface; gradual and long climb out.
Trail surface: 52 percent singletrack, 46 percent dirt road, and 2 percent paved road.
Terrain: Follow the ridge into a steeply carved canyon, grass-covered hills, oak and pine woodlands, hillsides thick with chaparral; picturesque pond and creek at the bottom.
Seasons: Best in spring and fall. Coe can be wicked hot in summer, although when it is foggy on the coast, the breeze makes it bearable. Ridable in winter, except when closed after storms.
Other trail users: Hikers, backpackers, equestrians, and an occasional vehicle on the dirt roads.

Canine compatibility: Dogs not permitted.
Land status: Henry W. Coe State Park.
Nearest town: Morgan Hill.
Fees and permits: $5.00 parking fee on weekends.
Schedule: Open 24 hours daily. Singletrack trails closed for 48 hours after rainfall over half an inch. Check with park rangers for status of trails. If you plan to extend the ride beyond China Hole, check ahead at the visitor center on the conditions at Coyote Creek.
Maps: USGS map: Mt. Sizer, CA.
State Park map: *Henry W. Coe State Park California, Trail and Camping Map* (2002), available for purchase at the visitor center.
Henry W. Coe State Park, *The Bike Map* flyer for trails in the northern section of the park, Coe HQ edition, available free at visitor center.
Trail contact: Henry W. Coe State Park, P.O. Box 846, Morgan Hill, CA 95038; (408) 779-2728; www.parks.ca.gov and www.coecore.org.

Finding the trailhead: From San Jose: Take U.S. Highway 101 south to Morgan Hill. Take the East Dunn Avenue exit and follow the signs east to Henry W. Coe State Park. It is 13 miles of narrow winding road. There are two parking lots, which can fill up on weekends and holidays. If the upper lot is full, a nice half-mile singletrack connects the lower lot to the visitor center. When both lots are full, they turn folks away. There is no other parking along the winding road leading up to the park. The ride starts at the visitor center at park headquarters, where there are restrooms and water.

How cool! China Hole in the early summer... ▶

Henry W. Coe Park: China Hole Out-and-Back

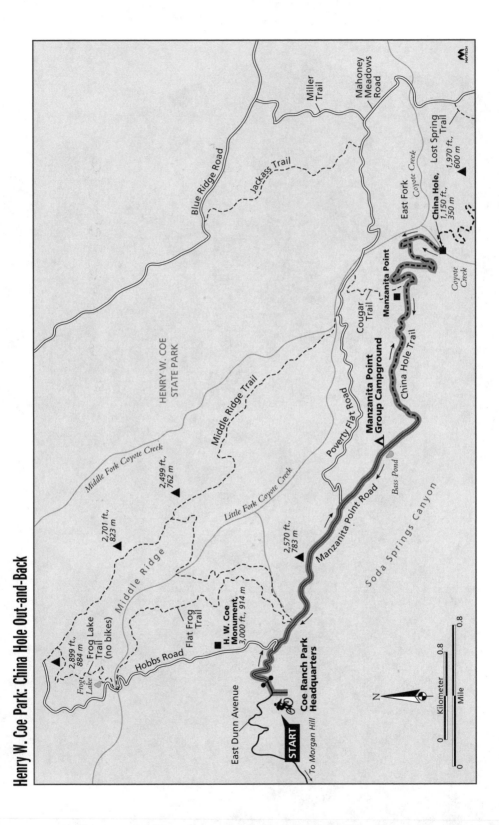

The Ride

Within 84,000 acres of wilderness, Henry W. Coe Park offers nearly 200 miles of dirt roads and singletrack trails for mountain biking. Practically none of them is easy. This is rugged open space and explains some of the popularity of the ride to China Hole. This is a good place for strong intermediate riders to get a taste of "Coe." You will see more traffic here than in most other places in the park. In winter and early spring, when the water is high in all the creeks, this is a good ride. There are no stream crossings unless you opt to ride beyond China Hole.

At first glance it is hard to get excited about a ride down into China Hole. You know what that means on the way out. Not to worry, the grade out is not as bad as it sounds. Half the ride is on the well-graded Manzanita Point Road to the group campground. From here you drop about 1,100 feet down a well-maintained single-track to Coyote Creek. The first mile weaves through woodlands of oaks and ponderosa pines. No flailing here, the poison oak makes a nice tunnel. At the actual Manzanita Point, you are riding out in the open through dense chaparral. The needlelike chamise can be rough on bare arms and legs. The charred manzanita stalks are remnants of a controlled burn. From here you get a view of the park's immense wilderness. The trail switchbacks down into Soda Springs Canyon and Coyote Creek below.

Once at the creek you have arrived at China Hole—the rock-flanked pool. This is a nice swimming hole (do not expect to do laps here) in spring and early summer. As the weather warms, the pool and creek get uninvitingly green and slimy. Bring a book, relax, and enjoy. On the way out the singletrack grade is manageable. Even though you are in and out of shade, this can be hot climb in summer. The ride out on the dirt road seems longer, although it is not quite as long as the singletrack.

Manzanita Point Group Campground is perched on the end of the ridge under the oaks and ponderosa pines. This makes a great base camp, offering a springboard for riding deeper into the wilderness. Reservations are on a first-come, first-served basis. Bring the support crew and spend some time. Spending a couple of days allows you to ride farther into the park. Each group can bring in one vehicle for supplies. (Read, plenty of water.) There is no potable water at the campground. Better yet, join Responsible Organized Mountain Pedalers (ROMP) on one of their work parties. Spend a day helping with trail maintenance, then enjoy the next day exploring the far reaches of this amazing wilderness.

Check at the visitor center before you start for an update on trail conditions. There are maps, water, and restrooms there but no food. The water at the headquarters is the only potable water in the park. Bring lots of water—a hundred-ounce hydration pack and a couple of water bottles. There are restrooms at Manzanita Point campground. If you are sensitive to poison oak, bring some preexposure lotion.

Some general notes on the trail: Despite the wilderness feel out here, do not ride off the legal trails. Stay off anything not posted as a trail or on the current map.

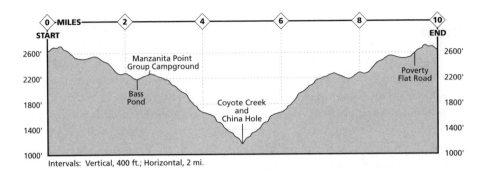

Intervals: Vertical, 400 ft.; Horizontal, 2 mi.

And, no, the singletracks are not for kiddy trailers! A misguided dad was seen walking down China Hole Trail with a wide-eyed kid in the back.

Miles and Directions

0.0 **START** from the visitor center at the park headquarters. Turn left (heading north) up paved East Dunn Avenue. After 200 feet turn right up paved Manzanita Point Road. Trailhead GPS: N 37 11 12.3, W 121 32 48.5.

0.1 Pass through the gate. The pavement quickly ends.

0.5 Veer right on Manzanita Point Road at the fork with Hobbs Road.

1.6 Veer right on Manzanita Point Road at the fork with Poverty Flat Road.

2.1 Veer left at the fork. The road to the right goes to Blue Oak Horse Camp. You will soon pass Bass Pond on the right and a series of roads taking off on the right to campsites. Stay to the left at all forks through here.

2.4 Just past Campsite 7 is a sign to China Hole. Turn left and head down the singletrack.

2.6 Stay left at the fork. The trail on the right goes back up to the campground.

3.5 Arrive at Manzanita Point. Cougar Trail drops down on the left to Poverty Flat. Stay to the right on China Hole Trail and ride down to the canyon floor. Just before arriving at the creek, ignore Mile Trail (no bikes) on the right.

5.0 Arrive at Coyote Creek and China Hole. Return the way you came. **Option:** Before turning back continue across the creek on China Hole Trail and explore. The trail on the other side is not very obvious. Cross downstream a few yards from where you arrived at the creek. Follow the trail toward Lost Spring Trail and Mahoney Meadows. The trail on this side of the creek is narrower, steeper, and less traveled than what you came down. It is about 2.1 miles to Lost Spring Trail. If you want more distance, turn left onto Lost Spring Trail for another 0.9 mile. A turnaround here gives you a 16-mile total round-trip.

6.5 Veer left on China Hole Trail at the junction with Cougar Trail.

7.6 Turn right onto Manzanita Point Road. Follow this the rest of the way back.

10.0 Arrive back at the park headquarters.

Ride Information

Local Information

The Pine Ridge Association, P.O. Box 846, Morgan Hill, CA 95038; (408) 779-2728; www.coepark.org.

Morgan Hill Chamber of Commerce, 17450 Monterey Road, Suite B, Morgan Hill, CA 95037; (408) 779-9444; www.morganhill.org.

Local Events and Attractions

Annual Events at Coe Park: Mother's Day Breakfast, Fall Tarantula Fest and Barbecue, Backcountry Weekend (April); Morgan Hill; (408) 779-2728; www.coepark.org.

Accommodations

Henry W. Coe State Park camping: For car accessed campground contact (800) 444-7275 or www.reserveamerica.com.

For group camping and bike camping/backpacking, call the park headquarters at (408) 779-2728. Camping is on a first-come, first-served basis. There is usually space available, except on weekends in spring and on holidays.

Holiday Inn Express, 17035 Condit Road, Morgan Hill; (408) 776-7676; www.hiexpress-morganhill.com.

Restaurants and Java Jolts

Dusty Trail Barbeque, 16490 Monterey Road, Morgan Hill; (408) 776-9072.

Starbucks, 17015 Walnut Grove, Morgan Hill; (408) 465-2107.

Group Rides

Coe mountain-biking Web site: www.coecore.homestead.com.

26 Henry W. Coe Park: Spike Jones-Grizzly Gulch Loop

Welcome to the world of Henry W. Coe Park! Here you will find some of the best singletrack in the Bay Area—and the most rugged riding. This ride offers a great introduction to the southern and more remote reaches of the park. Expect challenging singletrack to the top of a panoramic ridge. Suck in as much fresh air as you can. Enjoy narrow singletrack descents through a secluded canyon. Do not expect much traffic out here.

Start: From Hunting Hollow entrance to Henry W. Coe Park.

Distance: 12.7-mile loop.

Approximate riding time: 2 to 2.5 hours.

Difficulty rating: Difficult; strenuous climbs with steep, technical descents.

Trail surface: 53 percent singletrack, 17 percent dirt road, and 30 percent paved road.

Terrain: Rugged mountains, steep grass-covered hills and canyons, oak woodlands, meditation pond, creek crossings.

Seasons: Best in spring and fall. Hot and dry in summer; ridable in winter when trails are open, but the creek crossings make for a cold ride home.

Other trail users: Hikers and equestrians.

Canine compatibility: Dogs not permitted.

Land status: Henry W. Coe State Park.

Nearest town: Gilroy.

Fees and permits: $3.00 parking fee on spring and summer weekends.

Schedule: Open 24 hours daily. Singletrack trails closed for 48 hours after rainfall over half an inch. Check with park rangers for status of trails. Reservations are required for camping.

Maps: USGS map: Gilroy Hot Springs, CA. State Park map: *Henry W. Coe State Park California, Trail and Camping Map* (2002), available for purchase at the visitor center. Henry W. Coe State Park, trail map flyer of Southern End—Hunting Hollow & Coyote Creek Entrances, available at Hunting Hollow when stocked.

Trail contact: Henry W. Coe State Park, P.O. Box 846, Morgan Hill, CA 95038; (408) 779-2728; www.parks.ca.gov or www.coepark.org.

Finding the trailhead: From San Jose: Take U.S. Highway 101 south to Gilroy. Exit at Leavesley Road/California Highway 152 West and head *east* on Leavesley Road. After 1.8 miles turn left onto New Avenue and then right onto Roop Road. At the turnoff for Coyote Lake County Park, Roop becomes Gilroy Hot Springs Road. Stay on Gilroy Hot Springs Road to the Hunting Hollow entrance to Henry W. Coe Park. Turn right into the dirt parking lot. There are outhouses but no water or phone.

The Ride

Henry W. Coe State Park is one of the most bike-friendly parks in the Bay Area. Ride responsibly, and keep it that way. All the singletrack in the southern section of this park is open to bikers. However, if you venture far enough to the northeast, you will reach the Orestimba Wilderness, which is off-limits to bikes. As the park Web

The magnificent view from Steer Ridge Road near Wilson Peak changes with the seasons.

site says, "Most trails and roads are steep to very steep to ridiculously steep." Come to Coe for the singletrack, not fire roads. Somehow, grinding or pushing up a steep hill on singletrack is more bearable than it is on fire roads.

Compared with the western zone of the park near the visitor center, this southern area is even more remote. The locals who ride here are a hardy group. Among them are some of the staff at Specialized headquarters in Morgan Hill. Keep an eye out for some new equipment on these trails.

The ride begins at the southwest entrance to Henry W. Coe Park at Hunting Hollow. There is limited parking nearly 2 miles up the road at the Coyote Creek entrance, where you will ride onto the dirt. Vehicles are more secure at the Hunting Hollow parking lot, where there is a park ranger on weekends from March to June. For this loop the road ride gives you a bit of a warm-up before starting the climbs. Save the Coyote Creek entrance for the rides that go farther north into the park. There is no potable water at either entrance or along the trails. Bring water with you—and lots of it.

The Spike Jones Trail should make you smile as much as the 1940s musical comedian of the same name. This gorgeous singletrack meanders through shady oak woodlands before climbing up to the ridgetop meadows of tall grass. The ride

Henry W. Coe Park: Spike Jones–Grizzly Gulch Loop

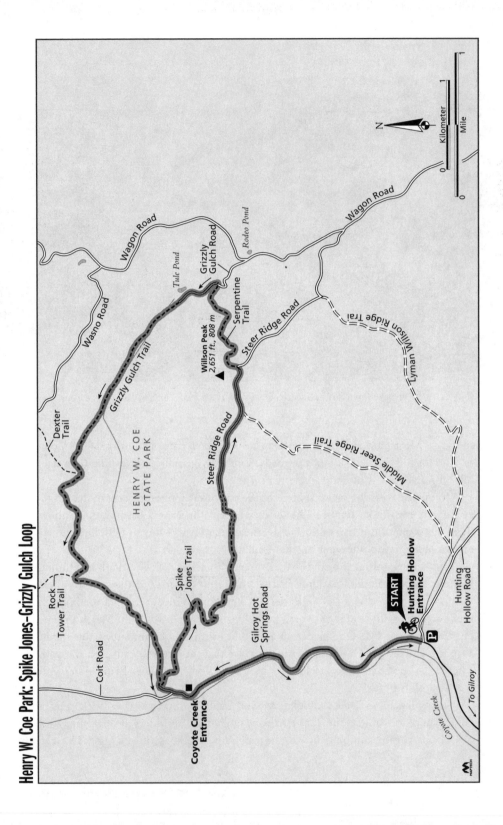

becomes steep and endless. If you need to, you will not be the first person to push your bike up this trail. The view along the ridge is worth it, as are the wildflowers in spring. Nearer the top you will connect with seldom-maintained Steer Ridge Road, which takes you on to the summit. From there you soon pick up Serpentine Trail (a fast + narrow = fun descent) to Grizzly Gulch Road. You pass Tule Pond as the road gradually narrows to a singletrack. This is a favorite trail, but you will probably not see any traffic. There are just too many trails for the few riders that make it out here.

There are several creek crossings along the Grizzly Creek Trail before it gradually heads up along the grassy contours of the canyon. The trail becomes loose, steep, and technical when it eventually drops down to cross the creek one last time. By then you are back into the shade of the oak woodland for a smooth ride back to the beginning of the Spike Jones Trail. You have returned from the wilderness.

As a general note on the area, the farther north you go from Hunting Hollow, the less equestrian traffic you will encounter. While the Lyman Willson Ridge Trail is a popular route out of Hunting Hollow, the hoofed traffic tends to tear it up in the wet season. If you come down that way, assume there may be a horse around every corner. The Lyman Willson Ridge Trail is also more exposed. There are some hefty creek crossings along the Hunting Hollow Road.

Despite the wilderness feel out here, do not ride off the legal trails. Stay off anything not posted as a trail or on the current park map.

Miles and Directions

0.0 **START** from Hunting Hollow entrance and parking lot. Turn right as you leave the parking lot, heading north up paved Gilroy Hot Springs Road. Parking lot entrance GPS: N 37 04 33.5, W 121 28 01.4.

1.9 Turn right at the end of the pavement (just before the bridge across Coyote Creek) and go around the gate at the Coyote Creek entrance to the park.

2.0 Turn right at the fork with Coit Road, following signs to Timm Trail toward Willson Camp.

2.1 Turn left onto Spike Jones Trail at the fork with Timm Springs #1 Trail.

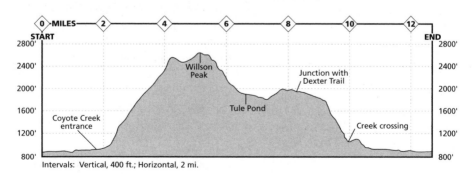

2.2 Veer right at the fork, staying on Spike Jones Trail. You will return from the left on Grizzly Gulch Trail at the end of the loop. Stay on the main singletrack trail, ignoring any faint side trails along the way.

4.3 Turn left onto Steer Ridge Road toward Willson Camp. This is a steep, overgrown, and rutted dirt road. It becomes dual track in sections.

5.2 Veer left on Steer Ridge Road at the junction with Middle Steer Ridge Trail on the right.

5.4 Veer right at the unsigned fork near the summit and outcropping of serpentine rock. The trail to the left goes to Willson Peak (2,651 feet).

5.5 Turn left onto Serpentine Trail to Rodeo Pond. The trail soon narrows from dual track to singletrack.

6.4 Turn left onto Grizzly Gulch Trail toward Tule Pond. The trail narrows to a dual track and eventually fades to a singletrack at Mile 7.0.

8.3 Veer left at the fork to stay on Grizzly Gulch Trail. The right uphill trail (Dexter Trail) goes to Kelly Lake.

9.3 Veer left on Grizzly Gulch Trail. The trail to the right is Rock Tower Trail to Jackson Field.

9.8 Veer left on Grizzly Gulch Trail at the fork with Cullen Trail.

10.5 Turn right onto Spike Jones Trail to Coyote Creek entrance. This completes the loop. Return the way you came.

10.7 Merge with Coit Road, continuing straight ahead.

10.8 Turn left onto paved Gilroy Hot Springs Road.

12.7 Arrive back at the Hunting Hollow parking lot.

Ride Information

Local Information
The Pine Ridge Association, P.O. Box 846, Morgan Hill, CA 95038; (408) 779- 2728; www.coepark.org.
Gilroy Visitors Bureau, 7780 Monterey Street, Gilroy, CA 95020; (408) 842-6436; www.gilroyvisitor.org.

Local Events and Attractions
Gilroy Garlic Festival, last full weekend in July; (408) 842-1625; www.gilroygarlicfestival.com.

Accommodations
Henry W. Coe State Park camping: For car-accessed campground contact (800) 444-7275 or www.reserveamerica.com. For group camping and bike camping, call park headquarters at (408) 779-2728. Camping is on a first-come, first-served basis. There is usually space available, except weekends in spring and on holidays.
Coyote Lake Campground, County of Santa Clara, Parks and Recreation Department, 298 Garden Hill Drive, Los Gatos; information (408) 355-2200; reservations (408) 355-2201; www.parkhere.org.

Restaurants and Java Jolts
Chevys Fresh Mex, 8440 Murray Avenue, Gilroy; (408) 847-2726; www.chevys.com.
Starbucks, Gilroy Outlet Center, 8375 Arroya Circle, Gilroy; (408) 846-9733; www.starbucks.com.

Group Rides
Coe mountain-biking Web site: www.coecore.homestead.com.

27 Henry W. Coe Park: Kelly Lake Loop

This ride is the heart of Henry W. Coe Park, taking you deep into the remote reaches of the wilderness. As with all rides in the park, steep climbs are a guarantee. However, the rewards are great—plenty of narrow singletrack, expansive views, wild creek crossings, a peaceful pond, long downhill runs, and lots of switchbacks. You return with a sense of solitude rarely attainable elsewhere in the Bay Area.

Start: From the Coyote Creek entrance to Henry W. Coe Park at the end of Gilroy Hot Springs Road.
Distance: 16.4-mile loop.
Approximate riding time: 3.5 to 4.5 hours.
Difficulty rating: Difficult; strenuous climbs with steep, technical descents; remote, as in you do not want to get hurt out here.
Trail surface: 70 percent singletrack, 22 percent dirt road, and 8 percent dual track.
Terrain: Rugged mountains, steep grass-covered hills and canyons, oak woodlands, secluded pond, plenty of creek crossings, challenging singletrack with rocks, ruts, and loose dirt.
Seasons: Best in spring and fall. Hot and dry in summer, cold and wet creek crossings in winter.
Other trail users: Hikers and equestrians.
Canine compatibility: Dogs not permitted.

Land status: Henry W. Coe State Park.
Nearest town: Gilroy.
Fees and permits: No fees or permits required.
Schedule: Open 24 hours daily. Singletrack trails closed for 48 hours after rainfall over half an inch. Check with park rangers for status of trails.
Maps: USGS maps: Gilroy Hot Springs, CA; Mississippi Creek, CA.
State Park map: *Henry W. Coe State Park California, Trail and Camping Map* (2002), available for purchase at the visitor center.
Henry W. Coe State Park, trail map flyer of Southern End—Hunting Hollow & Coyote Creek Entrances, available at Hunting Hollow when stocked.
Trail contact: Henry W. Coe State Park, P.O. Box 846, Morgan Hill, CA 95038; (408) 779-2728; www.parks.ca.gov.

Finding the trailhead: From San Jose: Take U.S. Highway 101 south to Gilroy. Exit at Leavesley Road/California Highway 152 West and head *east* on Leavesley Road. After 1.8 miles turn left onto New Avenue and then right onto Roop Road. At the turnoff for Coyote Lake County Park, Roop becomes Gilroy Hot Springs Road. Stay on Gilroy Hot Springs Road to the end. This is a couple of miles beyond the Hunting Hollow entrance to Henry W. Coe State Park. There is limited parking along the road. There is an outhouse up the trail but no drinking water or phone.

The Ride

This is Coe, where the climbs are steep, the descents challenging, and the country remote. If you are in shape, have fun and enjoy the singletrack adventure. This is some of the most remote riding in the Bay Area. Kelly Lake Loop takes you deep into Henry W. Coe State Park. You may want to check out one of the "shorter" rides in the park before venturing this far.

Kelly Lake—don't expect any shade here!

The ride begins up the fire road along Coyote Creek. At the crest of the first hill, you can look across to see historic Gilroy Hot Springs. The Nature Conservancy purchased this land in 2002 to preserve this area as open space. Time will tell what resources the state of California has to restore this once-private retreat and whether the hot springs will open to the public.

This ride does not linger on fire roads but soon takes off onto Coe's signature singletrack. The Anza Trail is a fun ride through the cool woodlands of oak and bay laurel. The switchbacks make for a gradual climb. Those wishing a shorter ride can do an out-and-back along the Anza and Grapevine Trail, turning around when it starts to hurt.

For those going the distance, this loop takes you *up* Jackson Trail. The woodlands give way to open meadows with scattered oaks—the Jackson Field. As you reach the ridge, the views open up to the south. On the clearest days you can see the Sierra Nevada Mountains and the Monterey Peninsula from the summit. Whatever the season, the view along the ridge is classic California landscape.

The drop down Kelly Trail is steep and loose—the decisive factor in riding the loop this direction. Kelly Lake is a pleasant pond but not a major destination. It is a landmark along the way. In summer, it gets hot in this canyon, and there is little shade. From here it is a steady dirt-road climb to the next great singletrack. The

Cross Canyon Trail is a narrow, fast descent into Kelly Cabin Canyon. As you drop into the canyon, buckeye and gray pine join the oaks to provide some shade. Depending on the season, the thistle can be unpleasant on bare legs. And the poison oak and ticks will reach more than your legs. The creek crossings are an adventure in themselves. It is not always obvious where the trail resumes on the other side. At one point the trail runs down the creekbed.

The 1.5-mile climb out of the canyon is smooth, nontechnical, and gradual. This is the north-facing side of the canyon, so there are some trees and brush. Once on the ridge, there is no lingering. The singletrack Grapevine Trail cuts through the grasslands and drops right back down to the shaded Anza Trail. Both trails are rocky in sections with some steep pitches, but this is a fun way to wrap up the ride. Once you have finished this loop, you can start designing your own routes through the Coe wilderness. Despite the wilderness feel out here, do not ride off the legal trails. Stay off anything not posted as a trail or on the current map.

Bring plenty of food, a full hydration pack, two bottles of water, and the official park map. In case of emergency bring iodine tablets or a water filter. You may want to stick in some extra tools for this ride, particularly a chain tool and an extra chain.

Miles and Directions

0.0 **START** from entrance gate at the end of Gilroy Hot Springs Road, heading into the park on the dirt road. Trailhead GPS: N 37 05 58.9, W 121 28 22.0.

0.1 Veer left at the fork onto Coit Road, heading toward Coit Camp. There is an outhouse to the right above the sheltered picnic area.

0.8 Glance at historic Gilroy Hot Springs on the left across Coyote Creek.

1.0 Turn right onto the singletrack Anza Trail to Grapevine Spring and Woodchopper Spring. After about 250 feet, turn left onto Anza Trail to Grapevine Spring. Ignore Cullen Trail at Mile 1.6.

2.0 Turn right onto Jackson Trail toward Kelly Lake. The climbing continues and gets steeper.

3.4 Turn left onto Jackson Road to Kelly Lake. The singletrack gives way to dual track. Stay on the main dual track along the ridge and continue UP along the ridge. Ignore side trails to Rock Tower Trail on the right (to Grizzly Gulch) and then on the left (to Coit Camp).

4.1 This is the last peak. Is it Jackson Peak, or was that the one before this? Does it matter? Take a moment to enjoy the view before dropping down into the canyon. Be forewarned—the downhill dual track has some ruts.

4.7 Turn right onto Wasno (as in, there "was no") Road to Kelly Lake.

5.1 Turn left onto the Kelly Lake Trail to, finally, Kelly Lake. This is very steep and loose single-track. Be glad you are doing the loop this direction.

6.0 Arrive at Kelly Lake. Cross the dam and take the squirrelly singletrack on the left down to the dirt road.

6.1 Turn right up Coit Road toward Coit Lake. There is an outhouse here. **Bailout:** Turn left onto Coit Road. This dirt road will take you back to the car, but not without a gradual climb of 600 feet—nothing by Coe standards.

Henry W. Coe Park: Kelly Lake Loop

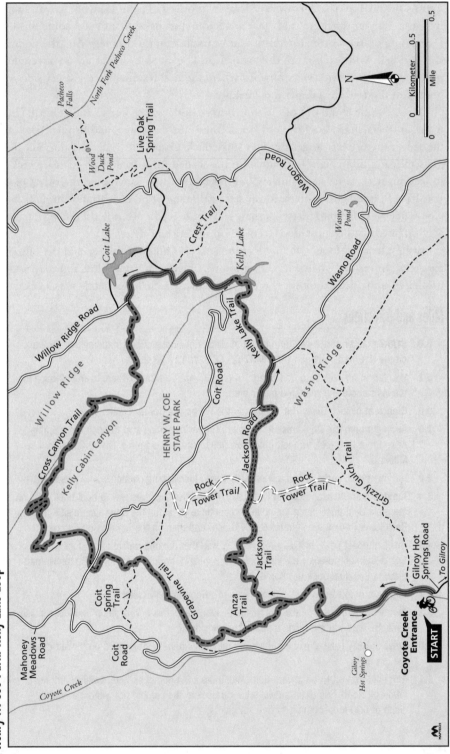

6.9 Turn left onto Willow Ridge Road.

7.4 Turn left onto the Cross Canyon Trail toward Mahoney Meadows.

9.1 You are on the canyon floor and making the first of more than a dozen river crossings—not all are ridable.

10.2 This is the last stream crossing before climbing out of the canyon and last chance on the trail to wash off the poison oak oil.

11.7 Go straight across Coit Road onto Grapevine Trail. The trail is dual track for about 250 feet before a fork. Take the singletrack 90 degrees to the left, just before the grass-high rock. There is no sign here, so it is a little confusing. Do not continue straight ahead on the singletrack out to the point. **Bailout:** This is another chance to bail onto Coit Road. Take a right and head back to the car.

12.3 Turn left at the T intersection onto Coit Spring Trail toward Kelly Lake.

12.4 Turn right downhill at the T intersection just before the fence. Although there may not be a sign, you are on Grapevine Trail.

13.4 Turn left onto Anza Trail toward Woodchopper Spring. There will be another sign several yards down the trail confirming that you are on Anza Trail. **Bailout:** Turn right on the shortcut to Coit Road, which will take you back to your car. But why pass up nice singletrack for a dirt road? It will only save you 0.8 mile.

14.4 Continue straight on Anza Trail at the junction with Jackson Trail. This completes the loop. You are now backtracking to the car.

15.3 Turn right on Anza Trail and then left onto Coit Road. This takes you back to the Coyote Creek entrance.

16.4 Arrive back at the pavement. Check for ticks and wash up as soon as you can.

Pacheco Falls Option

In spring the cascading falls along the North Fork Pacheco Creek are worth the ride. To reach Pacheco Falls follow the directions above to Mile 6.9. From that junction on Coit Road, turn right onto Crest Trail and follow for 1.1 miles. Turn left onto Wagon Road for 0.6 mile. Turn right onto Live Oak Spring Trail for about 1.1 miles. Turn right toward Wood Duck Pond and Pacheco Falls (0.9 mile). On the way to the falls, stop near Wood Duck Pond for a view of the cascade below. For the return backtrack on Live Oak Spring Trail to Wagon Trail. Depending on how you feel, you may want to opt for an easier (relatively speaking) return down Wagon

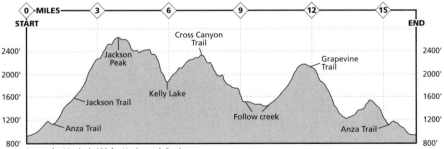

Intervals: Vertical, 400 ft.; Horizontal, 3 mi.

Road to take Lyman Willson Ridge Trail. This will take you back to the Hunting Hollow entrance. Ride the road back up to the Coyote Creek entrance.

Ride Information

Local Information
The Pine Ridge Association, P.O. Box 846, Morgan Hill, CA 95038; (408) 779-2728; www.coepark.org.
Gilroy Visitors Bureau, 7780 Monterey Street, Gilroy, CA 95020; (408) 842-6436; www.gilroyvisitor.org.

Local Events and Attractions
Gilroy Garlic Festival, last full weekend in July; (408) 842-1625; www.gilroygarlicfestival.com.

Accommodations
Henry W. Coe State Park camping: For car-accessed campground contact (800) 444-7275 or www.reserveamerica.com. For group camping and bike camping, call park headquarters at (408) 779-2728. Camping is on a first-come, first-served basis. There is usually space available, except weekends in spring and on holidays.
Coyote Lake Campground, County of Santa Clara, Parks and Recreation Department, 298 Garden Hill Drive, Los Gatos; information (408) 355-2200; reservations (408) 355-2201; www.parkhere.org.

Restaurants and Java Jolts
Chevys Fresh Mex, 8440 Murray Avenue, Gilroy; (408) 847-2726; www.chevys.com.
Starbucks, Gilroy Outlet Center, 8375 Arroya Circle, Gilroy; (408) 846-9733; www. starbucks.com.

Group Rides
Coe mountain-biking Web site: www.coecore.homestead.com.

COE EPIC ENDURO
This annual event may become the premier 10k of the mountain bike world—that is 10,000 feet of climbing in one day. The reward are obvious—10,000 feet of downhill. The route varies, but it usually covers between 45 and 60 miles. Be clear, this is not a race; it is an adventure ride. This is about personal challenges and pacing, and it is supposed to be fun. The first Coe epic was in 2001 when thirteen riders finished. Check out the route on the Web site (www.coecore.homestead.com), and try some sections. Will you become part of the Coe Core?

28 Soquel Demonstration Forest Loop

This secluded gem is tucked away in the Santa Cruz Mountains on the backside of the Forest of Nisene Marks. Enjoy a ridgetop view of Monterey Bay before dropping into Soquel Demonstration State Forest. Here you will find some of the most challenging and picturesque singletrack in the Bay Area. Maneuver through rocks, drops, logs, and steep shoots among the redwoods. Logs to ride and teeter-totters are there for the more skilled riders. The singletrack trails are for strong intermediate and advanced riders only. Access for emergency crews is limited.

Start: From the bridge and entrance to Soquel Demonstration State Forest on Highland Way.

Distance: 14.1-mile loop.

Approximate riding time: 2.5 hours.

Difficulty rating: Difficult; steady climbs, technically advanced singletrack with plenty of obstacles.

Trail surface: 53 percent dirt road, 34 percent singletrack, and 13 percent paved road (but all you will remember is the singletrack).

Terrain: Smooth dirt road through mixed woodlands to the ridge, cool view, singletrack along ragged ridge, steep descent through lush redwood forests.

Seasons: Best in spring, summer, and fall; muddy in winter. The park recommends waiting three days after rain before riding the trails. Spare these trails—no thrashing allowed.

Other trail users: Hikers and equestrians.

Canine compatibility: Leashed dogs permitted.

Land status: Soquel Demonstration State Forest.

Nearest town: Soquel.

Fees and permits: No fees or permits required.

Schedule: Open daily from dawn to dusk.

Maps: USGS maps: Laurel, CA; Loma Prieta, CA.

California Department of Forestry and Fire Protection, base map for Soquel Demonstration State Forest, available online at www.fire.ca.gov/php/rsrc-mgt_content/downloads/sdsf_basemap2.pdf.

Trail contact: Soquel Demonstration State Forest, 4750 Old San Jose Road, Soquel, CA 95073; (831) 475-8643; www.fire.ca.gov/php/rsrc-mgt_soquel.php.

Finding the trailhead: From San Jose: Take California Highway 17 south toward Santa Cruz. Near the top take the Summit Road exit and head southeast. Follow Summit Road as it becomes Highland Way. Nearly 10 miles from the highway, watch for a pullout near a bridge with a yellow railing. There is a small sign for Soquel Demonstration State Forest. Parking is available along Highland Way or across the bridge. The surrounding land here is private, but the dirt road (Hihn's Mill Road) is public access. There is no water at the trailhead. An outhouse is across the bridge and down Hihn's Mill Road about 0.2 mile.

The Ride

This is one of eight demonstration forests operated by the California Department of Forestry and Fire Protection (CDF). Demonstration forests are "working forests."

Scan the Santa Cruz Mountains from the ridge.

Here the CDF tests ways to improve the use of the forest, from timber production to environmental stewardship and recreation.

The state of California purchased this land in 1988. Prior to that, logging was the mainstay of the land. Two faults run through the forest, the San Andreas and Zayante, creating rugged and steep hillsides. Here you will find some of the most technically challenging singletrack in the Bay Area. The narrow trails offer plenty of obstacles: rocks, drops, steep shoots, and logs—many logs. The volunteer trail workers have had some fun here. If you cannot hop a log before you start this ride, you should be able to by the time you finish.

The loop begins on a narrow paved road through a mixed forest of redwoods, Douglas fir, oak, and madrone. At the crest of the paved road, you turn onto a smooth dirt road that takes you to the upper ridge of the Forest of Nisene Marks. The shade disappears near the summit as you ride past manzanita and live oak shrubs. On a clear day you can see Monterey Bay, Santa Cruz, and the surrounding mountains.

Once you enter Soquel Demonstration State Forest, the trail narrows, obstacles appear, and the terrain becomes rugged. The Ridge Trail is a fine path, winding through the woods and becoming especially brilliant as it goes deeper into the canyon and redwood forest. There are some steep uphill climbs, but all are very short. This loop takes you to the end of Ridge Trail and down Sawpit Trail, giving you the longest ride. However, there are four other trails coming off Ridge Trail; you can head down Corral Road, Sulphur Springs Road, Braille Trail (the most popular and insane), and Tractor Trail. At some point you should come back and ride them all. Most of these downhill runs are not very ridable uphill. However, it can be done. If you want to ride one uphill, try Sulphur Springs Road. Next try Tractor Trail. Neither is pleasant, but they are more ridable than the other two. You will understand the reason for the long roundabout route to the top on this loop.

Once you finish the downhill runs, it is a middle–chain ring climb out on Hihn's Mill Road, a dirt logging road. When selecting your own route through Soquel Demonstration Forest, know that the farther you go along the Ridge Trail, the more you have to climb out. The top of Sawpit Trail is nearly the same elevation as the bottom of Sulphur Springs Trail. This is the common dilemma—there is more exciting downhill than pleasant uphill. The downhill trails are not very long (about a mile and a half each). You can repeat the loops. Whichever way you go, you will get a good workout.

The heart of Soquel is remote. Not too many people get up there, except mountain bikers. Nonetheless, remember that hikers and equestrians have the right of way. The trails are sweet enough; there should be no need to venture off them. Staying on the designated trails also keeps you off private property.

Warning: If you biff badly and are hurt, it is a ruggedly painful struggle out. Do not expect your cell phone to work. It will take a while for help to arrive. This is a good place to ride with a partner. If you ride alone, then ride with extra caution.

If you like this place, volunteer to help with trail maintenance!

Miles and Directions

0.0 **START** from the pavement near the bridge and entrance to the demonstration forest. Ride up (southeast) Highland Way. Trailhead GPS: N 37 04.55, W121 51.03.

1.9 Turn right onto the dirt Buzzard Lagoon Road. (FYI: Highland Way becomes Eureka Canyon Road here and heads down toward Corralitos and Aptos.) This well-graded dirt road weaves in and out of state land.

2.9 Make a sharp right at the fork to continue toward the Forest of Nisene Marks. You are now on Aptos Creek Fire Road. Buzzard Lagoon Road continues straight ahead and drops down the wrong side of the mountain. Stay on the main dirt road; do not take any of the unmarked trails on the right. They are on private property.

4.1 Maneuver around the state park gate and continue the climb up Aptos Creek Fire Road.

5.1 This is the highest overlook of the Forest of Nisene Marks, at 2,500 feet. The road widens and the view of Monterey Bay is before you. Behind the view, or to the right as you came up the fire road, is the narrow singletrack entrance to Soquel Demonstration State Forest. There is a signboard here and map. Ride on; you are on the Ridge Trail. Ignore any vague trails you pass. All legal trails are signed. **Option:** There are five trails coming off

Soquel Demonstration Forest Loop

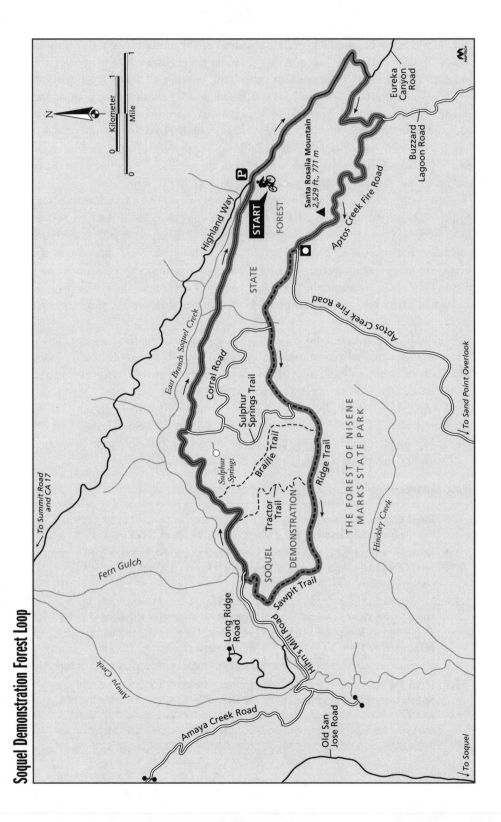

Ridge Trail that take you down to Hihn's Mill Road and back to the car. You can opt to take any of them.

5.8 Continue straight on Ridge Trail at the junction with Corral Road.

6.6 Continue straight on Ridge Trail at the junction with Sulphur Springs Road. The clearing is a helipad and one of the few places rescuers can get into the forest. If you have any doubts about riding the more technical trails up ahead, this is the place to head down. It is still a steep descent but for the most part a smooth dirt road.

7.1 Continue on Ridge Trail at the junction of Braille Trail, one of the most popular downhill runs. **Option:** If you cannot stand it any longer, close your eyes and feel your way down the Braille Trail. This trail offers more logs, seesaws, drops, and steep shots. Remember that the helipad is back up the trail a ways. There are bailout paths around most of the obstacles.

7.2 Just off the trail on the left, there is a picnic table and a view of Santa Cruz and the coast.

7.6 Arrive at the junction with Tractor Trail. Continue straight on Ridge Trail, where you will venture deeper into the woods and hone your log-hopping skills. There will be a gnarly descent and wicked uphill before the end of Ridge Trail, both relatively short. You can always bail onto Tractor Trail, another popular downhill. It is a steep start with some good jumps and turns.

8.6 Turn right and head down Sawpit Trail.

9.8 Turn right onto Hihn's Mill Road. This logging road takes you back to the parking area. You will pass the bottom of each downhill trail along the way out.

10.4 Pass the lower end of Tractor Trail on the right.

10.8 Pass bottom of Braille Trail on the right.

11.6 Continue up Hihn's Mill Road at the junction with Sulphur Springs Trail. **Option:** If you feel like another downhill run, you can grind your way up to the Ridge Trail from here. Turn right at the top and pick another trail to come down.

13.9 Arrive at the signboard, outhouse, and lower entrance to the demonstration forest. Continue past the gate and straight through the clearing.

14.1 Cross the bridge and arrive back at Highland Way.

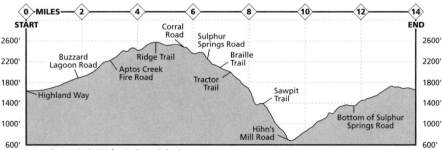

Intervals: Vertical, 400 ft.; Horizontal, 2 mi.

Option

Strong riders can skip the long, gradual climb to the Ridge Trail. Start with a ride down Hihn's Mill Road and turn left up Sulphur Springs Trail. Turn right onto Ridge Trail and pick your favorite trail back down to Hihn's Mill Road. Repeat loops as necessary.

Ride Information

Local Information

Stewards of Soquel, P.O. Box 1544, Aptos, CA 95001; www.soquelforest.org.
Trailworkers.com; www.trailworkers.com.
Santa Cruz State Parks, 600 Ocean Street, Santa Cruz, CA 95060; (831) 429-2850; www.santacruzstateparks.org.

Accommodations

The Forest of Nisene Marks camping: Westridge Trail Camp, first-come, first-served basis, call the park service for information at (831) 763-7064 or (831) 761-3487.
California State Parks camping: Henry Cowell Redwoods, 101 North Big Trees Park Road, Felton, (831) 438-2396; New Brighton Beach, 1500 Park Avenue, Capitola, (831) 464-6330; Seacliff Beach, 201 State Park Drive, Aptos, (831) 429-2850/685-6442/685-6500; and Manresa Beach, 400 San Andreas Road, La Seva Beach, (831) 724-3750/761-1795/429-2850; information www.parks.ca.gov; reservations (800) 444-PARK; www.reserveamerica.com.
Hostelling International Santa Cruz at Carmelita Cottages, 321 Main Street, Santa Cruz; (831) 423-8304; www.hi-santacruz.org.

Restaurants and Java Jolts

Surf City Coffee Company, 3070 Porter Street, Soquel; (831) 684-2750; www.surfcity coffee.com.
The Ugly Mug, 4640 Soquel Drive, Soquel; (831) 477-1341.

29 The Forest of Nisene Marks Out-and-Back

This ride offers something for all riding abilities. Ride through a regenerating redwood forest on a well-graded dirt road. The lower section offers a smooth and pleasant ride for beginners. Intermediate riders warm up before a long climb to Sand Point Overlook for a view of Monterey Bay and the surrounding Santa Cruz Mountains. Strong riders can continue on to the crest of the mountain, gaining 1,000 more feet of elevation. There are miles of downhill to enjoy on the way back.

Start: From the entrance to the Forest of Nisene Marks State Park.
Distance: 16.2 miles out and back.
Approximate riding time: 2 hours.
Difficulty rating: Moderate; nontechnical ride. Moderate climbing requires some stamina. There are options for beginners as well as strong advanced riders.
Trail surface: Well-graded dirt road, with option for 15 percent singletrack at the beginning and end of the ride.
Terrain: Shaded second-growth redwood forest, along Aptos Creek and up the rugged mountain to a lookout over Monterey Bay and surrounding mountains.
Seasons: Well-graded road offers year-round riding. Great place to beat the heat in summer.

Other trail users: Hikers, joggers, equestrians, and vehicles.
Canine compatibility: Leashed dogs permitted on Aptos Creek Road and in the picnic areas only.
Land status: The Forest of Nisene Marks State Park.
Nearest town: Aptos.
Fees and permits: $6.00 parking fee at the main entrance.
Schedule: Open daily sunrise to sunset.
Maps: USGS maps: Laurel, CA; Soquel, CA.
Trail contact: The Forest of Nisene Marks State Park, Aptos Creek Road, Soquel Drive, Aptos, CA 95003; (831) 763–7062; www.parks.ca.gov.

Finding the trailhead: From Santa Cruz: Head south on California Highway 1 to Aptos. Take the Seacliff Beach exit, turning left onto State Park Road. Turn right onto Soquel Drive and follow under the railroad trestle to Aptos Village. Make a left onto Aptos Creek Road and follow to the entrance station of the park.

Alternative parking: You can also start in Aptos Village. There is a parking area on the right at the beginning of Aptos Creek Road, just past the Aptos Station shopping area. Ride 0.8 mile up the paved road to the park entrance. Limited parking is also available at the Porter Family Picnic Area.

The Ride

The Forest of Nisene Marks is a living monument to the regeneration of nature. It is a "forest in the state of becoming." Like virgin forests throughout the Santa Cruz Mountains, it suffered severely from clear-cut logging. The mountain town of Loma Prieta cropped up and became one of the largest lumber mills in the area. After forty

The Forest of Nisene Marks Out-and-Back

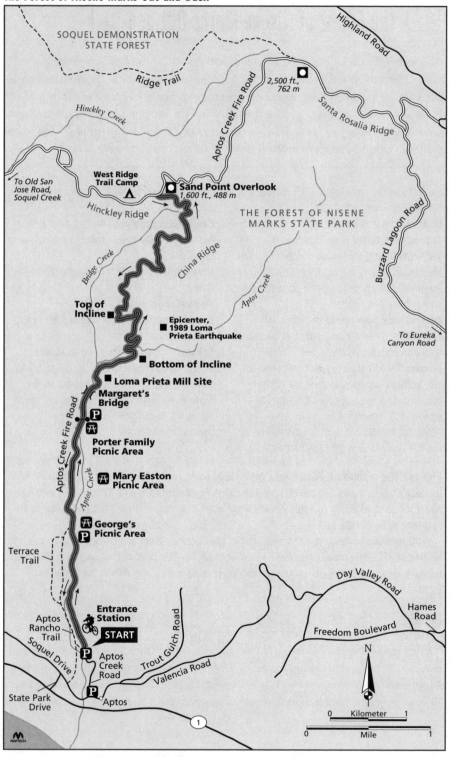

intense years the mill closed when "the red gold" was gone. Fire destroyed the last buildings in 1942, but the damage from the logging remains.

The park's name comes from the Marks family, Salinas Valley farmers who purchased the land in the 1950s. Nisene Marks was a mom who raised her children right. In 1963 her children donated most of today's park to the state of California, with stipulations to preserve the land in a natural state and name it in honor of their mother.

The best trails in the park are along the west side of Aptos Creek Road between the entrance and George's Picnic Area. This is an optional route for riders with at least intermediate technical skills. Here you will find narrow singletrack trails through dense groves of redwood, with some obstacles along the way. Heads up; these are popular trails for hikers, joggers, and equestrians as well. Riding in the park is a privilege; try to preserve it. As the master plan for the park evolves, check to make sure the lower trails are still open to bikes. No bikes are allowed on the east side of Aptos Creek Road (to the right going up). Beyond the steel bridge at George's Picnic Area, you can ride your bike only on the fire roads.

There are many ways to do this ride. The first half of the ride along graded Aptos Creek Road is great for beginners and children. You can stop at any of three picnic areas along the way before turning around. Margaret's Bridge is a pleasant destination and makes an easy 5-mile out-and-back. Similarly, you can ride to the last creek crossing at Mile 3.6 for a gentle 7.2-mile round-trip ride. Alternatively, you can drive to a picnic area and start from there.

The second half of the ride leaves the canyon floor and climbs through the rugged mountains of the park. This shift in terrain is dramatic evidence of the geologic upheaval along the California coast. Where would mountain biking be without plate tectonics? We would be flatlanders. As you strain to move your bike up the grade, imagine the force of nature pushing these mountains upward. You will pass the epicenter area for the 1989 Loma Prieta Earthquake, which collapsed freeways in Oakland and buildings in San Francisco and rocked the World Series. No bikes are allowed on the trail taking you closer to the epicenter. You can lock up your bike and hike it, but the evidence of the shifting landscape is all around you.

The first mile and a half of climbing is on the Incline; named for the narrow-gauge railroad line that hauled the massive timber down 600 vertical feet of hillside in less than a mile. Although this elaborate steam-powered winch and cable was short-lived (1912–1916), it hauled out twenty-four-million board feet of lumber. Once at the top of the Incline, the road levels off and follows an old railroad grade to Sand Point Overlook. On a clear day you can see Monterey Bay, the city of Santa Cruz, and the surrounding Santa Cruz Mountains.

This is an easy route to follow. The entire ride is in the shade of the forest, making this a great place to beat the summer heat. Aptos Creek offers a bonus for cooling off. Strong riders can continue to the crest of the mountain and connect with a loop through Soquel Demonstration State Forest for 30-some miles of strenuous riding.

Miles and Directions

0.0 **START** from the parking lot and entrance kiosk to the park where Aptos Creek Road becomes dirt. The entire out-and-back is on this road. **Technical option:** For some great singletrack start at the trailhead for Split Stuff Trail. This trailhead is to the left of the information board at the north end of the parking lot. As you start, stay to the right at several short junctions to get on Aptos Ranch Trail, which parallels the graded Aptos Creek Road. Follow this all the way to George's Picnic Area. Not all junctions will be marked, but the trail is rather intuitive. There will be several shortcuts up to the road. Try to stay on the main singletrack. Heads up, there is a 3-foot drop off a giant redwood root about 1 mile along the trail. This singletrack route adds only 0.1 mile to the featured ride. Trailhead GPS: N 36 59.10, W 121 54.16.

1.1 Pass Aptos Ranch Trail on the left and George's Picnic Area on the right. You will soon ride across the Steel Bridge and enter into upper section of the park. There are no legal singletrack trails for bikes above the bridge.

1.6 Pass Mary Easton Picnic Area.

2.2 The road forks for parking at the Porter Family Picnic Area. This is the last place to park and pee. The gate to Aptos Creek Fire Road is on the left.

2.7 Pass former site of Loma Prieta Sawmill on the left.

3.6 A bridge takes you over Aptos Creek and the climbing begins. Up ahead was the lower end of the Old Incline Railroad Line.

3.7 Pass the trail to the epicenter of the October 1989 Loma Prieta Earthquake—no bikes allowed. If you want to check it out, lock your bike and take a hike.

5.1 You have reached the top of the Incline and the steepest grade. The climbing continues to the top but is more gradual.

7.1 Continue straight where Big Slide Trail merges from the right—no bikes allowed.

8.1 Arrive at Sand Point Overlook (1,600 feet). Return down the way you came. **Option:** Continue 3.5 miles up Aptos Creek Fire Road to Santa Rosalia Ridge overlook at 2,500 feet. At the summit you can turn around. Or make a left turn onto Ridge Trail in Soquel Demonstration Forest for some of the best singletrack and an epic ride back to the car.

14.0 Pass Porter Family Picnic Area; watch for cars again.

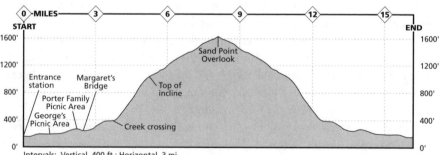

Intervals: Vertical, 400 ft.; Horizontal, 3 mi.

15.1 Pass George's Picnic Area. **Option:** Take a right onto the singletrack Aptos Ranch Trail. Watch for signs to the parking lot. If you go beyond 16.3 miles, you have overshot the parking lot.

16.2 Arrive back at the park entrance.

Loop Option

If you can't stand out-and-backs, don't mind riding the road (12 miles of pavement), and have strong stamina, try this beautiful 30-mile loop: From Aptos Creek Road head east on Soquel Drive. Very shortly, turn left onto Trout Gulch Road, then right onto Valencia Road. After 2.5 miles turn right onto Day Valley Road. Turn left onto Freedom Boulevard (carefully) and then left onto Hames Road. Ride 1.5 miles, and turn left onto Eureka Canyon Road in the town of Corralitos. Continue up Eureka Canyon Road for a little over 2 miles; turn left onto Rider Road, then right onto Buzzard Lagoon Road. Climb past homes, beyond the pavement, past the overlook at 2,100 feet, and to Aptos Creek Fire Road, nearly 5 miles. Turn left along the ridge to the overlook atop the Forest of Nisene Marks. Enjoy nearly 13 miles of downhill on Aptos Creek Fire Road back to the start.

Ride Information

Local Information

Santa Cruz State Parks, District Office, 600 Ocean Street, Santa Cruz, CA 95060; (831) 429-2850; www.santacruzstateparks.org.

Santa Cruz County Conference and Visitors Council, 1211 Ocean Street, Santa Cruz, CA 95060; (831) 425-1234 or (800) 833-3494; www.santacruzca.org.

Local Events and Attractions

Santa Cruz Beach Boardwalk, 400 Beach Street, Santa Cruz; recorded message (831) 426-7433; www.beachboardwalk.com.

Skyview Drive-In theater, 22605 Soquel Drive, Santa Cruz; (831) 475-3405.

Accommodations

The Forest of Nisene Marks camping, Westridge Trail Camp; first-come first-served basis; call the park service for information at (831) 763-7064 or (831) 761-3487.

California State Parks camping: New Brighton Beach, 1500 Park Avenue, Capitola, (831) 464-6330; Seacliff Beach, 201 State Park Drive, Aptos, (831) 429-2850/685-6442/ 685-6500; and Manresa Beach, 400 San Andreas Road, La Seva Beach, (831) 724-3750/761-1795/429-2850; information www.parks.ca.gov; reservations (800) 444-PARK; www.reserveamerica.com.

Santa Cruz KOA, 1186 Andreas Road, Watsonville; (831) 722-0551 or (800) 562-7701; www.koa.com.

Hostelling International Santa Cruz at Carmelita Cottages, 321 Main Street, Santa Cruz; (831) 423-8304; www.hi-santacruz.org.

Restaurants and Java Jolts

Cole's Bar-B-Q, 8059 Aptos Street, Aptos; (831) 662-1721.

The Britannia Arms, 8017 Soquel Drive, Aptos; (831) 688-1233.

The Farm Bakery, Cafe & Gifts, 6790 Soquel Drive, Aptos; (831) 684-0266.

30 Wilder Ranch Loop

Wilder Ranch State Park is a mountain biking playground. The park runs from the western slopes of the Santa Cruz Mountains to the bluffs overlooking the Pacific Ocean, a 1,800-foot drop in elevation. Here you will find miles of singletrack weaving in and out of thick redwoods and along grass-covered hillsides. Dirt roads add to the network, providing more than 35 miles of multiuse trails from which to choose. There are trails for all abilities, from the flat Old Cove Landing Trail for beginners to the Enchanted Loop for advanced riders. All this with a backdrop view of the coast.

Start: From the day-use parking lot at Wilder Ranch State Park.

Distance: 10.8-mile loop.

Approximate riding time: 1.5 hours.

Difficulty rating: Moderate; gradual grade with some short, challenging climbs. Singletrack includes some rocks, ruts, and drops—plenty of options for a wide range of ability.

Trail surface: 75 percent dirt road and 25 percent singletrack, with option for 65 percent singletrack loop.

Terrain: Grass-covered coastal mountain with oak woodlands, redwoods forests in the deep ravines, coastal breeze and views; options to ride the bluffs above the crashing Pacific Ocean.

Seasons: Year-round. Best in spring with wildflowers; can be dusty by end of summer, muddy in winter.

Other trail users: Hikers and equestrians.

Canine compatibility: Dogs not permitted.

Land status: Wilder Ranch State Park.

Nearest town: Santa Cruz.

Fees and permits: $6.00 parking fee.

Schedule: Open daily 8:00 A.M. to sunset. Be sure to call ahead to check trail status during winter. The park temporarily closes for up to 24 hours after significant rainfall. Some trails, particularly Enchanted Trail, close longer through the wet season.

Maps: USGS maps: Santa Cruz, CA; Felton, CA.
Wilder Ranch State Park map, available at the entrance and the interpretive center when open.

Trail contact: Wilder Ranch State Park, 1401 Old Coast Road, Santa Cruz, CA 95060; (831) 423-9703; www.parks.ca.gov.

Finding the trailhead: From Santa Cruz by car: Head north on California Highway 1/Mission Street out of Santa Cruz. The turnoff for the park is about 1.8 miles from Western Drive, the last signal in town. Turn left into Wilder Ranch State Park and veer left again to the park entry kiosk and day-use parking. The ride begins at the gate on the paved road heading down to the Cultural Preserve. The only restrooms and water in the park are here. (Note: There is some parking along CA 1 just before the turnoff to the park. Be forewarned; there have been problems with vandalism. The price of parking may be worth it.)

From Santa Cruz by bike: A paved county bike trail parallels CA 1 north of Santa Cruz. The path starts at Shaffer Street, 1 block north of Western Drive. Riding north for a little over a mile, the path takes you directly into Wilder Ranch Park. The path ends at Mile 0.3 below. Turn right into the tunnel and head for the dirt.

Breathtaking views of the Monterey Peninsula coast follow you down Wilder Ranch.

The Ride

Wilder Ranch State Park is located just north of the coastal community of Santa Cruz. The park runs from the crest of Ben Lomond Mountain down to the wave-scoured bluffs overlooking the Pacific Ocean. You get to ride between the two. Years of free-range biking have been "redirected" and preserved into some fine singletrack through the park. There are bridges now at all the stream crossings.

Ohlone Indians were early residents of the Wilder Creek watershed and enjoyed the natural bounty of the land and ocean. Once settlers arrived, the land was used for ranching, dairy operations, logging, and cement production. The last private residents were the Wilder family, who lived and worked the land for a hundred years. Development pressures in the 1970s led to the preservation of the land as a state park. Today the farm complex is a cultural preserve. The interpretive center offers a living history of the area, teaching about the people, plants, and animals in the park. Self-guided walking tours of Wilder Ranch are available at the interpretive center, along with weekend docent-led tours. (You can drop the kids here while you ride the trails; check for schedules.) Wilder Beach and estuary are closed to the public for habitat restoration.

Wilder Ranch Loop

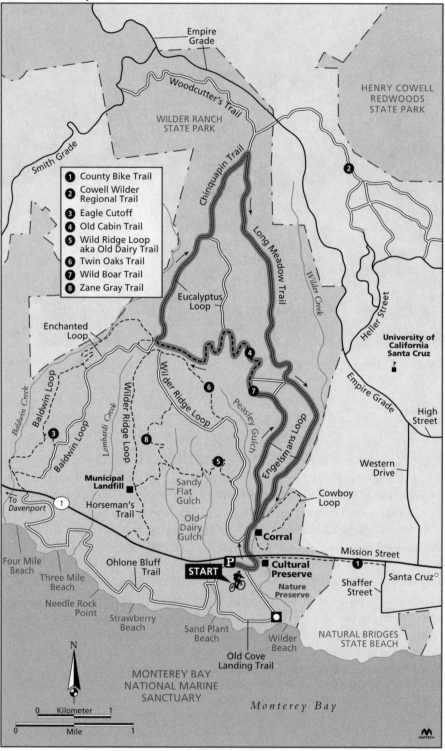

HENRY COWELL REDWOODS STATE PARK

Empire Grade

Woodcutter's Trail

WILDER RANCH STATE PARK

Smith Grade

Chinquapin Trail

Long Meadow Trail

Wilder Creek

Heller Street

University of California Santa Cruz

Empire Grade

High Street

Western Drive

1. County Bike Trail
2. Cowell Wilder Regional Trail
3. Eagle Cutoff
4. Old Cabin Trail
5. Wild Ridge Loop aka Old Dairy Trail
6. Twin Oaks Trail
7. Wild Boar Trail
8. Zane Gray Trail

Eucalyptus Loop

Enchanted Loop

Baldwin Creek

Baldwin Loop

Baldwin Loop

Lombardi Creek

Wilder Ridge Loop

Wilder Ridge Loop

Peasley Gulch

Engelsmans Loop

Cowboy Loop

Municipal Landfill

Sandy Flat Gulch

Old Dairy Gulch

Corral

To Davenport

Horseman's Trail

Mission Street

Santa Cruz

Ohlone Bluff Trail

START P

Cultural Preserve

Nature Preserve

Shaffer Street

Four Mile Beach

Three Mile Beach

Needle Rock Point

Strawberry Beach

Sand Plant Beach

Old Cove Landing Trail

Wilder Beach

NATURAL BRIDGES STATE BEACH

N

MONTEREY BAY NATIONAL MARINE SANCTUARY

Monterey Bay

Kilometer 0 — 1

Mile 0 — 1

MAPTECH

As for the trails, this is a mountain biker's playground. There is no "one" way through Wilder Ranch. This loop is an introduction to the park, and you will hopefully come back to create your own favorite route. Trails and loops are short enough that you can repeat your favorite sections as much as you want. This route gives a taste of some of the best singletrack (Wild Boar and Old Cabin Trails and a portion of Eucalyptus Loop) while also taking you to the top of the park for a long uninterrupted downhill ride, albeit on dirt road. However, many folks come to Wilder just for the singletrack. If that is you, skip straight to the singletrack option offered below. Enchanted Forest is the most technically challenging singletrack in Wilder—beautiful. Go clockwise. There are significant root drops going this way that would not be nearly as fun to ride up!

TIDBIT: Volunteer to help maintain the trails. Trail work is typically on the first Sunday of the month. Meet at the day-use parking area at 9:45 A.M. For more information and to confirm workdays, contact www.Trailworkers.com.

There are active mountain bike patrols in the park. Respect these folks; many of them work here because they love to bike—sweet assignment. Not only do they help maintain the trails but they are also advocates for bike access.

By the end of summer, some of the trails get dusty and sandy; no surprise that they get muddy in winter. Trail maintenance entails the spreading of gravel on eroded sections. Unfortunately, until the first rain washes the nasty grit into the sand, it is squirrelly to ride on and misery to land on.

The trails alone are not the only draw to the park. When you are not in the thick redwood and Douglas fir forests or the oak woodlands, there can be crisp coastal views. There can also be days when the rides are fog enshrouded and drippy wet.

Upper reaches of the Wilder Ranch are accessible from the junction of Chinquapin Trail and Empire Grade. You can ride up Empire Grade from CA 1 by going up Bay Street or Western Drive. However, this is more than 4 miles of climbing on narrow, paved road with little shoulder. Chinquapin Trail connects to a network of trails on the University of California Santa Cruz campus. From here you can access Henry Cowell Redwoods State Park via the U-Con Trail and Rincon Connector Trail. These trails are steep and can be slippery when wet. There is no bridge across the San Lorenzo River, making this connection impassable from November to April.

Miles and Directions

0.0 **START** from the day-use parking area and gate on the paved road heading down to the Cultural Preserve. Trailhead GPS: N 36 57.38, W 122 05.06.

0.1 Turn left and walk your bike through the farm complex.

0.3 The paved bike path from Santa Cruz comes in from the right. Continue straight through the tunnel. Pass the information board and veer left at fork to the corral.

0.5 This is a little confusing the first time through. Veer right at the first fork. This is just a shortcut around the signed intersection a few yards ahead to Wilder Ridge Loop on the left, where you would also go right.

0.6 Just past the bridge is an intersection. Go left up the short, steep grade onto Engelsmans Loop. At the end of the ride, you will complete the loop, coming down Engelsmans Loop straight ahead.

1.8 Turn left onto the singletrack Wild Boar Trail.

2.0 There will be a sharp bend to the right. The CLOSED TRAIL sign on the left is the top of the old Wagon Wheel Trail—long since gone.

2.3 Turn left onto Old Cabin Trail at a connector to Engelsmans Loop.

3.3 Turn left onto Eucalyptus Loop.

3.9 Keep to the right where a smaller trail comes in on the right through the trees.

4.2 Veer right where the trail forks.

4.4 Turn right at the junction with wider Eucalyptus Loop. **Option:** Turn left and follow the Give Me More Singletrack option below.

5.5 Reach a picnic table and panoramic view through the small stand of namesake trees. Turn left on Chinquapin Trail. All that remains is a gentle climb from here. **Option:** Continue straight to take Eucalyptus Loop down. You can then backtrack on Old Cabin, Wild Boar, and Engelsmans Trails. Better yet, explore a bit and find a new way back.

6.4 Turn right onto Long Meadow Trail for the downhill cruise. **Woodcutter's Trail Out-and-Back Option:** Continue straight up Chinquapin Trail 0.2 mile to Woodcutter's Trail. Turn left for a 3.4-mile round-trip down to Smith Grade and back up on a graded dirt road. At one time there were singletrack sections through here and the trail closed during winter. The trail has since been graded and widened to be rid-able year-round. **Access to UCSC and Henry Cowell Redwoods State Park Option:** Continue straight up Chinquapin Trail 0.4 mile to Empire Grade Road and across to the University of California's nature reserve. From here you can access trails on campus or drop into San Lorenzo River Canyon and on up into Henry Cowell Redwoods State Park.

6.7 Continue on the main road, ignoring a path sneaking off to the left.

8.6 Veer right at the sharp turn. Ignore the singletrack taking off to the left. If you stop and look back, you can see the rock-wall remains of an old limekiln once used for making cement.

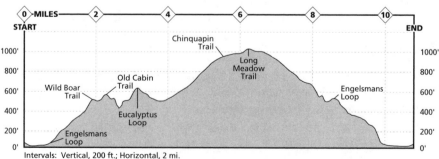

Intervals: Vertical, 200 ft.; Horizontal, 2 mi.

8.6+ Turn left onto Engelsmans Loop at the four-way intersection. **Option:** Turn right to Old Cabin Trail for another loop.

9.8 Stay to the left on the main road where an unsigned road merges from the right.

10.2 Continue straight at the four-way intersection, completing the loop. Cross the bridge and veer left at the fork, riding along the right side of the corral. Ride back through the tunnel. **Option:** Continue straight past the bridge to ride Wilder Ridge Loop and do some more exploring.

10.6 Continue straight through the cultural preserve. (The paved bike path to Santa Cruz turns to the left after the tunnel.)

10.7 Turn right onto the paved road up to the parking area.

10.8 Arrive back at the parking lot.

Give Me More Singletrack Option

At Mile 4.4 above turn left to take the Enchanted Loop. This takes you deep into the redwoods and up a grassy hillside. Ride this loop clockwise; the root drops and ruts are much more fun to go down than up. This is a gorgeous loop with a steep but short climb out of the canyon.

At the end of Enchanted Loop, turn right onto a short section of pavement and then head left on the wide Wilder Ridge Loop. (This may be confusing, since you will be at a fork where Wilder Ridge Loop goes both ways.) Turn when you come to Twin Oaks Trail for a rolling downhill run through the grasses. This trail can become a washboard in summer.

At the bottom of Twin Oaks Trail, turn right up a short steep section of Wilder Ridge Loop. Connect ahead with Zane Gray Trail on the left. This fun little run offers a panoramic view of the coast with some ruts and rocks. Try to ignore the view and stench of the landfill—it is just a reminder that our waste goes somewhere.

At the end of the Zane Gray Trail, take a left onto Wilder Ridge Loop, formerly Old Dairy Trail. Enjoy an easy meander along the edge of the grass terrace, skirting small tree-shaded canyons. This drops you back onto the wider beginning section of the Wilder Ridge Loop, which will take you back to the tunnel and cultural preserve. Repeat any or all sections as needed. The entire singletrack option is 12 miles and takes about ninety minutes to two hours.

Old Cove Landing and Ohlone Bluff Trails

This is an easy family ride along the bluffs overlooking the ocean. The popular dirt path is wide and flat and offers a great view of the rugged coastline. When trails are muddy in the upper reaches of the park, this trail is usually open. Bring extra layers of clothing; it is often windy out there. The entire out-and-back is about 14 miles and will eventually take you to a tunnel under CA 1 and to the bottom of Baldwin Loop Trail. This is a popular return path for riders coming down from the northern end of the park.

The ride starts from the day-use parking area. As you face the restroom, take the dirt path to the right before the fence and path to the cultural preserve. This is the beginning of the Old Cove Landing Trail. It soon merges left onto a wider path, crosses the railroad tracks, and follows the edge of the bluff north. Although a little confusing, Old Cove Land Trail is a nearly 2.5-mile loop back to the parking lot.

At Mile 1.6 the Old Cove Landing Trail comes to a steep ledge overlooking Sand Plant Beach. The main path turns inland. You can carefully maneuver down the cliff here, cross the beach, and ride up the steep singletrack on the other side. This connects to the Ohlone Bluff Trail, which continues up the coast and through fields of row crops. If the tide is too high, it may be difficult to cross the inlet. If you do not want to go down to the beach, it is nearly a mile's ride around the gulch. The trail inland goes through a farm complex. At Mile 2.0 turn left along the railroad tracks. At Mile 2.2 make a sharp left, leaving the track and riding along the edge of the field to the northern overlook of Sand Plant Beach. Continue along the bluff as far as you want.

You can also bail out at the railroad tracks back at Mile 2.0 and ride straight up to the paved entrance to the park. Turn right and head back to the day-use parking area, completing the Old Cove Landing Trail loop.

Ride Information

Local Information
Santa Cruz State Parks, District Office, 600 Ocean Street, Santa Cruz, CA 95060; (831) 429-2850; www.santacruzstateparks.org.
Santa Cruz County Conference and Visitors Council, 1211 Ocean Street, Santa Cruz, CA 95060; (831) 425-1234 or (800) 833-3494; www.santacruzca.org.

Local Events and Attractions
Wilder Ranch State Park Cultural Preserve, docent-led tours of the historic farm and interpretive center; (831) 426-0505.
Natural Bridges State Beach, 2531 West Cliff Drive, Santa Cruz; (831) 423-4609; www.parks.ca.gov.
Santa Cruz Beach Boardwalk, 400 Beach Street, Santa Cruz; recorded message (831) 426-7433; www.beachboardwalk.com.

Accommodations
California State Parks camping: Henry Cowell Redwoods, 101 North Big Trees Park Road,
Felton, (831) 438-2396; New Brighton Beach, 1500 Park Avenue, Capitola, (831) 464-6330; Seacliff Beach, 201 State Park Drive, Aptos, (831) 429-2850/685-6442/ 685-6500; and Manresa Beach, 400 San Andreas Road, La Seva Beach, (831) 724-3750/761-1795/429-2850; information www.parks.ca.gov; reservations (800) 444-PARK; www.reserveamerica.com.
Hostelling International Santa Cruz at Carmelita Cottages, 321 Main Street, Santa Cruz; (831) 423-8304; www.hi-santacruz.org.

Restaurants and Java Jolts
Carpo's Westside, 2018 Mission Street, Santa Cruz; (831) 427-1880.
Coffeetopia, 1723 Mission Street, Santa Cruz; (831) 425-6583; www.coffeetopia.com.
Cafe Brazil, 1410 Mission Street, Santa Cruz; (831) 429-1855.

31 Big Basin-Butano Loop

Starting deep within the majestic redwood forest of the coastal range, this ride takes you over the mountain and down to the rolling grasslands near the coast. The return ride over the summit offers magnificent views of the Pacific coastline and the canyons of Butano State Park. This is a long loop requiring stamina. While most of the dirt is well-graded road, there are steep descents through ruts and loose gravel requiring some technical confidence. There are several options on this ride, including a moderate out-and-back for strong beginners willing to work for some smooth downhill.

Start: From the beginning of Gazos Creek Road in Big Basin Redwoods State Park.
Distance: 27.3-mile loop.
Approximate riding time: 3.5 to 4.5 hours.
Difficulty rating: Difficult; the climb is steady and moderate, and steep descents have ruts and loose gravel; strenuous only for the distance.
Trail surface: 79 percent dirt and 21 percent paved roads.
Terrain: Lush redwood forests, rugged coastal mountains, deep ravines, grassy hills, ridgetop vistas, constantly changing landscape.
Seasons: Year-round. Muddy in the damp ravines through winter; cool place to ride in summer, although it can get warm on the exposed ridges.
Other trail users: Hikers, equestrians, and vehicles.

Canine compatibility: Dogs not permitted.
Land status: Big Basin Redwoods and Butano State Parks.
Nearest town: Boulder Creek.
Fees and permits: $6.00 parking fee.
Schedule: Open 6:00 A.M. to 10:00 P.M. daily.
Maps: USGS maps: Big Basin, CA; Franklin Point, CA; Ano Nuevo, CA.
Mountain Parks Foundation and California State Parks, *Big Basin Redwoods Park Map* (1999), available for purchase at the park headquarters.
Trail contacts: Big Basin Redwoods State Park, 21600 Big Basin Way, Boulder Creek, CA 95006; (831) 338-8860; www.parks.ca.gov or www.bigbasin.org.
Butano State Park, 1500 Cloverdale Road, Pescadero, CA 94060; (650) 879-2040; www.parks.ca.gov.

Finding the trailhead: From San Jose: Take Interstate 280 to the Saratoga Avenue exit. Follow Saratoga Avenue southwest through Saratoga as it becomes Big Basin Way/California Highway 9. Wind up the hill out of Saratoga for about 7 miles and cross Skyline Boulevard/California Highway 35. Continue down CA 9 for 6 miles to a junction. Go straight at the split, following the signs to Big Basin Redwoods State Park. This narrow, winding road is California Highway 236 (Big Basin Highway), which takes you into the park. Just past the park headquarters, turn right at the kiosk onto North Escapes Road. Drive toward the picnic areas, past the museum and store. Park on the right, about 0.3 mile up North Escape Road and across from the bridge. There are restrooms and water here. Although unsigned here, the road across the bridge is the beginning of Gazos Creek Road.

The Ride

It is hard to imagine 1884, when there were twenty-eight sawmills operating in Big Basin and the adjoining San Lorenzo Valley. Giant redwoods were turned into thirty-four-million board feet of lumber per year. The Sempervirens (meaning "ever-living") Club launched the first major campaign to preserve the redwood forest. This led to Big Basin's becoming the first California state park in 1902. Twenty-five years later, the newly named Big Basin Redwoods State Park gave birth to the state system that now encompasses nearly 300 parks. Still under the preservation efforts of today's Sempervirens Fund, the park continues to expand.

If you have never been on a long ride, this is a good one to start with. The grade is moderate, and the scenery is constantly changing. You can also start the loop from the coastal side at Gazos Creek or Butano State Park.

The ride begins deep within the redwood forest not far from the park headquarters. Beginning on the east end of Gazos Creek Road, you will follow this well-marked dirt road over the mountain and down toward Gazos Creek Beach. As you reach the summit, the forest thins into oaks, Douglas fir, manzanita, and toyon. Once past Sandy Point Line Shack, you quickly drop into the lush canyon of ferns and more redwoods along Gazos Creek. The descent is steep and sometimes rutted with sections of loose gravel. The road wallows in mud during winter and spring, which explains the deposits of gravel. Too bad, this distracts from an otherwise smooth downhill run.

Gazos Creek Road follows the picturesque creek all the way to the coast. As the road levels out, it becomes paved but remains a shaded and rather quiet ride. It is hard to imagine the creek dammed as a holding pen for logs during the late 1890s.

Once you head north on Cloverdale Road, traffic picks up and you have to be alert. The forest has given way to grassy fields along the berry- and poison oak–lined roadway. On the weekends watch out for motorcycles racing through here. Less than a mile past the entrance to Butano State Park, you are back on the dirt and steadily climbing Butano Fire Road. Considering the 2,100-foot elevation gain, this is not bad. The fire road is tame on this side of the mountain, with a few sections of sandstone. The steeper gradient is near the summit when you may be losing some steam. You skirt the northern reaches of Butano State Park, also known for its redwood stands deep within the canyon. The road weaves in and out of cool forests, which give way to thinner and shorter stands of pine. The view opens up along the dry higher ridges as you rise above the typical cloud layer. Enjoy the view of the watershed below and the coast beyond.

Just past a dirt airstrip, you are back into the trees. Enjoy a short break in the climb before the final ascent to the summit on China Grade (2,265 feet). After the

◀ *How do you take a picture of a giant redwood?*

Big Basin-Butano Loop

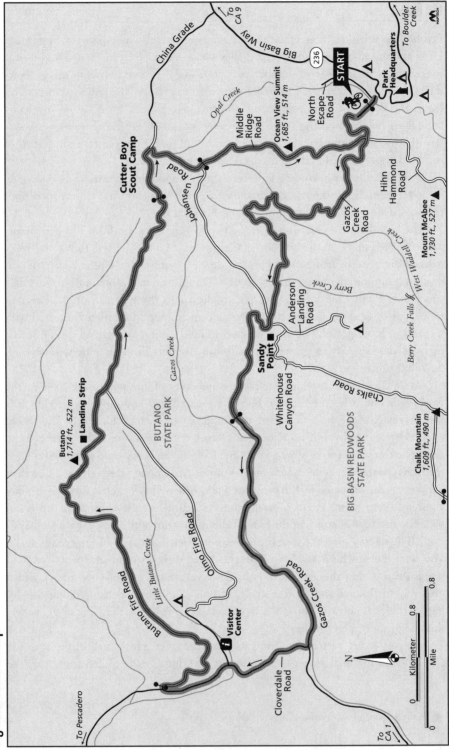

To CA 9

China Grade

Big Basin Way

START

236

Park Headquarters

To Boulder Creek

Opal Creek

Ocean View Summit
1,685 ft., 514 m

Middle Ridge Road

North Escape Road

Cutter Boy Scout Camp

Johansen Road

Hihn Hammond Road

Gazos Creek Road

Mount McAbee
1,730 ft., 527 m

West Waddell Creek

Berry Creek

Berry Creek Falls

Anderson Landing Road

Butano
1,714 ft., 522 m

Landing Strip

BUTANO STATE PARK

Gazos Creek

Sandy Point

Whitehouse Canyon Road

Chalks Road

BIG BASIN REDWOODS STATE PARK

Chalk Mountain
1,609 ft., 490 m

Butano Fire Road

Little Butano Creek

Olmo Fire Road

To Pescadero

Visitor Center

Gazos Creek Road

Cloverdale Road

To CA 1

N

Kilometer   0   0.8   0.8
Mile   0   0.8

climb, Johansen Road is a smooth and welcome descent to Middle Ridge Road. As you hammer the short climbs on the roller-coaster ridge, be glad you are going down this trail rather than up. Where the roadbed is sandstone, watch for sand traps at the bottom of the quick descents. Try to look up for a quick panorama at Ocean View Summit. Chances are you have not seen much traffic for a while, but keep an eye out for hikers and other trail users as you get closer to park headquarters.

There is no legal singletrack for bikes along this loop. If you see a sign that says otherwise, check with the rangers. The NO BIKE signs are "altered" from time to time.

Miles and Directions

0.0 **START** at the beginning of Gazos Creek Road at its junction with North Escape Road. There is no sign here; the bridge is your cue. Cross the bridge over Opal Creek and ride straight through the picnic area. Trailhead GPS at the junction of Gazos Creek and North Escape Roads: N 37 10.33, W 122 13.19 (GPS readings are very tough to get here).

0.1 Ride around the gate and continue on Gazos Creek Road. The paved road becomes gravel at 0.2 mile.

0.9 Continue straight on Gazos Creek Road at the fork with Middle Ridge Trail on the right. (You will complete the loop at this point.)

0.9+ Ignore the second fork with Middle Ridge Road on the left. **Side trip:** Turn left and follow Middle Ridge Fire Road to Hihn Hammond Road. Turn right to Mount McAbee Overlook (1,730 feet) and a view of Waddell Creek Canyon below. It is about 2 miles to the overlook from Gazos Creek Road, with moderate climbing.

6.1 Ride around the locked gate. There is an unsigned T intersection up ahead with Whitehouse Canyon Road on the left. Veer right to continue on Gazos Creek Road. Ride past the Sandy Point Line Shack on the right. Just past the fenced private property, Johansen Road merges from the right. Continue straight on Gazos Creek Road, dropping steeply into lush Gazos Creek Canyon. Watch for vehicles, nasty loose gravel, and ruts.

8.2 Pass through a gate just before the road becomes paved. Continue straight on Gazos Creek Road. Ignore the driveway to the right leading to the Pescadero Conservation Alliance Mountain Camp.

11.5 Turn right onto Cloverdale Road and watch for traffic. **Side trip:** You have come this far; consider a lunch break at the beach. Turn left and ride about 2 miles to Gazos Beach at the junction with California Highway 1.

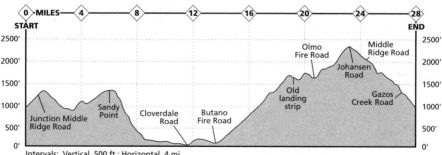

Intervals: Vertical, 500 ft.; Horizontal, 4 mi.

12.6 Pass entrance to Butano State Park on the right. There are water and restrooms inside the park.

13.5 Turn right onto a short uphill drive leading to a locked gate. Although unsigned, this is Butano Fire Road. Lift your bike over the gate, heeding the DON'T CLIMB ON THE GATE sign, and ride on. Follow this dirt road to the top of the mountain, passing several hiking-only trails into Butano State Park along the way.

16.1 Veer right at the unmarked fork.

18.6 Continue straight across the dirt airstrip.

19.1 Pass Butano Trail Camp on the right–NO BIKES.

19.5 Continue straight pass Olmo Fire Road on the right.

22.5 Climb over the locked cable across the road. Ride through the dirt parking area and turn right onto China Grade.

23.1 Turn right onto Johansen Road.

23.9 Turn left onto Middle Ridge Road.

24.0 Ride around the locked gate and continue on Middle Ridge Road. Pass several hiking-only trails on the left.

26.3 Turn left back onto Gazos Creek Road.

27.2 Ride around the gate and back into the picnic area.

27.3 Cross the bridge and arrive back at your vehicle.

Sandy Point Out-and-Back Option

The 12-mile out-and-back ride on Gazos Creek Road to Sandy Point is a non-technical ride for strong beginners.

Middle Ridge Loop Option

Turn right up Middle Ridge Road (Mile 0.9) for a more strenuous 12-mile loop. (As for the AUTHORIZED VEHICLES ONLY sign, that means you.) Trust your gut on this one: If you like to climb, go for it. If you have any hesitation, skip it. Once you get to the top of Middle Ridge Road, turn left down Johansen Road. This is a pleasant descent to Sandy Point and the junction with Gazos Creek Road. Make two left turns, returning down Gazos Creek Road to your starting point.

Chalk Mountain Side Trip Option

From the intersection at Sandy Point (Mile 6.1), turn left onto Whitehouse Canyon Road to Chalks Road. About 0.5 mile past Chalk Mountain (1,609 feet) is a spectacular view of the coast. On a clear day you can see north to the Marin Headlands and south to Monterey Bay. The out-and-back to this vista point is about 8.5 miles and strenuous. The ride along the ridge is exposed. It may be hot or bitterly cold! Bring plenty of water.

Ride Information

Local Information

Current Big Basin weather:
www.bigbasin.org/weather.

Santa Cruz State Parks, 600 Ocean Street, Santa Cruz, CA 95060; (831) 429-2850; www.santacruzstateparks.org.

Mountain Parks Foundation, 525 North Bog Trees Park Road, Felton, CA 95018; (831) 335-3174; www.mountainparks.org.

Santa Cruz County Conference and Visitors Council, 1211 Ocean Street, Santa Cruz, CA 95060; (800) 833-3494; www.santacruz.org.

Local Events and Attractions

Henry Cowell Redwoods State Park, 101 North Big Trees Park Road, Felton; (831) 438-2396; www.parks.ca.gov.

Accommodations

Campgrounds: Big Basin Redwoods State Park, Henry Cowell Redwoods State Park, Butano State Park; reservations (800) 444-7275; www.reserveamerica.com.

Big Basin Tent Cabins, (800) 874-8368 or (831) 338-4745; www.calparksco.com.

Sanborn Park Hostel, 15808 Sanborn Road, Saratoga; (408) 741-0166; www.sanborn parkhostel.org.

Restaurants and Java Jolts

Boulder Creek Brewery and Cafe, 1304 State Highway 9, Boulder Creek; (831) 338-7882; www.bouldercreekbrewery.com.

Blue Sun Cafe, 13070 State Highway 9, Boulder Creek; (831) 338-6441; www.bluesuncafe.com.

32 Waddell Creek Out-and-Back

This is a pleasant ride along Waddell Creek, the coastal access for Big Basin Redwoods State Park. In a coastal range of steep climbs and quick descents, this is one of the easier rides into the woods. The trail meanders along the cool and lush creek among cottonwoods, alders, redwoods, and ferns. Bring a lock for the bike rack at the end and take the fifteen-minute hike to picturesque Berry Creek Falls. The elevation at the bike rack is only 300 feet, but there are some gradual ups and downs along the way.

Start: Across California Highway 1 from Waddell Beach.
Distance: 11.4 miles out and back.
Approximate riding time: 1.5 hours.
Difficulty rating: Easy; nontechnical but still warrants fat tires.
Trail surface: 90 percent graded dirt road, 7 percent paved road, and 3 percent single-track.
Terrain: Lush creek canyon of oaks, cottonwoods, alders, and redwoods; a Pacific Ocean beach on one end, a hike to a waterfall on the other.
Seasons: Year-round, although best in late spring, summer, and fall. As with many trails, it can be very muddy in winter.

Other trail users: Hikers, vehicles, and equestrians.
Canine compatibility: Dogs not permitted.
Land status: Big Basin Redwoods State Park.
Nearest town: Davenport.
Fees and permits: No fees or permits required.
Schedule: Open 6:00 A.M. to 10:00 P.M. daily.
Maps: USGS maps: Franklin Point, CA; Ano Nuevo, CA.
California State Parks, *Big Basin Redwoods Park Map* (1999).
Trail contact: Big Basin Redwoods State Park, 21600 Big Basin Way, Boulder Creek, CA 95006; (831) 338–8860.
Rancho del Oso office; (831) 427–2288; www.parks.ca.gov or www.bigbasin.org.

Finding the trailhead: From Santa Cruz (by car): Take CA 1 north about 17 miles to Waddell Beach. The trailhead is across the highway (east) of the beach. Park at the beach or along the highway. There is no water at the trailhead. There is an outhouse at the beach and up the trail 0.3 mile near the horse camp. The only potable water on the trail is there as well.

From Santa Cruz (by bus): Bus service is available to Waddell Beach. For the schedule contact Santa Cruz Metropolitan Transit District, 370 Encinal Street, Suite 100, Santa Cruz, CA 95056; (831) 425–8600; www.scmtd.com.

The Ride

Most people visit Big Basin Redwoods State Park near the park headquarters—at 1,000 feet near the headwaters of Waddell Creek and accessed from the other side of the mountain. This ride begins at the Rancho del Oso entrance on the southwest tip of the park where Waddell Creek reaches the ocean.

Grizzlies once lived in the deep ravines of these mountains. Although long since wiped out by hunters, legends and names remain. Rancho del Oso means Ranch of

Waddell Creek Out-and-Back

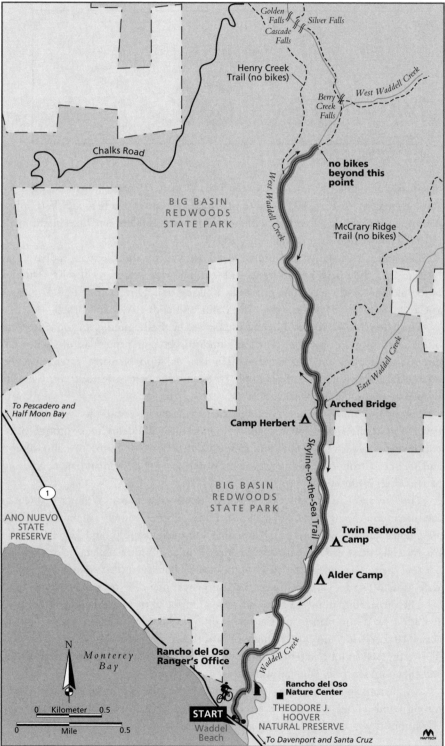

Golden Falls
Silver Falls
Cascade Falls

Henry Creek Trail (no bikes)

West Waddell Creek

Berry Creek Falls

no bikes beyond this point

Chalks Road

McCrary Ridge Trail (no bikes)

BIG BASIN REDWOODS STATE PARK

West Waddell Creek

East Waddell Creek

Arched Bridge

Camp Herbert ⛺

To Pescadero and Half Moon Bay

Skyline-to-the-Sea Trail

BIG BASIN REDWOODS STATE PARK

1

ANO NUEVO STATE PRESERVE

Twin Redwoods Camp ⛺

⛺ **Alder Camp**

N

Monterey Bay

Rancho del Oso Ranger's Office

Waddell Creek

Rancho del Oso Nature Center ■

0 Kilometer 0.5

0 Mile 0.5

START

Waddel Beach

THEODORE J. HOOVER NATURAL PRESERVE

To Davenport and Santa Cruz

MAPTECH

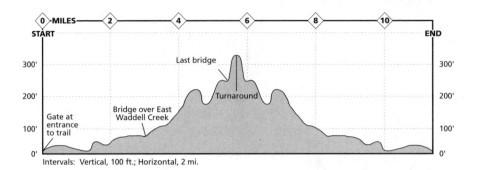

Intervals: Vertical, 100 ft.; Horizontal, 2 mi.

the Bear. The name of the creek comes from William Waddell, an early landowner and logger who died in 1875 because of complications from a bear attack. (He lost an arm in the attack.) Every year there is an annual Halloween hike in the park called "The Missing Arm of William Waddell."

The trail is well signed and simple to follow; you stay on the main trail as far as bikes can go. Side trails are off limits to bikes. The ride begins on the western end of the Skyline-to-the-Sea Trail, primarily a hiking trail. This 32-mile trail originates at Castle Rock State Park, traverses Big Basin, and ends at Waddell Beach.

The Theodore J. Hoover Natural Preserve is at the beginning of the ride. One of the few freshwater marshes remaining undisturbed along the coast of California, this is a great place for bird-watching. Rancho del Oso Nature Center is on the other side of the wetland and accessible by bike at the next road south on CA 1. It is open to the public on weekends.

You pass several farms and homes in the first 2 miles, so watch for vehicles along here. Most of the ride meanders along cool and lush Waddell Creek through oaks, cottonwoods, alders, redwoods, and ferns. Waddell Creek is home to coho salmon and steelhead trout—no fishing, though. Watch for giant salamanders, newts, and banana slugs in the wet season.

This can be a great family ride. The trail rises from the coast to about 320 feet at the turnaround point. Beginners will notice that it is not entirely flat, but the climbs are gradual and the descents fun. Kid trailers can make this, although where the trail has washed out, it may be barely wide enough (if at all) for a trailer. Three miles up the trail there is a singletrack detour with some hairpin turns that some may need to walk. Watch for ruts, particularly on the last quarter of a mile near the end.

The turnaround point for bikes is a pleasant place to picnic and enjoy the stream. Bring a lock if you plan to do the fifteen-minute hike up to Berry Creek Falls, at about 10 feet wide and 30 feet high, one of the largest waterfalls in the Bay Area. This is the first of four waterfalls along the creek. The next ones are Silver, Cascade, and then Golden Falls. You can walk as far as you like.

An obvious spot to check out at the end of the ride is popular Waddell Beach. Strong winds and surf make this a renowned spot for kite-boarding. Consider the conditions if you feel like swimming.

Miles and Directions

0.0   **START** from the gate at the trailhead to Skyline-to-the-Sea Trail. The gate is always closed but unlocked. Trailhead GPS: N 37 05 50.2, W 122 16 46.1.

0.3   Veer left on the paved road past the Rancho Del Oso Ranger Office and the information board. Pass through the gate and follow the Skyline-to-the-Sea Trail signs. The road becomes graded dirt. Ignore all side trails; they are marked PRIVATE or NO BIKES ALLOWED.

1.1   Continue straight and cross the bridge. Veer to the left past the bridge, passing two private roads on the right.

2.8   The dirt road is washed out. Follow the detour along a short, sweet singletrack with switchbacks.

3.2   You have a choice here, depending on your mood and the season: Veer right on the path just before the creek and cross on the bridge. Alternatively, continue straight and ford the creek. Both ways meet up on the other side of East Waddell Creek. This creek drains most of Big Basin, which explains the high, fancy bridge. Bypass McCrary Ridge Trail up ahead on the right.

5.7   Arrive at the bike rack and end of the trail for riding. Return the way you came. **Side trip:** It is a half-mile (fifteen-minute) walk up to Berry Creek Falls. The trail starts to the right of the information board and crosses the creek.

11.4   Arrive back at CA 1 and the parking lot.

Ride Information

Local Information

Santa Cruz State Parks, 600 Ocean Street, Santa Cruz, CA 95060; (831) 429-2850; www.santacruzstateparks.org.
Mountain Parks Foundation, 525 North Bog Trees Park Road, Felton, CA 95018; (831) 335-3174; www.mountainparks.org.

Local Events and Attractions

Rancho Del Oso Nature and History Center, Waddell Creek Association, 3600 Highway 1, Davenport; (831) 427-2288; www.parks.ca.gov (search Waddell Creek Association).
Ano Nuevo State Reserve, New Years Creek Road, Pescadero; www.parks.ca.gov (search Ano Nuevo State Preserve and/or Park).

Accommodations

Waddell Creek trail camps, Big Basin Redwood State Park; (831) 338-8861 between 10:00 A.M. and 5:00 P.M.; www.parks.ca.gov (search Waddell Creek—Rancho Del Oso, Big Basin Redwoods State Park).

Butano State Park campground; reservations (800) 444-7275; www.parks.ca.gov.
Pigeon Point Lighthouse Hostel, 210 Pigeon Point Road, Pescadero; (650) 879-0633 or (800) 909-4776; www.norcalhostels.org.
Costanoa, 2001 Rossi Road, Pescadero; (650) 879-1100 or (800) 738-7477; www.costanoa.com (bike rentals and some private singletrack trails for guests only).

Restaurants and Java Jolts

Arcangeli Grocery Co. and Norm's Market, 287 Stage Road, Pescadero; (650) 879-0147; www.pescaderobakery.com or www.arcangeli grocery.com.
Taqueria de Amigos, 1999 Pescadero Road (at the gas station), Pescadero; (415) 879-0232.
Whale City Bakery, Bar and Grill, 490 State Highway 1, Davenport; (831) 423-9803.

In Addition

Tips for Mountain Biking with Kids

The time has finally come when the kids have progressed from rear-mounted child seats, kiddie trailers, and training wheels to two wheels. Now their fun begins. Most kids love the dirt, and parents don't have to worry about traffic.

The key to a winning ride is to know your kids. Tailor the ride to their individual needs. This will depend on their age, ability, endurance, and temperament. In general, when introducing kids to mountain biking, stick to the smoother trails, gradual grades, shorter trips, and places with interesting stops along the way. Kids are naturals on the trail. Their smaller bike frames and lower center of gravity enable them to make sharp turns more easily than many adults can. The following tips will get you and your child off to a good start.

1. **Helmets are mandatory.** That's the law in California for all children under eighteen years of age. Make it cool—their cool. Let them decorate their helmets. Stickers work fine, especially decals from bike shops and races.

2. **Make sure they have an approved bike helmet that fits correctly.** It's time to master the art of adjusting helmets, which will constantly need adjusting as kids grow. Chances are you will need to do it for all their friends as well. Here's how:

- Adjust the straps so that the helmet does not move around on the head.
- The helmet should cover the forehead, with about one finger width of space above the eyebrow. That means it is flat atop the head, not tilted back.
- The chinstrap should be comfortably snug. (This is not a muzzle.)
- The front and back straps should form a V just below the ear.
- If you need more help, check out www.bhsi.org.

3. **Ride the right bike.** Make sure the bike is the right size and in good working condition. Teach them how to tune it up. Kids don't like chain suck any more than adults do. Adjust the seat.

4. **Wear comfortable clothes.** Some kids really get into the look and attire. Others won't be seen in spandex. Padded shorts may not look cool, but they serve an important purpose. Kids can wear them under regular shorts if necessary. You don't want to hear about a sore butt ten minutes into a ride.

5. **Wear sunscreen and lip balm.** Bring the lip balm; it can soothe chafing in the middle of a ride.

6. **Bring plenty of water and food.** Kids get hungry much faster than adults do. It's amazing how much they can eat on a ride.

7. **Give them a whistle.** Teach them that three blasts mean help—and to keep it quiet otherwise.

8. Keep it fun and interesting. Don't be so vested in a ride that you can't change the plan or turn around. You are building memories—hopefully good ones.

9. Learn how to deflect whining with distractions. This is not the time or place for power plays. This may require a massive exercise in deep breathing—just don't let them see you doing it. If possible, find water. Take the kids down to the creek, let them get wet (if it is warm enough), and let them skip rocks. It's a law of nature: Even the most disgruntled riders usually perk up when they can play with rocks and water.

10. Relax. Enjoy the slower pace and frequent stops. This is not a workout. If you want them to wait for you when they blast by you in a few years, you had better wait for them now.

11. Know your kids. If your kids are leaders, let them lead. Don't ride their rear wheel to make them go faster. It may make them get off their bike altogether. If your child prefers to follow unwatched, let him or her straggle. No matter how slow you have to go, it is better than a complete stop; consider this good trials training.

12. Bring a friend, the right friend. If you have an alpha male, adding a competitive friend may pick up the pace for a faster ride. On the other hand, you could have a meltdown and mutiny miles from the car or home.

13. Timing is critical. Head back to the barn while they still have half their energy left. When it's gone, they are done. This may take practice, but learn it quickly.

14. Teach trail etiquette, respect for other trail users, and zero-impact biking. These are our future land stewards and mountain biking ambassadors.

Grab the kids and hit the dirt.

Honorable Mentions

Note: Helmets are required for all riders on all these trails; but of course helmets should be worn on all rides for safety.

K Santa Teresa Park

Tucked away in the southeastern corner of San Jose, the Santa Teresa Hills offer some fine singletrack and a quick workout. The grass-covered hills rise from 210 feet near the golf course to 1,155 feet at Coyote Peak. The access road takes you halfway up the hill, but the trails rise and fall throughout the park. This is a moderate ride, with technical sections and some good climbs. The view is expansive, with Mount Hamilton on the horizon. Since there is little shade, ride in the mornings during the hot summer. Evenings are inviting, but this is a popular spot for hikers and equestrians as well.

There are many ways to ride these hills. A good introduction starts from the Bernal Road parking area: Head southwest on Mine Trail to the switchbacks on Stile Ranch Trail. At the bottom head up Fortini and Mine Trails to Hidden Springs Trail. Turn right and head up toward Coyote Peak via the right fork onto Coyote Trail. Return down Rocky Ridge Trail and expect some rugged singletrack. At the bottom return to the start on Mine Trail, completing a nearly 7-mile loop. Cross Bernal Road (north side of the park) and do the Bernal Hill Loop clockwise, adding 2 miles.

From the Santa Clara Valley, exit either U.S. Highway 101 or California Highway 85 at Bernal Road. Head west 1.3 miles, crossing Santa Teresa Boulevard, passing the golf course, and winding up the hills into the park. There is an entrance fee; parking, water, and restrooms are available at the Pueblo Day Use Area. Otherwise park at the small parking area at the end of the public access on Bernal Road. Check for trail closures, especially along Rocky Ridge Trail. Maps are available at the trailheads and online. The ranger station is located at nearby Hellyer County Park; (408) 225–0225; www.parkhere.org.

L Almaden Quicksilver Park

Scattered mining remnants barely allude to what was once the richest mercury (quicksilver) mining area in California. Today all the mine shafts are sealed. Oaks, chaparral, and grasses have reclaimed these hills. Catch this park in spring, when the wildflowers are brilliant. All the bike trails in the park are nontechnical fire roads. For a 10-mile loop, start from the Hacienda Staging Area and ride Mine Hill Road 3 miles to the summit at Bull Run. Despite nearly 1,100 feet of climbing, the grade is moderate and there is some shade. You can enjoy the view of the adjoining Sierra

Azul Open Space Preserve and Mount Umunhum. Continue on Mine Hill Road to the end of the line for bikes. At this point turn right to return on Randol Trail. The last section of the loop backtracks on Mine Hill Road to the parking lot.

In San Jose take California Highway 85 to the Almaden Expressway and exit south. Go 4.5 miles and turn right onto Almaden Road. Follow Almaden Road 3 miles, passing through the historic town of New Almaden. The Hacienda Staging Area is on the right. Trails are subject to closure after rain. Be sure to check online or call ahead.

New trails are opening to bikes in this park! Bikes can now enter the park from Mockingbird Hill Lane off Almaden Road and at the new Wood Trail parking area on Hicks Road. The new Wood Trail (a section of the Bay Area Ridge Trail) offers an easier entrance to Almaden Quicksilver Park, as well as a connection to the adjoining Sierra Azul Open Space Preserve. For more information contact the ranger station at (408) 268–3883; www.parkhere.org.

M Sierra Azul Open Space Preserve

This is the local workout guaranteed to build up those legs. Views of the Santa Clara Valley and the Santa Cruz Mountains distract from the pain. Plus, anything that steep gives good downhill. Watch for traffic; you are not alone out here. The chaparral-covered hills offer no shade; it sizzles in summer.

Start at Lexington Reservoir, ride east on Alma Bridge Road to the first Sierra Azul (Blue Mountain Range) gate (SA22). This is the trailhead for Limekiln Trail, more commonly called Overgrown Trail. Ride up this shaded, wide singletrack for 1.4 miles and turn left at the junction onto the much wider Priest Rock Trail (2,600 feet at the upper end.) Alternatively, you can continue straight up Limekiln Trail to Mount El Sombroso (2,999 feet). Both routes will take you to Kennedy Trail, where you turn left for a wickedly steep downhill into a residential neighborhood. Once on the pavement, turn left onto Kennedy Road through Los Gatos. Turn left again onto Los Gatos Boulevard, which becomes Main Street. Turn left onto the Los Gatos Creek Trail just before the freeway overcrossing and follow it up to the Lexington Reservoir. Some prefer to start on Kennedy Trail and go clockwise—pick your poison. It is a relentless fire road climb in that direction, but then there is no easy way on this mountain.

From southbound California Highway 17, take the Bear Creek Road exit, cross over the highway, and go 0.4 mile north on CA 17 to Alma Bridge Road. Drive across the dam to the parking area at Lexington Reservoir County Park (parking fee); www.parkhere.org. The trails are in the Midpeninsula Regional Open Space District; (650) 691–1200; www.openspace.org. A map is available online.

St. Joseph's Hill Open Space Preserve

Enjoy a quick escape through grassland, chaparral, and woodlands just outside Los Gatos. The top of St. Joseph's Hill (1,250 feet) offers a view of the Santa Clara Valley, Lexington Reservoir, and the Santa Cruz Mountains. Although the trails are rather steep, the climbs are not very long. This is an easy to moderate ride; the preserve is only 268 acres. This is a good place to build up some stamina. Since this is a popular spot for hikers and equestrians, too, things can get crowded on weekends and evenings in summer. Once you've explored St. Joseph's Hill, ride on up to Lexington Reservoir and ride the lower trails on Sierra Azul Open Space Preserve.

Take California Highway 17 to Los Gatos; exit on California Highway 9–Los Gatos/Saratoga Avenue and head east. Turn right on Los Gatos Boulevard, which becomes Main Street. The high school is on the right and is a convenient place to park. From here head west on Main Street and turn left onto College Avenue. Turn right onto Jones Road; the trailhead is at the end of the road. About 0.7 mile up Jones Trail, turn left to climb toward the top of the hill. A counterclockwise loop up Manzanita Trail and back down Novitiate Trail takes you to the peak and encircles the upper hill. Without exploring any other trails, this is nearly a 5-mile ride. For more information contact the Midpeninsula Regional Open Space District; (650) 691–1200. There is a map online at www.openspace.org.

The Peninsula

Welcome to the Peninsula, as in the San Francisco–San Mateo Peninsula. With the Santa Cruz Mountains running the length of the Peninsula, local riders have easy access to some amazing rides. California Highway 35 follows the ridgeline of the mountains and is a starting point for a host of rides. Views of both the Pacific Coast and San Francisco Bay follow riders along the ridges and to the peaks. The terrain drops steeply on either side of the mountain range, dipping into dense redwood forests in the ravines on the damp western slopes.

The Midpeninsula Regional Open Space District (MROSD) operates most of the accessible open-space land along the ridge. Created in 1972, this independent special district manages twenty-six open-space preserves, securing nearly 50,000 acres into public land. The district has been more open to mountain biking than some other land stewards, offering some truly inspiring singletrack treks into the woods.

Not all Peninsula riding is on the ridge. You can ride along the coastal bluff south of Pacifica before bagging North Peak, or you can ride through local parks on the lower foothills above San Francisco Bay. There is riding for all levels of ability throughout the year. The coastal climate and forests provide comfortable summer riding.

Although the city of San Francisco gets short shrift in this guide, there is mountain biking there for those willing to brave some concrete and traffic. Tempting as it is to piece together some loops through the city, liabilities and the onerous task of getting approval of property owners has quashed the effort. Not all is pavement in the City by the Bay; there are dirt tracks in Golden Gate Park, Land's End, and the Presidio. Moreover, where there are cities, there will always be urban assault—and I will take heat for that statement. Surf the Web for suggested rides through San Francisco.

For local advocacy and stewardship, check out www.sfmtb.com. This is a loose-knit and dedicated group of riders.

If you want to meet other mountain bikers, check out the monthly Critical Mass rides; www.critical-mass.org or http://bapd.org/gcrass-1.html. Sometimes mountain bikers hear the calling to ride the streets.

33 Saratoga Gap–Long Ridge Loop

This is some of the most easily accessible singletrack in the Bay Area. The price is sharing the trail with lots of other bikers, hikers, and equestrians, especially on weekends. Much of the ride is in the cool shade of oak, madrone, and Douglas fir woodlands. Whenever you leave the trees for the grass-covered ridge, you have a panoramic view of the Santa Cruz Mountains and the Pacific Ocean before you. This ride is just plain fun.

Start: From Saratoga Gap Trail at the intersection of California Highways 9 and 35.
Distance: 10.1 miles out and back with a loop.
Approximate riding time: 1.5 to 2 hours.
Difficulty: Moderate; modest climbing—nothing long. Ragged singletrack requires skill, steep descent not for the timid.
Trail surface: 70 percent singletrack and 30 percent dirt road.
Terrain: Undulating ridge, oak woodlands, Douglas fir forests, grass-covered hillsides, coastal views, steep ravines.
Seasons: Brilliant in spring with wildflowers and in fall with clear views. The shaded trails can be a respite from the summer heat; sections close in winter.
Other trail users: Hikers and equestrians.
Canine compatibility: Dogs not permitted.
Land status: Midpeninsula Regional Open Space Park District.

Nearest town: Saratoga.
Fees and permits: No fees or permits required.
Schedule: Open daily from dawn (half hour before sunrise) to dusk (half hour after sunset). The Long Ridge and Peters Creek Trails close in the wet season, as do portions of the Bay Area Ridge Trail.
Maps: USGS maps: Mindego Hill, CA; Cupertino, CA.
Midpeninsula Regional Open Space District map, *Southern Skyline Region—Open Space Preserves,* available at the trailhead and online.
Trail contact: Midpeninsula Regional Open Space Park District, 330 Distel Circle, Los Altos, CA 94022; (650) 691-1200; www.openspace.org.
Trail regulations: Helmets are required at all times. The speed limit is 15 mph, 5 mph when passing other trail users.

Finding the trailhead: From San Jose: Take Interstate 280 to the Saratoga Avenue exit. Follow Saratoga Avenue southwest through Saratoga as it becomes Big Basin Way/CA 9. (Big Basin Way becomes Congress Springs Road but remains CA 9.) Wind up the hill out of Saratoga for about 7 miles to Skyline Boulevard/CA 35. The trailhead and limited parking are on the right side of CA 9 just before the intersection. A larger lot is on the left at the Saratoga Gap Vista Point and is accessed from Skyline Boulevard. No water or restrooms are available.

Saratoga Gap–Long Ridge Loop

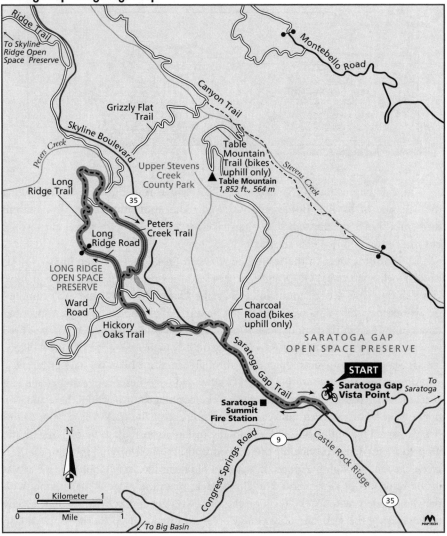

The Ride

Word is out on the singletrack trails through the Saratoga Gap and Long Ridge Open Space Preserves. These extremely popular trails are easily accessible for mountain bikers in the San Jose area. This is a good loop for intermediate riders. Advanced riders can use this as a starting point for longer rides north through adjoining open-space preserves or down into Stevens Creek Canyon. Beginners should start at the Long Ridge Open Space Preserve, skipping the obstacles along the Saratoga Gap Trail. Much of this ride follows the Bay Area Ridge Trail.

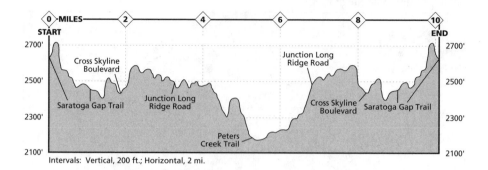

Intervals: Vertical, 200 ft.; Horizontal, 2 mi.

The ride begins on the Saratoga Gap Trail, which runs through the trees along the east side of Skyline Boulevard. Scattered rocks, root drops, and a few hairpin turns mix things up through here and make for a fun ride. Not much flat terrain, but the climbs and descents are short.

After crossing over to the Long Ridge Open Space Preserve, the mixed woodland of oak, madrone, and Douglas fir gives way to grassy hillsides and expansive views of the Santa Cruz Mountains and Pacific Ocean. In spring and early summer, massive displays of wildflowers add to the picture. An all-too-short singletrack looks down onto Portola Redwoods State Park and Butano Ridge beyond. If you ventured west on a side trip down Ward Road, you would come to the edge of Portola Redwoods State Park. However, there is no through access for bikes on state property.

After riding the open ridge, Long Ridge Road becomes a sweet singletrack and veers into the woods. In winter you have to be content to turn around here and skip this section. Wet-season closures are in effect to protect the trail surface from excessive damage. This undulating trail eventually makes a short climb before an extreme drop to Peters Creek. Once on the canyon floor, the trail meanders along the lush creek canyon, through meadows, and past an old farm site. In fall look for ripe apples in the remnants of an orchard. The climb back up to the ridge is manageable with the well-graded switchbacks. Back on the ridge you get another glimpse of the view before leaving the west side of Skyline Boulevard to wrap it up on the Saratoga Gap Trail. On weekends in summer there is a hot dog and drinks stand in the parking lot to greet you at the end of the ride.

Parts of this ride parallel Skyline Boulevard, which itself is popular for motorcycles and sports cars. Keep this in mind when making the road crossings. Moreover, just as you feel you are away from it all in the woods, the drone of motorcycles racing in the background may draw you back to reality.

With no shortage of fire roads in the Bay Area, the singletrack trails in the open-space preserves are refreshing! Kudos go to the Midpeninsula Regional Open Space District, Responsible Organized Mountain Pedalers (ROMP), and Mountain Bikers of Santa Cruz (MBOSC) for their advocacy and trail work. Other open-space managers please take note.

Miles and Directions

0.0   **START** from the trailhead for the Saratoga Gap Trail and head north. Trailhead GPS: N 37 15.310, W 122 07.166.

1.7   This intersection marks the entrance to Upper Stevens Creek Park on the right. Cross the fire road and continue straight (somewhat left) to stay on Saratoga Gap Trail. (FYI: The trail to the right is the top of Charcoal Road, a great climb out from Stevens Canyon. Bikes are allowed uphill only on this trail.)

2.0   Carefully cross Skyline Boulevard onto Hickory Oaks Trail. This quickly turns into a fire road entering the Long Ridge Open Space Preserve.

2.2   Turn left at the fork onto the singletrack. Savor this section; it is over way too soon.

2.5   Veer left back onto the fire road.

3.1   Veer right at the fork with Ward Road, following the singletrack toward Long Ridge Road.

3.3   Merge straight onto the wider Ward Road.

3.4   Continue straight at the intersection onto Long Ridge Road. You will complete the loop here, coming up from the right on Peters Creek Trail.

3.8   Veer right to stay on Long Ridge Road, which soon turns right into a great singletrack run. This trail gate is closed throughout the winter.

4.6   Continue straight on Long Ridge Road, crossing the fire road leading to Peters Creek Trail on the right.

5.3   After a *steep* downhill run, continue straight on Peters Creek Trail. **Options:** A left turn at the junction offers several choices. (1) Turn left again in about 0.1 mile and head farther north on the Bay Area Ridge Trail. This will take you into Skyline Ridge Open Space Preserve and beyond. (2) Take the right fork in 0.1 mile toward Grizzly Flat parking. Cross Skyline Boulevard and enjoy a long descent down Grizzly Flat Trail. At the bottom turn right onto Canyon Trail. After 0.3 mile turn up Table Mountain Trail and Charcoal Trail for a long 3-mile ride back to the Saratoga Gap Trail.

5.7   Veer left at the junction.

5.9   Veer right to stay on the main trail. The unsigned trail to the left cuts over to Skyline Boulevard.

6.3   Veer right and pass a small pond on the left—private property. Cross over a bridge and ride up the singletrack switchbacks.

6.7   Turn left back onto Ward Road, completing the loop part of the ride. The rest is backtracking.

6.8   Veer right at the fork to Hickory Oaks Trail.

7.0   Turn left onto the dirt road.

7.6   Turn right up the singletrack.

7.8   Turn right onto the dirt road and follow it back to Skyline Boulevard.

8.1   Cross Skyline Boulevard and pick up the singletrack back to Saratoga Gap.

8.4   Continue straight across the fire road.

10.1   Arrive back at the trailhead on CA 9.

Ride Information

Local Information

Saratoga Chamber of Commerce, 14485 Big Basin Way, Saratoga, CA 95070; (408) 867-0753; www.saratogachamber.org; Saratoga Community Home Page: www.saratoga-ca.com.

Accommodations

Sanborn Park Hostel, 15808 Sanborn Road; (408) 741-0166; www.sanbornparkhostel.org.
Camping Big Basin Redwoods State Park, 21600 Big Basin Way; reservations (800) 444-7275; www.reserveamerica.com.

Big Basin Tent Cabins; (800) 874-8368 or (831) 338-4745; www.calparksco.com.

Restaurants and Java Jolts

Blue Rock Shoot, 14523 Big Basin Way, Saratoga; (408) 868-1613.
International Coffee Exchange, 14471 Big Basin Way, Saratoga; (408) 741-1185.
Florentine Restaurant, 14510 Big Basin Way, Saratoga; (408) 741-1784; www.florentine.net.

TRICKY SWITCHBACK TURNS
Here are some tips to keep you on your bike as well as on the trail from expert Blair Lombardi. Blair won the 1990 Veteran National Cross Country Championship and was a member of the U.S. National Team at the 1990 World Championships in Durango, Colorado. She is an elite-level coach for USA Cycling and, to all those who know her, the Goddess of Balance.

- Always look in the direction of the turn.
- As you ride up through switchbacks, scoot your hips forward on your saddle as the terrain angle increases. Conversely, as you ride down through switchbacks, stay off your saddle. Shift your weight back as the terrain becomes steeper.
- Keep your elbows bent and your arms flexible.
- Whether going up or down through switchbacks, approach them in the center of the trail. Just before you reach the apex, steer away from the turn and skirt the outside edge of the trail. When your front wheel has passed the apex, steer into the turn and exit in the center of the trail.

34 Black Mountain–Stevens Canyon Loop

Check out sweeping views and sweet singletrack. Nothing is free. There is a price: the paved grind to the top of Black Mountain. Get strong; build those charging-rhinoceros legs. Otherwise, score a friend to shuttle you near the top for the descent into Stevens Canyon. This is a convenient ride for Peninsula bikers who are sitting on paydirt. Five thanks to those who have fought hard for these trails, for this open-space jewel in our backyard.

Start: From the intersection of Stevens Canyon and Mount Eden Roads.
Distance: 17.9-mile loop.
Approximate riding time: 2.5 hours.
Difficulty: Difficult; interminable climb, sections of narrow singletrack with loose rocks and roots.
Trail surface: 57 percent paved road, 28 percent dirt road, and 15 percent singletrack.
Terrain: A mountain shrouded in oak woodlands, vineyards, chaparral, and grassland; view from the top, deep canyon, creek to cross; almost more pavement than knobby tires can stand.
Seasons: Year-round; creek crossing can be dicey in winter.
Other trail users: Hikers, equestrians, and vehicles.
Canine compatibility: Dogs not permitted.
Land status: Midpeninsula Regional Open Space District and Stevens Creek County Park.
Nearest town: Cupertino.

Fees and permits: No fees or permits required.
Schedule: Open daily from dawn (half hour before sunrise) to dusk (half hour after sunset).
Maps: USGS maps: Cupertino, CA; Mindego Hill, CA.
Midpeninsula Regional Open Space District map, *Southern Skyline Region—Open Space Preserves,* available online.
Trail contacts: Midpeninsula Regional Open Space Park District, 330 Distel Circle, Los Altos, CA 94022; (650) 691–1200; www.openspace.org.
Santa Clara County Department of Parks and Recreation, Stevens Creek County Park, 11401 Stevens Canyon Road, Cupertino, CA 95014; (408) 867–9959.
Upper Stevens Creek County Park; (408) 867–9959; www.parkhere.org.
Trail regulations: Helmets are required at all times. The speed limit is 15 mph, 5 mph when passing other trail users.

Finding the trailhead: From San Jose: Take Interstate 280 north to Cupertino. Exit on the Foothill Expressway/Foothill Boulevard and head south. Foothill Boulevard becomes Stevens Canyon Road. Nearly 3 miles from the freeway, pass the dam to Stevens Creek Reservoir and drive around the right (west) side of the reservoir. Pass Montebello Road on the right and begin tracing the first leg of the ride. Turn right at the junction of Mount Eden Road (1.4 miles from Montebello Road) and park up ahead on the left at the Stevens Creek County Park–Canyon Picnic Area. Water, restrooms, and a telephone are available here. Since there are several places to park along here, mileage for the ride begins at the intersection of Stevens Canyon Road and Mount Eden Road.

Check out this west view when you reach the peak of Black Mountain.

There are several other places to park and begin this ride. Starting at the Canyon Picnic Area stacks most of the road riding at the beginning of the ride and ensures there is no climbing at the end. Parking at the dam is closest; there is usually an outhouse, but there is no water. There is also a county park on the lake just past Montebello Road. There is no parking on Montebello Road or Stevens Canyon Road beyond the county parks; the sheriff diligently enforces this.

The Ride

How does a loop with 10 miles of road riding make it into a mountain biking guide? The view along Monte Bello Ridge and the singletrack descent into the canyon and along Stevens Creek are worth it. Since there is no parking on Montebello Road or the upper end of Stevens Canyon Road, there is little escaping the pavement— unless, that is, you are lucky enough to score a shuttle ride to the top of Montebello Road.

The ride begins along the road at the lower end of Stevens Creek and follows the reservoir before heading up Montebello Road. Half a mile up the road, you pass Picchetti Ranch and Winery on the left. This historical landmark is an open-space preserve with a grassy picnic area, orchards, and an operating winery. Wine tasting is available throughout the week; check their Web site for hours.

In all, this steep twisty road takes you 5 miles through oak-covered hillsides, past vineyards and palatial homes before finally hitting the dirt. This climb is a popular route for road bikers, but mountain bikers clearly have the better way down. Once you enter the Monte Bello Open Space Preserve, it is another mile and a half before reaching the top of Black Mountain. The 2,200 feet of climbing is great training; however, it is a butt-numbing ride. Riding out of the saddle occasionally will help.

Views of the South Bay unfold during your climb, but once on top, the full panorama opens up. To the west you look down into Stevens Creek Canyon, across to Skyline Ridge, and beyond to the Pacific Ocean. Even if it is foggy, the rolling "cat claws" give a classic bay view of their own. To the north you can see San Francisco and Mount Tamalpais; to the east, radio transmission stations.

This ride is about delayed gratification, and the ride down is the payoff. You are riding grass-covered hillsides with views at every corner, often at eye level with red-tailed hawks. Smooth singletrack on the Old Ranch and Bella Vista Trails takes you down into Stevens Creek Canyon.

Once onto the canyon floor, it is not all downhill. Stevens Creek runs along the San Andreas Fault—source of the 1906 San Francisco earthquake. This active fault has twisted things around, so you will not find a level, weathered canyon; there are still short sections of uphill. Canyon Trail starts out as a wide dirt road that narrows to singletrack past Grizzly Flat Trail. The trail gets dusty and soft in late summer and fall. After the exposed ridge you may welcome the shaded canyon's predominantly oak, madrone, and bay laurel woodland with pockets of Douglas fir. Nearing the end, you will have to ford Stevens Creek. This can be refreshing most of the year. But during winter's high water, it can be dicey and hazardous. Given the limited parking near the trailheads, there are not many hikers through here. Most of the traffic in the heart of this ride will be other mountain bikers.

After you leave the open-space preserve, you soon hit the pavement again. The ride ends with a shaded road ride along Stevens Creek back to the parking area.

Monte Bello, the "beautiful mountain," lends itself to epic rides. There are many options for connecting with the other open-space preserves. By starting from Page Mill Road or Skyline Boulevard, you can put together a loop without the road ride.

Miles and Directions

0.0 **START** from the junction of Stevens Canyon Road and Mount Eden Road. Head north on Stevens Canyon Road, back toward the reservoir and dam. Intersection GPS: N 37 16.51, W 122 04.22.

1.4 Turn left onto Montebello Road.

6.3 Continue straight on the paved road at an entrance to the Monte Bello Open Space Preserve. **Option:** If you are anxious to hit the dirt, turn left onto Waterwheel Creek Trail. This overgrown dirt road rejoins the featured ride at Mile 7.2 and is only about 0.7 mile

Black Mountain–Stevens Canyon Loop

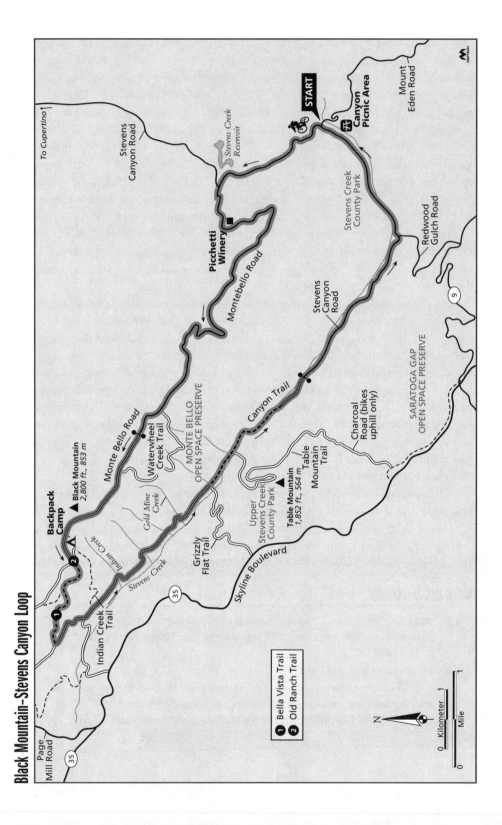

To Cupertino

Page Mill Road

35

Stevens Canyon Road

Stevens Creek Reservoir

START

Canyon Picnic Area

Mount Eden Road

Picchetti Winery

Stevens Creek County Park

Redwood Gulch Road

9

Backpack Camp

Black Mountain 2,800 ft., 853 m

Monte Bello Road

Waterwheel Creek Trail

MONTE BELLO OPEN SPACE PRESERVE

Canyon Trail

Stevens Canyon Road

SARATOGA GAP OPEN SPACE PRESERVE

Charcoal Road (bikes uphill only)

Gold Mine Creek

Indian Creek

Grizzly Flat Trail

Stevens Creek

Upper Stevens Creek County Park

Table Mountain 1,852 ft., 564 m

Table Mountain Trail

Indian Creek Trail

Skyline Boulevard

35

2

1

1 Bella Vista Trail
2 Old Ranch Trail

N

0   Kilometer   1

0   Mile   1

MAPTECH

longer. This starts out as a feel-good trail until you realize you are losing more than 400 feet of hard-earned elevation you will soon have to make up.

6.6 Continue straight around the gate into the open-space preserve. You are no longer on Montebello Road but are now on Monte Bello Road, where the pavement becomes broken and soon turns to dirt.

7.2 Stay on the main road. Waterwheel Creek Trail merges from the left.

8.1 Arrive at the summit of Black Mountain (2,800 feet). Despite all the hardware up here, do not expect cell phones to work. Continue north down the other side.

8.3 Continue straight at the fork. **Shortcut:** Turn left down Indian Creek Trail. This wide, steep trail drops you to Mile 10.8. Turn left onto Canyon Trail.

8.4 Continue straight at the fork. The trail to the left goes to Black Mountain Backpack Camp; reservations required. There are restrooms and a telephone there but no potable water.

8.7 Cross the main road at the intersection to pick up Old Ranch Trail. This meandering singletrack takes you to Bella Vista Trail.

9.2 Turn left onto Bella Vista Trail for a smooth singletrack descent into the canyon. Keep a heads-up for rattlesnakes along here. If you come upon one too quickly, the only place to bail is over the edge.

10.0 Make a sharp left onto the wide Canyon Trail. You will soon pass a bench on the right, before a short uphill climb to the left.

10.5 Continue straight where Stevens Creek Nature Trail takes off on the right. This trail takes you up to Skyline Boulevard or to White Oak Trail. It is closed during the wet season.

10.8 Veer right where Indian Creek Trail drops in from the left.

12.8 Continue straight where Grizzly Flat Trail heads uphill on the right. Canyon Trail begins to narrow for some sweet singletrack as you leave the open-space preserve and cross into Upper Stevens Creek County Park.

13.1 A sign announces that you are now leaving the city of Palo Alto! Okay, where was the welcome to Palo Alto sign? Veer left at the fork to stay on Canyon Trail. The right fork goes up Table Mountain Trail (uphill traffic only) to Saratoga Gap Trail. Along Canyon Trail you will cross Stevens Creek a couple of times. Depending on the season, it can be a challenge to stay dry. Gradually, old sections of asphalt begin to appear along with a few homes, and then you are on the paved Stevens Canyon Road.

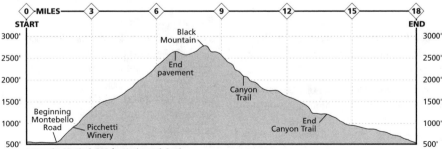

Intervals: Vertical, 500 ft.; Horizontal, 3 mi.

Wrap up this loop with a little cyclocross action.

14.4 Pass around the gate and start watching for cars.

16.3 Go straight at the stop sign where Redwood Gulch Road begins on the right.

17.9 Arrive back at the intersection of Stevens Canyon and Mount Eden Roads.

Option to Reduce the Amount of Road Riding

Start this ride from the other direction as an out-and-back from Stevens Canyon Road. Ride up Canyon Trail as far as you like.

Ride Information

Local Information

Cupertino Chamber of Commerce, 20455 Silverado Avenue, Cupertino, CA 95014; (408) 252-7054; www.cupertino-chamber.org.

Local Events and Attractions

Picchetti Winery, 13100 Montebello Road, Cupertino; (408) 741-1310; www.picchetti.com.

Accommodations

Black Mountain Backpack Camp, contact Midpeninsula Regional Open Space District, 330 Distel Circle, Los Altos, CA 94022; (650) 691-1200; www.openspace.org.

Sanborn Park Hostel, 15808 Sanborn Road, Saratoga; (408) 741-0166; www.sanborn parkhostel.org.

35 Skyline Ridge Loop

This scenic ride connects four open-space preserves along Skyline Boulevard between San Mateo and Santa Clara Counties. The ride offers sweeping singletrack through grassy ridgetops and oak woodlands. The changing views include the Santa Cruz Mountains, the Pacific Ocean, and San Francisco Bay. Spring wildflowers are a bonus. The climbs are manageable; anything steep is short-lived. Most climbs are rewarded with some singletrack—ah, except for the last climb home. There are many options to shorten or expand this loop to suit your talent and desire.

Start: From Russian Ridge Open Space Preserve parking lot on Alpine Road at Skyline Boulevard.
Distance: 12.3-mile loop.
Approximate riding time: 2 to 2.5 hours.
Difficulty: Moderate; modest grade with a few challenging climbs, well-packed singletrack with minor obstacles.
Trail surface: 45 percent singletrack, 45 percent dirt road, and 10 percent paved road.
Terrain: Undulating ridge, woodlands, grass-covered hillsides, coastal and bay views, steep wooded ravines.
Seasons: Year-round. Best in spring for the wildflowers and fall for the clear views. Exposed ridges can be windy and foggy in summer.
Other trail users: Hikers and equestrians.
Canine compatibility: Dogs not permitted on all the trails.

Land status: Midpeninsula Regional Open Space District.
Nearest town: Palo Alto.
Fees and permits: No fees or permits required.
Schedule: Open daily dawn (half hour before sunrise) to dusk (half hour after sunset); Skid and White Oak Trails are closed in the wet season.
Maps: USGS map: Mindego Hill, CA. Midpeninsula Regional Open Space District map, *Southern Skyline Region—Open Space Preserves,* available online and usually at the trailhead.
Trail contact: Midpeninsula Regional Open Space Park District, 330 Distel Circle, Los Altos, CA 94022; (650) 691-1200; www.openspace.org.
Trail regulations: Helmets are required at all times. The speed limit is 15 mph, 5 mph when passing other trail users.

Finding the trailhead: From San Francisco or San Jose: Take Interstate 280 to Los Altos Hills. Exit on Page Mill Road and head west for about 8.5 miles. Cross Skyline Boulevard (California Highway 35) onto Alpine Road. Immediately turn right into the parking area for Russian Ridge Open Space Preserve. There is an outhouse but no water.

The Ride

There is no time to get bored on this loop. While the directions may seem cumbersome, once you find your way around, the ride should flow. It is easy to take a wrong turn, but armed with the maps provided at most preserve trailheads, you should not have to go too far to get back on track—or better yet, find your own path.

Skyline Ridge Loop

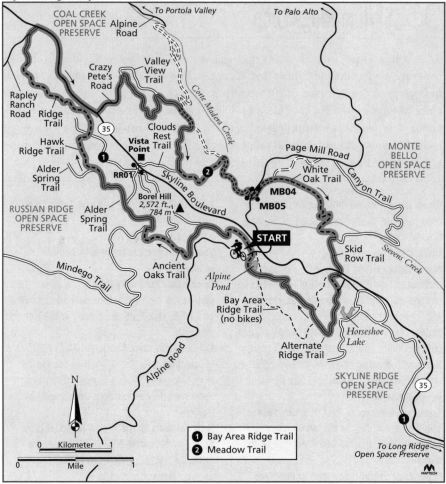

Skyline Boulevard is a winding road running along the ridge of the Santa Cruz Mountains. This loop tours four of the open-space preserves along both sides of Skyline Boulevard: Russian Ridge, Coal Creek, Monte Bello, and Skyline Ridge. The county line between San Mateo and Santa Cruz Counties runs through the middle of this ride.

The ride begins in the Russian Ridge Open Space Preserve on a section of the Bay Area Ridge Trail. From the grassy ridges you look over the top of Portola Redwoods State Park and Butano Ridge to the Pacific Ocean beyond. Ancient Oaks Trail is a sweet singletrack drop through lush oak woodland. Exposed twisting fire roads connect to singletrack Hawk Ridge Trail and more Ridge Trail. This is one of the finer sections of the Bay Area Ridge Trail for bicyclists. The spring wildflowers through here are some of the Bay Area's best. You can lap around Russian Ridge and never cross Skyline if you want. On its own this makes a good ride for strong beginner and intermediate riders. If the singletrack is intimidating, you can move over to the fire roads.

You can also avoid the mile ride along Skyline Boulevard by cutting across the middle of Russian Ridge Open Space Preserve at Gate RR01 and Vista Point. From here you can ride into Coal Creek Preserve on Clouds Rest Trail. However, you'll miss some nice singletrack that way.

To stick with the featured ride, next you cross over to the east side of Skyline Boulevard and enter Coal Creek Open Space Preserve. Crazy Pete's Road drops into a tall canopy of oak, madrone, and laurel. Quick views of the bay peek through the trees. The trail is dusty and loose in summer and fall, with some ruts. The old Alpine Road is a popular direct connection to the open-space for locals in Portola Valley. Once an old thoroughfare to Page Mill Road, Alpine Road has long since become overgrown and is nearly singletrack in spots.

Monte Bello is the third open-space preserve on this loop and offers a great switchbacking ride on White Oak Trail. Starting on a grassy meadow, this singletrack quickly drops into lush forest at the headwaters of Stevens Creek. With another short climb out of the canyon, you cross over to the west side of Skyline Boulevard and enter Skyline Ridge Open Space Preserve. This is the last open-space preserve on the loop. If you have had enough climbing, you can bail and ride the road back to the start. Otherwise, it is a fire-road climb over the hill and down past Alpine Pond. Before the climb you pass Horseshoe Lake—a quick side trip.

There are many ways to explore these open-space trails; this is merely an introduction. The easy access makes this a popular area for local riders. Design epic rides by joining these preserves with Long Ridge and Saratoga Open Space Preserves to the south and Upper Stevens Creek County Park.

Miles and Directions

0.0 **START** from the Ridge Trail at the north side of the Russian Ridge parking lot. Trailhead GPS: N 37 18.55, W 122 11.19.

0.5 Turn left at the fork to Ancient Oaks Trail. **Side trip:** Turn right for a quick out-and-back to Borel Hill (2,572 feet). This 0.6-mile detour is a mild climb and offers a great panoramic view of the San Francisco Bay with Stanford University below.

0.9 Turn right onto the singletrack Ancient Oaks Trail.

1.2 Veer left at the fork to stay on Ancient Oaks Trail, which drops to Mindego Trail.

1.6 Turn right onto Mindego Trail, a wide fire road.

1.9 Turn left onto Alder Spring Trail to Hawk Ridge Trail.

2.4 Turn right at the fork, heading uphill on the singletrack Hawk Ridge Trail.

2.9 At the intersection, go straight onto the Ridge Trail toward Rapley Ranch Road. (**Bailout:** Turn right and return along the Ridge Trail to the start, completing a nearly 5-mile loop of Russian Ridge Open Space Preserve.) This fine singletrack takes you into the woods before meandering back to the east side of the hill for more sweeping views of the coast. You will pass a wooden platform on the left—if you had the time, this would be a nice place to spend it. The trail crosses a private gravel road several times. Lacking signs, these intersections may make you wonder which way to go—but just cross over to pick up the singletrack on the other side.

4.1 Reach the end of the singletrack. Turn left onto the gravel road.

4.4 Go around the gate and turn right onto the wide, graded Rapley Ranch Road.

4.5 Turn right and ride along Skyline Boulevard, hugging the edge of the road.

5.4 Turn left onto Crazy Pete's Road. There are several private drives along here, but they are clearly marked. Although this looks like a sleepy road, keep a heads-up for cars. The pavement ends after 0.3 mile.

5.8 Reach a gated entrance and trailhead for the Coal Creek Open Space Preserve. Turn right at the fork onto Crazy Pete's Road. The left trail is Valley View, which rejoins Crazy Pete's Road below. Try it next time through.

6.5 Veer right at the junction with Valley View Trail. Crazy Pete's Road becomes singletrack.

6.8 Turn right onto Alpine Road, the old thoroughfare to Page Mill Road.

7.0 Make a sharp right turn uphill and through another gate. This rather unpleasant half-mile climb will soon be history. **Shortcut:** If you are not up for the climb, skip this loop and continue straight on Alpine Road. You will miss a pleasant singletrack run down Meadow Trail.

7.5 Turn left onto Meadow Trail.

8.0 Veer right at a fork with a nondesignated trail.

8.1 Turn right back onto Alpine Road.

8.6 Cross Page Mill Road, go around locked gate MB05, and enter Monte Bello Open Space Preserve. Turn left onto the trail along the fence and over the hill. If this trail has been plowed up, turn left before the gate and ride Page Mill Road to the next gate on the right, MB04.

8.8 Turn right on the short paved section past the gate. Very shortly, turn left at the beginning of the large grass parking area on the right.

8.9 Turn right onto White Oak Trail. This starts doubletrack and soon becomes singletrack.

10.1 Turn right onto Skid Row Trail toward Skyline. **Option:** When not closed in the wet season, the trail to the left takes you down across Stevens Creek and connects to Canyon Trail. Turn left at Canyon Trail and ride up to Page Mill Road. Just before the road, turn left and

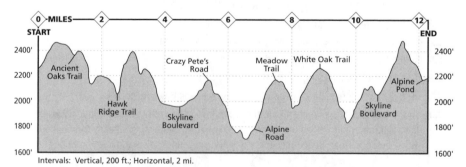

Intervals: Vertical, 200 ft.; Horizontal, 2 mi.

ride a series of dirt paths paralleling Page Mill Road. Turn left back onto White Oak Trail to repeat the section you just rode, making a great 3.5-mile loop.

10.4 Leave Monte Bello Open Space Preserve and cross Skyline Boulevard. Turn right at the gravel road to the parking area for Skyline Ridge Open Space Preserve. At the information board go left onto the singletrack Ridge Trail toward Horseshoe Lake. The trail to the right is the hiking-only section of the Bay Area Ridge Trail. **Bailout:** If you do not feel like more climbing, you can turn right onto Skyline Boulevard and ride the road back to Alpine Road. Turn left; the parking lot to Russian Ridge is on the right.

10.7 Turn right at the gravel road, ride past the accessible parking lot on the left, and pass through the gate onto a dirt road.

10.8 Turn right at the fork, heading uphill on the Ridge Trail—Alternate Route, meaning this is the way bikers and equestrians go. You will cross the hiking-only segment up ahead. There are several side trails coming off the main dirt road; stay to the right at each of them. **Option:** Turn left here and ride around Horseshoe Lake. You can pick up the Ridge Trail and head south to Long Ridge Open Space Preserve. There is a bit of a hill to climb to get there. Once over the hill the Ridge Trail will take you to Peters Creek Trail.

11.6 Continue straight, ignoring the side trail on the right.

11.7 Turn right at the T intersection.

11.9 Make a sharp left just before the ranger facility, then a quick right at the first fork. You will cross the hiking-only segment of the Ridge Trail again. Stay left of the earthen dam when you get to the Alpine Pond, which you will not see yet. The trail circling the pond is for hikers only.

12.1 Veer right at the fork below the dam, ignoring Old Page Mill Trail, which turns left past the big rock. Ride straight up to the other side of the pond. Catch a glimpse of the pond as you cross the bridge. Veer left at the fork past the bridge. This may sound complicated, but it is the only way bikes are allowed.

12.3 Cross Alpine Road; you are back at the parking lot where you started.

Kids' Option

Horseshoe Lake offers a nice multiuse trail for young children. The trail is short, lending itself to laps.

Ride Information

Local Events and Attractions
David C. Daniels Nature Center, located on Alpine Pond; (650) 691-1200.

Accommodations
Portola Redwoods State Park campground, 9000 Portola State Park Road, #F, La Honda; reservations (800) 444-7275; www.reserveamerica.com.

Hidden Villa Hostel (fall through spring only), 26870 Moody Road, Los Altos Hills; (650) 949-8648; www.hiddenvilla.org.

Restaurants and Java Jolts
Alice's Restaurant, 17288 Skyline Boulevard, Woodside; (650) 851-0303.

In Addition

Sharing the Trail with Horses

The multiuse trail signs are clear: Everyone makes way for the horses. With the average horse weighing in at 1,000 pounds, this is a wise rule. Hikers come second in the pecking order, meaning that bicyclists must yield to both horses and hikers. Across the country organizations representing each user group have debated what this really means. Here is a summary of what they've come up with:

- Get inside the head of a horse. It helps to understand that horses are creatures of prey. They have evolved an acute flight-or-fight response to danger.

- Horses do not like surprises. Make sure they know you are there, that you are human, and that your bike is not a predator. A lone bike lying by the side of the trail may appear to a horse as a hungry animal.

- Always keep a heads up for other trail users. Slow down when the line of sight is poor, for example, blind corners and hills.

- Slow down or stop when approaching a horse from any direction. Be cautious. Move out of the way of an oncoming horse. When approaching a horse from behind, remember horses are easily spooked.

- Speak up to alert the rider and to assure the horse you are a person. This doesn't have to be loud; a horse has extraordinary hearing and will hear you even if the rider does not. In some areas bells may work, but your voice is better. People, not bells, feed horses.

- Horseback riders will let you know what you can safely do around their horses and suggest the best way to pass.

- Wait for a wide spot in the trail to pass; give them wide berth. If the trail is narrow, go to the lower side of the trail while the horse passes. Horses are often leery of unfamiliar things that are taller than they are. Pass slowly and steadily, while talking to the horse.

With all the pressures on the wide-open spaces, equestrians and bikers have much to gain by working together for trail access. Conversely, they have much to lose by going it alone. Both groups share a love of the outdoors on their respective steeds. Joint trail rides, trail maintenance projects, and social functions connecting horse and bike groups have been extremely successful. Responsible Organized Mountain Pedalers (ROMP) sponsors annual ROMP and STOMP rides, "stomp" referring to the horses. Joint relays have also been held, with equestrians and cyclists switching mounts midcourse. There may be a future here in the adventure-racing arena. All of this has greatly improved perceptions between the groups.

Horses and cyclists meet all the time on the trail without incident. As with many activities, a few isolated incidents have disparaged both sides. As cyclists, we have a responsibility to continue to do our part. Consider this: every person you meet on the trail is a potential lobbyist for or against mountain bike access. Based on your encounter, which way will they cast their vote?

36 Old Haul Road Out-and-Back

Take a gentle ride through the mixed woodlands and redwood forests along Pescadero Creek. Once a rail line for hauling giant redwoods to the sawmill, Old Haul Road is now a well-graded dirt road. Overall, the grade is gradual. The steepest terrain is at the end: A 2-mile trek in and out of Portola Redwoods State Park offers a look at some redwood giants. This can be a pleasant family outing and an introduction to riding on the dirt.

Start: From the trailhead at Hoffman Creek on Wurr Road.
Distance: 13.4 miles out and back.
Approximate riding time: 1.5 to 2 hours.
Difficulty: Easy; not completely flat, wide dirt road.
Trail surface: 88 percent dirt road and 12 percent paved road.
Terrain: Old railroad grade through a mixed oak woodland and redwood forest along Pescadero Creek; paved service road inside Portola Redwoods State Park, giant redwoods nearby.
Seasons: Good year-round. Cool, shady ride in the heat of summer.
Other trail users: Hikers, equestrians, and vehicles (within Portola Redwoods State Park only).
Canine compatibility: Dogs not permitted.
Land status: San Mateo County Park and Portola Redwoods State Park.

Nearest town: Loma Mar.
Fees and permits: No fees or permits required.
Schedule: Open daily 8:00 A.M.; closing time varies from 5:00 to 8:00 P.M. throughout the year. Check the Pescadero Creek County Park Web site for current schedule.
Maps: USGS maps: La Honda, CA; Mindego Hill, CA; Big Basin, CA.
Pescadero Creek County Park map, San Mateo County Parks and Recreation.
Trail contacts: Pescadero Creek County Park, Loma Mar; (650) 879-0238; www.eparks.net (search parks, then Pescadero Creek). This includes a weather link. The nearest ranger is at Memorial County Park, 9500 Pescadero Creek Road, Loma Mar, CA 94021; (650) 363-4021.
Portola Redwoods State Park, 9000 Portola State Park Road, #F, La Honda, CA 94020; (650) 948-9098; www.parks.ca.gov.

Finding the trailhead: From San Francisco: Take Interstate 280 to the Woodside Road (California Highway 84) exit and go west (right). Follow Woodside Road through town, up the hill, across Skyline Boulevard (California Highway 35), and down through La Honda—about 20 miles of slow, winding road. Turn left onto Pescadero Road; veer right on Pescadero Road at the fork with Alpine Road. Turn left onto Wurr Road just before Memorial Park. Hoffman Creek Trail Head and parking area is 0.2 mile down the road on the left, just before the narrow bridge.

The Ride

This ride takes you through the canyon of Pescadero Creek Park on well-graded Old Haul Road. You will follow the sounds of the creek but rarely see it. A side trip

It's a smooth cruise through the lush redwoods. ▶

Old Haul Road Out-and-Back

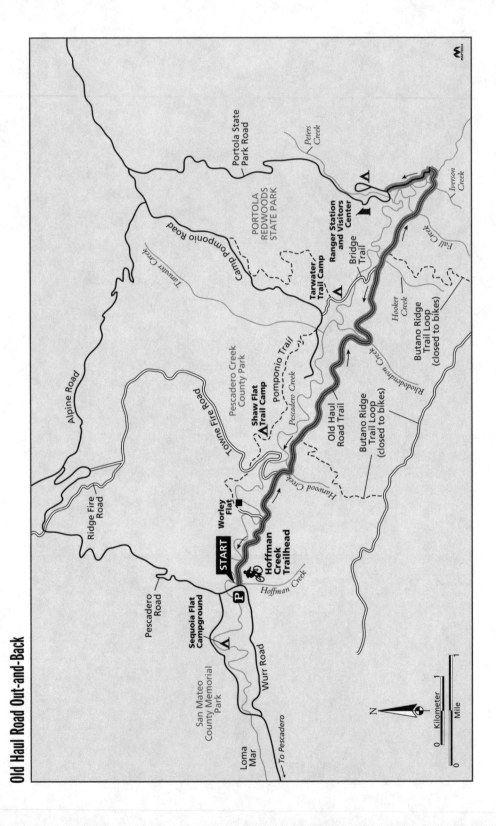

on Bridge Trail takes you down to the creek and a pleasant spot to picnic. The entire ride is through a forest of coastal redwoods, Douglas fir, live oak, and laurel. When inland areas are roasting in the summer heat, this is a cool, shady place to ride.

This is a good ride for beginners. While this can be a great family ride, not all will make it to the end. Overall, the grades are gentle; the high point is only 610 feet. However, this is not a flat ride; there is a quick, steep pitch within the first mile. Old Haul Road Trail is hard packed and graded, with an occasional section of pavement. Watch for patches of fresh-laid gravel—there is enough to warrant fat tires. The trail is well marked; do not venture off on unsigned trails. There are no legal singletrack trails for bikes in either park.

Old Haul Road is a remnant of the heydays of logging throughout the San Mateo and Santa Cruz Mountains. From the early 1920s to 1950s, a forty-two-ton locomotive traveled this railroad bed, taking the majestic coastal redwoods to the sawmill. Other remnants of this era are the enormous redwood stumps sprouting rings of second-growth trees.

Before turning back the last mile takes you for a quick glimpse of Portola Redwoods State Park. As soon as you turn off Old Haul Road, the trail plunges. At the bottom, before the gate and pavement, is a pile of scattered timber on the right. This is all that remains of the 1860s log cabin of Scandinavian immigrant Christian Iverson. Considered the first settler in the area, Iverson was the local Pony Express rider and bodyguard. A historic landmark for years, the cabin collapsed during the 1989 Loma Prieta earthquake.

A service road takes you through group picnic areas and to the ranger station and visitor center. Giant old-growth redwoods are worth the short climb. Unfortunately, the biggest trees are away from the biker's reach. If you bring a lock, you can leave your bike at the visitor center and hike the short Sequoia Nature Loop. There is water and a restroom at the visitor center. To see a tree 16 feet in diameter, you have to hike up to the northern tip of the park on Peter's Creek. Here you will find some of the biggest trees in northern California.

In the 1970s the U.S. Army Corps of Engineers proposed damming Pescadero Creek from Shaw Flat to the state park. Local opposition doomed the project, and

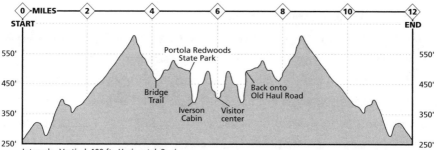

Intervals: Vertical, 100 ft.; Horizontal, 2 mi.

the creek remains free-flowing. Untapped deposits of natural gas and oil underlie the canyon, and strong odors of natural gas occasionally bubble up near Hoffman Creek. Other than the multiuse trail system and primitive camps, there are no services in Pescadero Park. Be sure to bring water; there is no water or restroom at the trailhead.

Miles and Directions

0.0 **START** from Hoffman Creek Trail Head on Old Haul Road. Proceed through the gate onto the main dirt road. About 50 yards from the information board and map, there is an unsigned trail veering to the left. Continue straight on the main road. There are several similar unsigned trails taking off to the left; ignore them all. Stay on the well-signed Old Haul Road until Portola Redwoods State Park. Trailhead GPS: N 37 16.262, W 122 17.079.

0.4 Veer left, following the sign to Old Haul Road.

0.6 Proceed through the gate.

0.7 Veer right at the fork with Pomponio Trail.

1.4 Veer right at the fork with Towne Trail to Shaw Flat Trail Camp.

4.2 Continue straight where Bridge Trail merges from the left. **Side trip:** Turn left onto Bridge Trail toward Tarwater Camp for an out-and-back to Pescadero Creek. This is a quick descent to the bridge and a moderate but steady climb back out. In summer this is a place to cool off, skip stones, and picnic. The round-trip is nearly a mile and takes about ten minutes of riding. Kids may balk at the climb out, about 130 feet rise in elevation.

5.3 Turn left off Old Haul Road into Portola Redwoods State Park. This is a well-signed junction. The descent into the state park is extremely steep. At the bottom of the hill, just before the gate, is the earthquake-damaged Iverson Cabin—a meager woodpile. Ride

COASTAL REDWOODS Rides along the Bay Area's coastal range weave in and out of redwood groves. There is something magical about riding through these coastal redwoods, *Sequoia sempervirens*. It is a combination of their size, age, uniqueness, and splendor. These coastal beauties are the tallest trees in the world, growing up to 360 feet tall and 20 feet in diameter. Obviously, these are old trees. Left alone, the average redwood would live for 500 to 1,000 years. The oldest known is roughly 2,000 years old.

Coastal redwoods are native to a narrow strip of land running from Monterey to the southwest corner of Oregon. Redwoods thrive in the cool foggy summers and mild winters. The fog of summer condenses on their needles and drips to earth, providing up to 10 inches of water to these trees and their lush understory. Surprisingly, these giants have a shallow root system—another reason you will find them in the moist ravines, out of the wind. There is a humbling quietness riding among these giants. Stop once in a while and listen.

past the gate, onto the pavement, and through the park's service center. **Bailout:** Do not go down unless you feel like climbing out. Turn around and head back. (FYI: Old Haul Road is closed to bikes up ahead.)

6.1 Continue straight through the group area.

6.2 Arrive at the ranger station and visitor center, where there are restrooms and water. Return the way you came.

7.2 Turn right, back onto Old Haul Road.

8.3 Veer left at the fork with Bridge Trail.

13.4 Arrive back at Hoffman Creek Trail Head and parking area.

Ride Information

Local Information

Santa Cruz State Parks, District Office, 600 Ocean Street, Santa Cruz, CA 95060; (831) 429-2850; www.santacruzstateparks.org.
San Mateo County Convention and Visitors Center, 111 Anza Boulevard, Suite 410, Burlingame, CA 94010; (650) 348-7600; www.sanmateocountycvb.com.

Local Events and Attractions

Apple Jacks Tavern, 8790 La Honda Road, La Honda; (650) 747-0331; www.geocities.com/sunsetstrip/4495.
Coastside Country Rodeo; www.driscoll ranches.com.

Accommodations

Portola Redwoods State Park campground, 9000 Portola State Park Road, #F, La Honda; reservations (800) 444-7275; www.reserve america.com.

Pescadero Creek and Memorial County Parks camping, 9500 Pescadero Creek Road, Loma Mar; (650) 363-4021. No reservations for family camping at Memorial Park and trail camps at Pescadero Creek's Shaw Flat and Tarwater. These are available on a first-come, first-served basis.
Hidden Villa Hostel (fall through spring only), 26870 Moody Road, Los Altos Hills; (650) 949-8648; www.hiddenvilla.org.

Restaurants and Java Jolts

Loma Mar Store, 8150 Pescadero Road, Loma Mar; (650) 879-3294; closest place for drinks and snacks.
Alice's Restaurant, 17288 Skyline Boulevard, Woodside; (650) 851-0303.
Taqueria de Amigos, 1999 Pescadero Road (at the gas station), Pescadero; (415) 879-0232.

37 Arastradero Preserve

Views of San Francisco Bay peak over the grassy hillsides and through the oak woodlands. A network of multiuse trails offers beginner and intermediate riders a taste of mountain biking without the mountain. Enjoy sweet singletrack winding through the hills. Short climbs take you away from much of the foot traffic and to views of San Francisco Bay. Learn some of the first lessons of mountain biking—how to explore on your own, navigate through a network of trails, know when to turn around, and find your way home. This is a safe place to get lost.

Start: From main parking lot to Arastradero Preserve on Arastradero Road.

Distance: As much as you want.

Approximate riding time: Until you have had enough.

Difficulty: Easy to moderate; smooth, wide trails for beginners, short but sweet singletrack. Stronger riders can repeat loops; some technical bumps and jumps at the upper end of the park.

Trail surface: Dirt roads, dual track, and singletrack.

Terrain: Rolling grass-covered hills, oak woodlands, meandering creeks, cool reflection ponds.

Seasons: Year-round. Best in spring with the wildflowers; can be hot in summer. Some trails closed in winter.

Other trail users: Hikers, runners, and equestrians.

Canine compatibility: Leashed dogs permitted.

Land status: City of Palo Alto.

Nearest town: Palo Alto.

Fees and permits: No fees or permits required.

Schedule: Open daily 8:00 A.M. to sunset.

Maps: USGS maps: Palo Alto, CA; Mindego Hill, CA.

City of Palo Alto; Arastradero Preserve Trail maps are usually available at the main parking lot and trailhead.

Trail contact: City of Palo Alto, Foothills Park Ranger Station, 3000 Page Mill Road, Los Altos Hills, CA 94022; (650) 329-2423; www.city.palo-alto.ca.us/ross/nature preserve/arastradero.html.

Finding the trailhead: From San Francisco or San Jose: Take Interstate 280 to Palo Alto; exit onto Page Mill Road and head west. Take the first right onto Arastradero Road. The parking lot is about a half mile on the right. If the parking lot is full, head for the Park & Ride on Page Mill Road near I-280.

The Ride

Arastradero Preserve is an easily accessible 609-acre open-space preserve near the junction of Page Mill Road and I–280. Nestled between Portola Valley and Los Altos Hills, the preserve offers a combination of open grasslands, oak woodlands, and rolling hills with Bay views along the ridge. There is a small lake (no swimming) and a couple of streams where the trees gather, making cool shelters in summer.

Keep up your speed through the Bowl—the other side is steeper than it looks.

The area was a working ranch until the early 1970s. When plans were drawn for a large housing development, an alarm went off in the city of Palo Alto. Intent on keeping the foothills open, the city purchased the property in 1976. The park's master plan called for restoring and protecting the native grassland and oak woodlands. As in much of California, nonnative grasses and weeds had over taken the foothills. Today a stewardship program is at work removing the thistle (yes!) and other invasive weeds, as well as planting native grasses and oaks. Sorry, poison oak is native and will most likely stay. You will see caged oak saplings, diligently watered by volunteers until they are established. The preserve has become an outdoor education program on ecology and natural history. What is evolving is an oasis of natural habitat to roam. Kudos to the city of Palo Alto for including mountain bikes!

There are 10.2 miles of multiuse trails available to mountain bikers, all carefully managed. Some trails are closed in winter. Most of the trails are well packed, but watch for fresh-laid gravel. This is a good place for beginners to get the feel of riding on the dirt, maneuvering narrow singletrack, and climbing short hills. More advanced riders can explore the upper reaches of the preserve and do multiple laps of favorite singletrack trails. Elevations range from 275 feet near the park entrance to 750 feet on the Bowl Loop.

Arastradero Preserve

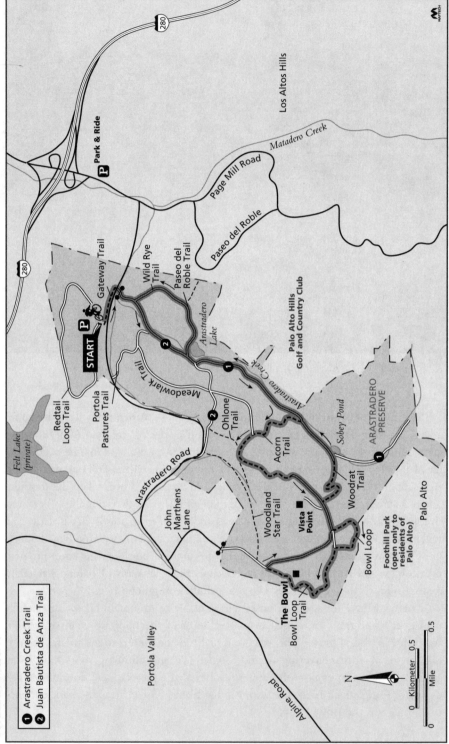

Arastradero feels like a neighborhood playground. Detailed directions of a great loop would leave you stopping at each intersection, often every quarter of a mile. Instead, keep your head up and explore on your own. Bring a map and a good sense of direction, and follow your nose. Well-signed trails make it easy to find your way around, except along the western ridge and Bowl Loop. However, this adds to the sense of exploration. Repeat your favorite trails—repeat the entire park! Locals come here for a quick ride before or after (and sometimes during) work.

Highlights of the preserve include the Acorn Trail, Woodrat Trail, and Bowl Loop. Weather and trail conditions permitting, these are all fun singletrack. At the north end of the Bowl Loop, there is what looks like a small drained reservoir. The sides are steeply graded and the bottom flat. Technically competent riders can ride in and out of the Bowl. If you can manage the speed down, it will take you up the other side.

Beginners can ride Arastradero Creek Trail as an out-and-back, about 4 miles round-trip. Venture onto the side roads along the way as you see fit. The following is a 5.5-mile option for moderate riders. Strong beginners can try this; there are many places to bail or turn around. Intermediates will ride it faster, smoother—and several times.

Miles and Directions

Suggested Route

- Starting from the main parking lot, take Gateway Trail to Juan Bautista de Anza Trail. Parking lot GPS: N 37 23.13, W 122 10.29.
- At the lake turn left onto Arastradero Creek Trail.
- Turn right onto Acorn Trail.
- At the first junction go straight on Meadowlark Trail. (The city may reconfigure these trails over time.) Turn left up the ridge on Meadowlark Trail at the first opportunity (may be unsigned). Ride up the ridge to the Bowl Loop Trail.
- Ride the Bowl Loop Trail clockwise, checking out the Bowl at the end. Shaved legs take a major hit from the star thistle in the dry season.
- Return back Meadowlark Trail.
- Turn right onto Woodrat Trail. Enjoy the switchbacks and watch out for the giant poison hemlock.
- Turn left at the bottom, returning along Arastradero Creek Trail.
- Ride past the lake, turning right on Paseo del Roble Trail to Wild Rye Trail. Return to the parking lot. This ride takes about 50 minutes, more if you play around the Bowl for a while.

Calm and shady, Arastradero Lake.

Ride Information

Local Information
City of Palo Alto, 250 Hamilton Avenue, Palo Alto, CA 94301; (650) 329-2100; www.cityof paloalto.org.

Restaurants and Java Jolts
Alpine Inn, 3915 Alpine Road, Portola Valley; (650) 854-4004.

38 El Corte de Madera Creek Loop

This popular open-space preserve offers miles of high-quality singletrack for the strong and technically adept rider. Thirty-six miles of trails weave through mixed evergreen forests, across dry ridges of chaparral, and down into lush redwood-lined canyons. Technical downhill runs pair with less rewarding climbs back up the hillside. The terrain is constantly changing and at times rugged. This crazy-eight loop is merely an introduction to the preserve; it takes several trips to fully explore all the trails and pick a route best suited to your riding preference.

Start: From Skeggs Point Trailhead on Skyline Boulevard, 150 yards north of Skeggs Point parking lot and overlook.
Distance: 14.3-mile loop.
Approximate riding time: 3 hours.
Difficulty: Difficult; challenging climb; technical singletrack with rocks, drops, ruts, and roots.
Trail surface: 60 percent singletrack and 40 percent dirt road (often overgrown).
Terrain: Steep wooded canyons, chaparral-covered slopes near the ridges, dense Douglas fir and redwood forests, rugged trails with just about everything.
Seasons: Best in summer and fall. Many of the lower trails are closed during wet conditions.
Other trail users: Hikers and equestrians.
Canine compatibility: Dogs not permitted.
Land status: Midpeninsula Regional Open Space District.

Nearest town: Woodside.
Fees and permits: No fees or permits required.
Schedule: Open daily from dawn (half hour before sunrise) to dusk (half hour after sunset). Giant Salamander Trail and most trails west of El Corte Madera Creek are closed in the wet season. Call the Open Space District for the status of trails in winter and spring.
Maps: USGS map: Woodside, CA. Midpeninsula Regional Open Space District map, *El Corte de Madera Creek Open Space Preserve,* available online and usually at the trailhead.
Trail contact: Midpeninsula Regional Open Space District, 330 Distel Circle, Los Altos, CA 94022; (650) 691-1200; www.open space.org.
Trail regulations: Helmets are required at all times. The speed limit is 15 mph, 5 mph when passing other trail users.

Finding the trailhead: From San Francisco: Head south on Interstate 280 to California Highway 92. Take CA 92 west toward Half Moon Bay. Turn south onto Skyline Boulevard (California Highway 35) and drive about 8.5 miles. The Skeggs Point parking lot and overlook is on the left. Heading this direction (south), you cannot make a left turn from Skyline Boulevard. Just continue south until you find a safe place to turn around. There is an outhouse at the parking lot, but no water. To reach the trailhead ride about 150 yards north of the parking area along Skyline Boulevard. The Skeggs Point entrance to the preserve is on the west (left) side of road, at the gate. Be careful; this is a blind corner.

No riding through the creeks on North Leaf Trail—use the bridge.

The Ride

Welcome to the singletrack world. El Corte de Madera Creek Open Space Preserve is a local mountain biking mecca situated on the west side of Skyline Boulevard above Woodside. Miles of quality singletrack draw bikers to the steep canyons and rugged trails—there is little flat riding here. This area is also called Skeggs Point, named for the popular overlook and parking area where the ride begins. Strong riders with at least intermediate technical skills will enjoy this ride the most. Long faces and sliced knees tell the tales of unsuspecting riders dragged into the canyons by coaxing friends.

Although the trails are well signed, bring a map. After twisting and turning all over the hillside, it is easy to become disoriented. Bring plenty of water on this ride; there is none on the trail.

The ride begins on the ridge and drops down and around the creek-carved canyons below. Most of the ride is in the shade of mixed evergreen forests, dense redwoods, and lush riparian habitat. There are plenty of ruts, rocks, stumps, and trunks to dodge as you pick your way through the maze of trails. There is little time to get bored here.

El Corte de Madera Creek Loop

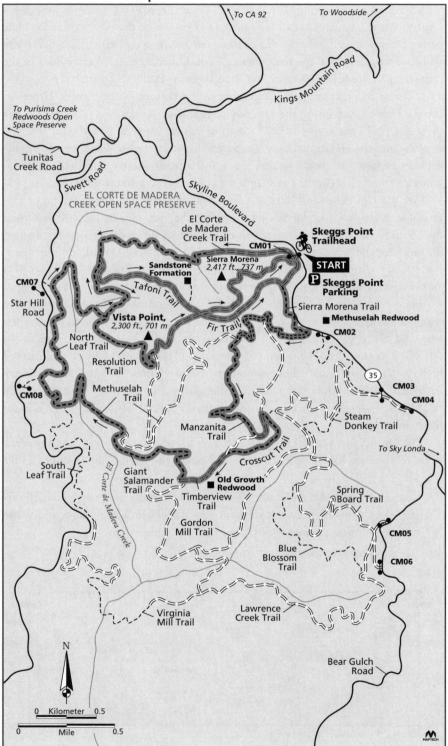

To CA 92
To Woodside

Kings Mountain Road

To Purisima Creek
Redwoods Open
Space Preserve

Tunitas
Creek Road

Swett Road

Skyline Boulevard

EL CORTE DE MADERA
CREEK OPEN SPACE PRESERVE

El Corte
de Madera
Creek Trail

CM01

Skeggs Point
Trailhead

START

Sandstone
Formation

Sierra Morena
2,417 ft., 737 m

P Skeggs Point
Parking

CM07

Tafoni Trail

Sierra Morena Trail
Methuselah Redwood

Star Hill
Road

Vista Point,
2,300 ft., 701 m

Fir Trail

CM02

North
Leaf Trail

35

Resolution
Trail

CM03

CM04

CM08

Methuselah
Trail

Steam
Donkey Trail

To Sky Londa

Manzanita
Trail

South
Leaf Trail

El Corte de Madera Creek

Crosscut Trail

Giant
Salamander
Trail

Old Growth
Redwood

Spring
Board Trail

CM05

Timberview
Trail

Gordon
Mill Trail

Blue
Blossom
Trail

CM06

Virginia
Mill Trail

Lawrence
Creek Trail

Bear Gulch
Road

N

0   Kilometer   0.5

0   Mile   0.5

MAPTECH

There are many options for riding El Corte de Madera, and everyone has a favorite route. This circuitous loop offers an overview of the northern and middle parts of the preserve. With 35 miles of designated trails open to mountain bikes, you will have to come back to check them all out. Other singletrack to explore in the southern part are Steam Donkey and Blue Blossom Trails—both are steep.

It is easy to pick a popular singletrack to the bottom of the canyon. However, there is little agreement on the best way to ride back up. You just cannot do all the great downhill runs in one ride. The math is simple: Every time you go down, you must reclaim the elevation. Enjoy the downhill and try not to think about the ride back up. Despite the great downhill, this is still a cross-country ride; there are speed limits on the trails. Leave the downhill rig at home; it is a heavy push out.

Like most of the coastal redwood forestland, this area was once a victim of logging. The preserve's steep terrain kept loggers at bay for a while. Nevertheless, from the 1860s to the turn of the twentieth century, eight different mills operated along the creekbeds here. Modern logging continued to 1988, when creation of the open-space preserve brought it to a halt. The canyons are regenerating and redwood trees are emerging once again, making for a cool ride along the canyons.

There was a time when off-road motorcycles and mountain biking had free range in this area. During the early years of the preserve, the policy was to leave the area wild. Since then, many of the early trails have either been closed or smoothed out. Now mountain biking is allowed on nearly all the officially signed and marked trails. While many lament those gone-but-never-forgotten trails, mountain biking has remained here while it has not in other parks. The local bicycle trails council ROMP (Responsible Organized Mountain Bike Pedalers) deserves special credit for their efforts here.

The Open Space District is looking at ways to reduce sedimentation in the creek to protect aquatic habitat. For our part, to preserve the salmon (and mountain bike access):

- Stay on designated trails at all times. Encourage others to do the same. All off-trail use is a misdemeanor. Riding on closed trails doubles the fine, and violators must appear in court. Bike patrols and radar are out there.

- Avoid riding in extremely wet conditions.

Intervals: Vertical, 200 ft.; Horizontal, 2 mi.

- Ride in control, observe the posted speed limit, and avoid locking up your brakes.
- Helmets are required. Actually, the salmon do not care about that, but the district and your loved ones do.

Miles and Directions

0.0 **START** from the Skeggs Point Trailhead on Skyline Boulevard, 150 yards north of Skeggs Point parking lot and overlook. Trailhead GPS: N 37 24.40, W 122 18.22.

0.1 Turn right at the fork onto El Corte de Madera Creek Trail for a smooth and quick descent. (At the end of the ride, you will return from the left on Tafoni Trail.)

0.8 Veer left and cross the bridge over El Corte de Madera Creek. Welcome to the singletrack world. The climb here is gradual.

1.7 Veer right at the fork, staying on El Corte de Madera Creek Trail. (You will be back to this spot later for the final climb of the day up Tafoni Trail.)

2.3 Turn left at the T intersection onto Resolution Trail. The last 0.3 mile of this sweet single-track is through exposed manzanita, where it is rocky and steep. Although you have the right-of-way, watch for downhill riders.

2.7 Remnants of an airplane crash are on the right. On October 28, 1953, the *Resolution*, a British DC–6 airplane, crashed into these hills, killing all nineteen onboard. Besides being disrespectful, it is illegal to remove any artifacts you may find along the way.

3.4 Turn left onto the wider Fir Trail. Although not a constant climb, you will be working your way up to Sierra Morena Trail.

3.5 A short trail leads up to Vista Point on the left. **Side trip:** Turn left for 0.2 mile of quick out-and-back. From under the shade of madrone trees, you can see the coastal mountains and Pacific Ocean below—on a clear day anyway.

3.7 Veer right to stay on Fir Trail at the intersection with Tafoni Trail on the left. (You will see this spot again later.) **Bailout:** Turn left onto Tafoni Trail back to Skyline Boulevard and the starting point.

3.9 Veer left on Fir Trail at the fork with a connector to Methuselah Trail. **Shortcut:** Skip the smooth downhill singletrack on Sierra Morena Trail and a grind up Methuselah Trail. Turn right for a 0.1-mile breeze to the junction at Mile 5.2 below and at the top of Manzanita Trail.

4.3 Turn right onto the Sierra Morena Trail, paralleling Skyline Boulevard. **Bailout:** Turn left and ride Fir Trail back to the Skeggs Point trailhead.

4.8 Make a sharp right turn onto Methuselah Trail. **Side trip:** Take a quick break to check out a giant redwood. Turn left and ride to gate CM02. This is another parking spot and entrance to the preserve. Cross Skyline Boulevard and follow the fenced path to Methuselah Redwood. Here you will see one of the rare survivors from the heydays of logging. This 1,800-year-old tree has a 14-foot diameter above the burls.

5.2 Turn right at the fork with Timberview Trail to stay on Methuselah Trail. This is not a pleasant climb.

5.6 Turn left onto Manzanita Trail. Sections of this singletrack are steep, rocky, and eroded. For a moment you will leave the shaded forest for the exposed manzanita-covered ridge.

6.7 Turn left down Timberview Trail.

6.9 Turn right onto Crosscut Trail—the rare level trail in this preserve. This is a narrow, smooth, and beautiful singletrack through the forest. It is just not long enough.

7.0 Stay right at the fork to Gordon Mill Trail.

7.5 Bear left, returning to Timberview Trail. **Side trip:** Get close with an old-growth redwood. Look for a sign ahead on the left at Mile 7.7. This lone 14-foot diameter tree is 70 yards off the Timberview Trail.

7.8 Turn right onto Giant Salamander Trail. This is a fun ride with steep drops, sharp rises, roots, ruts, and stumps. In the wet season watch out for salamanders—the rare ones can be over a foot long. They do not jump out of the way very well.

8.8 Turn left onto Methuselah Trail, a dirt road that soon becomes singletrack. Within a half mile you come to El Corte de Madera Creek, the lowest elevation of the ride. Efforts are under way to reduce siltation in this perennial creek, which is threatening the habitat of the endangered steelhead salmon. Cross on the rocks, as not to disturb the sediments. Waters can be high in winter and the trail closed for crossing. Continue up the packed singletrack on the other side of the creek.

9.4 Cross the bridge; veer right at the fork to continue on Methuselah Trail.

10.0 Turn right onto North Leaf Trail for more singletrack meandering along the contour of the hillside. The trail to the left heads up to Star Hill Road and gate CM08.

10.7 Turn right onto El Corte de Madera Creek Trail and drop down to the creek. At the creek turn right at the pump house and continue a gradual climb up the other side.

11.6 You are back at the junction with Resolution Trail, having completed a big loop. Turn left to stay on El Corte de Madera Creek Trail.

12.2 Turn right onto Tafoni Trail for the last loop. The trail will widen up ahead and alternate steep climbs with smooth descents. **Side trip:** At mile 13.0 you will come to a footpath on the left leading to the sandstone formation. This large and interesting rock outcropping gives the trail its name. Years of weathering create Tafoni sandstone structures—pockmarked holes and caves cut into the sandstone boulders. Stash the bike and walk 0.2 mile to an observation deck. Do not expect to climb on the rocks.

13.1 Veer left to stay on Tafoni Trail at the junction with Fir Trail. Enjoy the downhill—there will be three short spurts of climbing before you finish. Check out the banking along the road cuts. Near the end you will continue straight where El Corte de Madera Creek Trail drops down on the left.

14.3 Arrive back at the Skeggs Point Trailhead. Turn right and carefully ride Skyline Boulevard back to your car.

Ride Information

Local Information

San Mateo County Convention and Visitors Bureau, 111 Anza Boulevard, Suite 410, Burlingame, CA 94010; (650) 348-7600; www.sanmateocountycvb.com.

Local Events and Attractions

Kings Mountain Art Show—Labor Day weekend. Kings Mountain Community Center/Fire Station, 13889 Skyline Boulevard, Woodside; www.kingsmountainartfair.org.

Restaurants and Java Jolts

Alice's Restaurant, 17288 Skyline Boulevard, Woodside; (650) 851-0303.

39 Purisima: Whittemore Gulch Out-and-Back

Starting from the ridge overlooking Half Moon Bay, this ride takes you down the western slopes of the Santa Cruz Mountains. Smooth singletrack begins in the moss-draped forest of tan oak, madrone, and Douglas fir. Spectacular views of the Pacific Ocean open up as the trail switchbacks down the brush-covered hillside before quickly dropping into a moist redwood forest. Riding this as an out-and-back maximizes the singletrack, but there are other ways to climb out of Purisima Creek Canyon—not all of them pleasant.

Start: From the main entrance to Purisima Creek Redwoods Open Space Preserve on Skyline Boulevard.

Distance: 7 miles out and back.

Approximate riding time: 1.5 hours.

Difficulty: Moderate to difficult; mostly smooth trail, some steep loose sections, long climb out of the canyon.

Trail surface: 23 percent dirt road and 77 percent singletrack.

Terrain: Steep wooded canyons, chaparral-covered slope along the ridge, dense Douglas fir and redwood forest along the creeks.

Seasons: April to November. Whittemore Gulch is closed in winter; a cool place to escape the heat of summer.

Other trail users: Hikers and equestrians.

Canine compatibility: Dogs not permitted.

Land status: Midpeninsula Regional Open Space District.

Nearest town: Woodside (Skyline Boulevard entrance) and Half Moon Bay (Higgins Purisima Road entrance).

Fees and permits: No fees or permits required.

Schedule: Open daily dawn (half hour before sunrise) to dusk (half hour after sunset). Whittemore Gulch Trail is closed in the wet season, typically December to March, but depending on the weather it may still be closed in April or May. Call the open-space district for current trail conditions.

Maps: USGS map: Half Moon Bay, CA. Midpeninsula Regional Open Space District map, *Purisima Creek Redwoods Open Space Preserve,* available online and usually at the trailhead.

Trail contact: Midpeninsula Regional Open Space District, 330 Distel Court, Los Altos, CA 94022; (650) 691-1200; www.open space.org.

Trail regulations: Helmets are required at all times. The speed limit is 15 mph, 5 mph when passing other trail users.

Finding the trailhead: Skyline trailhead from San Francisco: Head south on Interstate 280 to California Highway 92. Take CA 92 west toward Half Moon Bay. Turn south onto Skyline Boulevard (California Highway 35) and drive about 4.5 miles. The parking lot and main entrance to Purisima Creek Redwoods Open Space Preserve is on the right. There is an outhouse but no water.

Higgins Purisima Trailhead Option

From Half Moon Bay: Head south on California Highway 1 for 1 mile and turn left onto Higgins Purisima Road. The parking lot is on the left just beyond a bridge and before the road bends back toward CA 1 on Purisima Creek Road. There is an outhouse at the trailhead, but no water. Trailhead GPS: 37 26.15, W122 22.13.

The Ride

Purisima Creek Redwoods Open Space Preserve offers an escape to the western slopes of the Santa Cruz Mountains overlooking Half Moon Bay. In Spanish *purisima* means "the most pure," and it is not a bad way to describe Whittemore Gulch Trail. Winter closings help preserve this trail, which is well signed and easy to follow.

There is a variety of terrain here. The ride begins in a dry oak, madrone, and Douglas fir woodland. After an initial rough drop, the trail smooths out and things get greener. As signaled by the moss hanging from the trees, this can be a drippy, wet fog zone. Once onto the Whittemore Gulch Trail, the singletrack and switchbacks begin. As the chaparral takes over, the view opens up of the deep forest, coastal hills, and Pacific Ocean below. Enjoy the views before the quick descent drops you into the redwood forest.

TIDBIT: Throughout the wet season, banana slugs come out in the redwood forests from Big Sur to the Oregon border. As the mascot for the University of California at Santa Cruz, they even come out for the games. Sometimes these bright-yellow slugs can be as long as 10 inches, giving new meaning to slime! Practice your agility by avoiding these favorite treats of the salamander.

By the early 1900s clear-cutting had removed nearly all the giant 1,000-year-old redwoods in this area, leaving stumps 10 to 20 feet in diameter. It is hard to imagine there once were seven mills along these creek banks. Today's redwood groves are second-growth, having sprouted from the mother tree in "family circles" or "fairy rings." An understory of ferns, berries, and wildflowers gives a Tolkienesque feel to the lower reaches of the ride. Even in summer it is cool and moist down here. That can translate into thick mud. You will be riding over exposed roots, winding around trees, and following the fern-covered creek banks. Heads up as you approach the lower ends of Whittemore Gulch Trail—there will likely be more uphill traffic.

Since there is a trailhead at both ends of this ride, you can easily start from either direction. If you prefer to start out climbing and extra driving does not bother you, you can launch from the end of Higgins Purisima Road (430 feet) and climb to the top (2,025 feet). If you go this way, you can also turn around at the junction with the Bay Area Ridge Trail (1,780 feet) and miss the last grind up to Skyline Boulevard.

Doing Whittemore Gulch Trail as an out-and-back maximizes the singletrack run. Unfortunately this popular trail can get crowded on weekends. To help keep traffic down and preserve bike access on the singletrack, consider returning up

The Whittemore Gulch out-and-back produces smiles with its spectacular views and great singletrack.

Purisima: Whittemore Gulch Out-and-Back

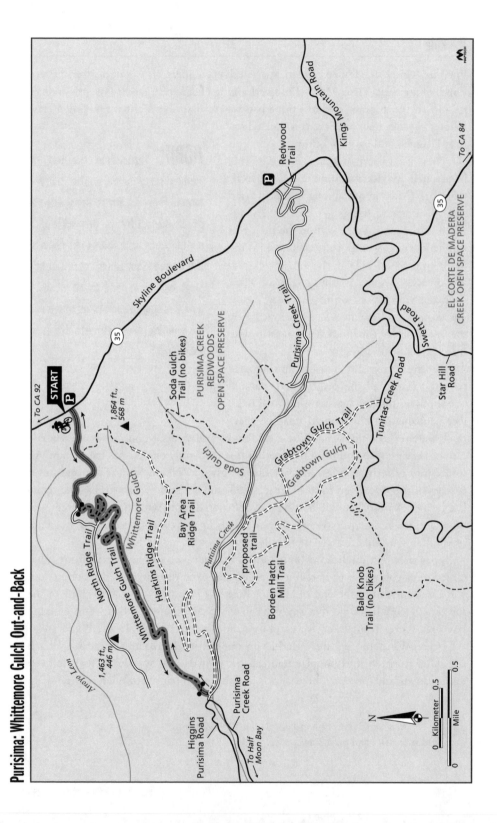

Purisima Creek Trail or the grueling Harkins Ridge Trail. If you take Harkins Ridge Trail, your reward will be a short but nice singletrack near the top.

Once you reach the bottom of the canyon near the Higgins Purisima Road trailhead, there are other, wider trails to explore in the preserve. Just be sure to save some steam for the ride out. The Borden Hatch Mill–Grabtown Gulch loop off Purisima Creek Trail used to be a side trip for strong riders. Any traffic thins out up there, and the fire roads become overgrown. Unfortunately a bridge washout closed the lower portion of Grabtown Gulch Trail. Plans are under way to reroute the trail. When reopened, this may once again be a challenging loop with sharp turns, water structures, and groping poison oak.

Strong riders can connect with El Corte de Madera Creek Open Space Preserve for a longer epic ride.

Miles and Directions

0.0 **START** from the North Ridge Trail trailhead. Wake up—this is a surprisingly steep start with loose rocks and ruts. Trailhead GPS: N 37 27.00, W 122 20.19.

0.3 Continue straight at the junction with Harkins Ridge Trail. The trail flattens out a bit here.

0.8 Turn left onto the singletrack Whittemore Gulch Trail. This gate is closed during the wet season.

1.3 Veer sharply to the left, staying on Whittemore Gulch Trail. The trail to the right is a connector to the North Ridge Trail.

3.4 Pass through the lower gate on the trail that is closed in the wet season. Veer right, passing the Harkins Ridge Trail on the left.

3.5 Cross the bridge over Purisima Creek and arrive at the lower trailhead. Turn around and return up Whittemore Gulch Trail. **Option:** If you prefer loops to retracing your tracks, return up Harkins Ridge Trail or Purisima Creek Trail. Purisima Creek Trail is the easier way out. However, if you avoid pavement at all costs and do not mind pushing up some painfully steep sections, take Harkins Ridge Trail. This route is not for beginners. In addition to being strenuous, this trail has ruts and loose rocks. **Side trip:** Head up Purisima Creek Trail for a mile and turn right up Borden Hatch Mill Trail. This somewhat overgrown fire road takes you away from most other trail users. As an out-and-back it is a constant uphill climb and a ripping descent back through the redwoods.

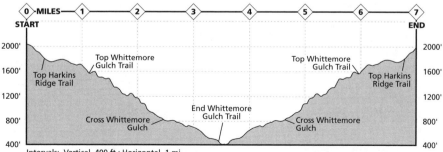

Intervals: Vertical, 400 ft.; Horizontal, 1 mi.

6.2 Turn right onto North Ridge Trail.

6.7 Continue straight past the junction with Harkins Ridge Trail. Endure the last and worst bit of the climb.

7.0 Arrive back at the parking lot.

Wet Season Option

When Whittemore Gulch Trail is closed, take Harkins Ridge Trail down and return up the Purisima Creek Trail. At the top of Purisima Creek Trail, turn left to ride paved Skyline Boulevard back to the start.

Connect with El Corte de Madera Creek Open Space Preserve

From Purisima Creek Trail take the Borden Hatch Mill Trail uphill and turn left at the junction with Bald Knob Trail. Turn right onto Grabtown Gulch Trail, which takes you to paved Tunitas Creek Road. Turn left and climb to Star Hill Road; turn right onto Star Hill Road. Ride more pavement until you come to gate CM07 on the left. This side entrance to the North Leaf Trail in El Corte de Madera Creek Open Space Preserve is down an unmarked fire road and not an easy gate to find. If you find yourself at gate CM08, do not despair. Head down to the junction of Methuselah and North Leaf Trail. If it is winter, check with the open-space preserve to see what trails are closed.

Ride Information

Local Information

Town of Woodside, 2955 Woodside Road, Woodside, CA 94062; (650) 851-6790; www.ci.woodside.ca.us.

Half Moon Bay Coastside Chamber of Commerce and Visitors Bureau, 520 Kelly Avenue, Half Moon Bay, CA 94019; (650) 726-8380; www.halfmoonbaychamber.org.

Local Events and Attractions

Kings Mountain Art Show—Labor Day weekend. Kings Mountain Community Center/Fire Station, 13889 Skyline Boulevard, Woodside; www.kingsmountainartfair.org.

Accommodations

Half Moon Bay State Park Beach Campground, 95 Kelly Avenue, Half Moon Bay; (650) 726-8820; www.parks.ca.gov; reservations (800) 444-7275; www.reserveamerica.com.

Point Montara Light House and Youth Hostel, Sixteenth Street at California Highway 1, Montara; (650) 728-7177; www.norcalhostels.org.

Restaurants and Java Jolts

Half Moon Bay Coffee Company, 20 Stone Pine Road, Half Moon Bay; (650) 726-3664; www.hmbcoffeeco.com.

40 McNee Ranch Out-and-Back

Enjoy gentle coastal singletrack before climbing to North Peak on Montara Mountain. This is a steady climb, strenuous in sections, but the view and downhill run are worth it. When the fog clears, it is a 360-degree view of the entire Bay Area, from Mount Tamalpais to Mount Diablo, with the crashing waves of the Pacific Ocean straight below. Accomplished downhillers may find alternative routes to the bottom.

Start: From the parking lot for McNee Ranch–Montara State Beach, east of California Highway 1 and across from Gray Whale Cove Beach.

Distance: 10 miles out and back.

Approximate riding time: 1.5 to 2 hours.

Difficulty: Difficult; strenuous climb. Mildly technical if you stay on the dirt road, extremely technical if you explore the single-track; options for a moderate ride.

Trail surface: 46 percent motley trail of broken asphalt and dirt varying from singletrack to a narrow road, 36 percent well-maintained dirt road, and 18 percent singletrack.

Terrain: Exposed, steep mountain covered with chaparral; continuous view.

Seasons: Year-round. Best spring and fall; can be bitterly cold in winter and foggy in summer.

Other trail users: Hikers, equestrians, and service vehicles.

Canine compatibility: Leashed dogs permitted.

Land status: McNee Ranch State Park.

Nearest town: Montara.

Fees and permits: No fees or permits required.

Schedule: Open daily 8:00 A.M. to sunset.

Maps: USGS map: Montara Mountain, CA. McNee Ranch–Montara State Beach map, available from the state park office in Half Moon Bay.

Trail contact: Half Moon Bay State Park Office, Half Moon Bay, CA 94019; (650) 726-8819; www.parks.ca.gov.

Finding the trailhead: From San Francisco: Head south on CA 1 (Gabrillo Highway) through Pacifica. Follow the highway 3 miles past the last signal in Pacifica. Just past Devil's Slide, turn left (east) into the parking lot signed for MCNEE RANCH–MONTARA STATE BEACH. This is across from Gray Whale Cove Beach, although there may be no signs for the beach. There is no water or restroom available at the parking lot.

From San Jose: Take Interstate 280 to California Highway 92 and drive west to Half Moon Bay. Turn north onto CA 1. The trailhead is about 8 miles north of Half Moon Bay and on the right. From this direction you will pass the southern entrance to McNee Ranch State Park at Martini Creek. Although you can start here, there is not much parking and you will miss the Gray Whale Cove Trail.

The Ride

Pick a clear day for this ride so that you can enjoy the views. Never mind that it gets wicked cold up there when the fog or rain sets in. This ride exposes you to the elements. Coastal scrub, coastal chaparral, and marine chaparral cover the mountain. Said simply, there are many bushes and few trees, although there is a cool tree tunnel

on the lower section of Old San Pedro Mountain Road. There are few trail signs along the way, so study the map at the trailhead and bring these directions with you.

The ride begins on the meandering Gray Whale Cove Trail above CA 1. In late winter you may spot whales migrating north along the coast. Unless the maintenance crew has been out, you may need your helmet here to fend off the face-slapping and handlebar-grabbing wild mustard. The poison oak is not as aggressive, but it is just as thick. In spring the wildflowers are particularly beautiful.

The next leg of the ride is up Old San Pedro Mountain Road. This was once the main thoroughfare for cars traveling between San Francisco and Half Moon Bay. This twisty connector passes between San Pedro and Montara Mountains. Today much of the weathered old road is overgrown or slipped away, narrowing at times to singletrack. The surface is a mixture of broken asphalt and dirt.

After splitting off from Old San Pedro Mountain Road, the road is generally smooth and well graded, providing access to service vehicles for the agencies and companies with communication towers and equipment at the top. It also becomes extremely steep. The first wall is not formidable, just long. There are pockets of sand to contend with and some slick sandstone farther up near the top. The good news is that the granite and sandstone drain well in winter. This is also why the area is prone to mudslides and slippage.

Once you reach North Peak, try to ignore the cluster of towers, repeaters, and discs. If it is a clear day, check out the next peaks to bag—Mount Tamalpais to the north, Mount Diablo to the east, the Mount Hamilton range to the southeast, and the Santa Cruz Mountains to the south. While it may take you an hour to reach the top, it will take you half that to get back.

On the way up you will pass several interesting singletrack trails disappearing into the brush. Stop and check them out for the ride down. For now, and until there are problems, it is okay to ride all roads and trails in McNee Ranch unless posted otherwise. When picking a line down, do consider the erosion problems some of these trails create. Ride softly and enjoy it while you can. If you do venture off the main road, ride with a friend or at least tell someone where to look if you do not show up after dark. If you encounter any serious carnage, you will have to rely on the next downhill junkie to pick up your pieces or relay for help. That may be hours—or days.

The Peninsula Open Space Trust owns the adjacent land to the south of the McNee Ranch. Although currently closed to the public, plans call for this land to become part of the Golden Gate National Recreation Area. Time will tell whether this translates into more trails accessible to bikes or not.

When you finish the ride, you may want to walk (no bikes allowed) across the street to wash off the poison oak in the ocean. Caution: The surf can be dangerous,

◀ *Grab a view of Montara State Beach through pampas grass.*

McNee Ranch Out-and-Back

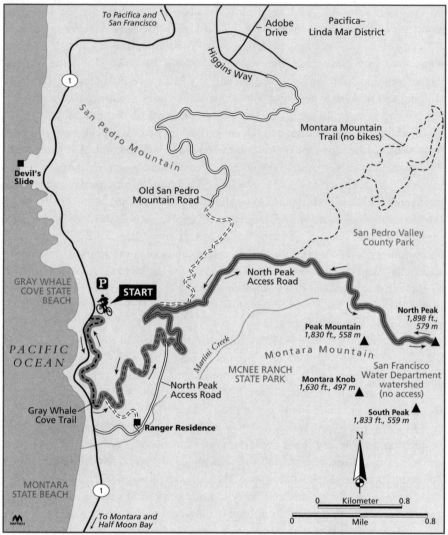

with riptides and sleeper waves. On a brighter note the beach has a history of being clothing optional.

As an easy option, enjoy the moderate lower portion of the mountain with a shorter out-and-back. For a longer moderate ride, stay on Old San Pedro Mountain Road and head north toward Pacifica as far as you like.

Miles and Directions

0.0 START from the south end of the parking lot for Montara State Beach–McNee Ranch. The singletrack trail begins through the wooden fence and past an information board.

Although there are no trail signs, this is the Gray Whale Cove Trail and is on the posted map. The initial climb quickly levels off. Trailhead GPS: N 37 33.46, W 122 30.46.

0.7 Stay to the right along the cliff. If you know the way, the trail to the left will eventually drop you down to Old San Pedro Mountain Road.

0.8 Turn left where the bike route sign points, although unless it is a new sign it may be completely illegible. The NO BIKES sign on the trail ahead is clearer.

0.9 Turn left onto Old (and weathered) San Pedro Mountain Road. Do not expect a sign. (Note: A right turn takes you down to the ranger's house and the park entrance at Martini Creek. There is an outhouse 0.3 mile in this direction.)

1.9 Continue straight up the hill where the dirt road merges from the right. From here to the top the road is well graded and wide for service vehicles commuting to the peak.

2.5 Singletrack trails appear on the right then left. Heed the NO BIKES sign on the left. Continue up Old San Pedro Mountain Road.

2.5+ Veer right on the main road. The broken road to the left is a section of the original road that curves around the hill. You will rejoin it at the next junction.

2.6 Veer right on the main road at the unmarked fork. You are now on the North Peak Access Road. You will soon come to the "wall." **Option:** Old San Pedro Mountain Road continues to the left. It will take you to Pacifica and is an alternative way into the park. This is also an easier option for anyone wanting to ride farther but not into the serious grind ahead on the right.

3.3 Arrive at the top of the wall, but not the end of the climbing.

3.7 Veer right where Montara Mountain Trail comes in on the left. No bikes are allowed anyway, but this goes down to San Pedro Valley County Park. A second short wall is coming up.

4.5 Continue straight at the saddle where an old road and cluster of trails turn off on the right.

4.7 Turn right at the fork leading to the first peak of antennas on the left.

4.9 Continue straight at the intersection of dirt roads. Ride up the hill through the S turn. The road passes through an old barbed-wired fence and by a cluster of antennas on the left. Just past the communication building is a small parking area; take the loose singletrack up to the peak.

5.0 Arrive at the top of North Peak, Montara Mountain (1,898 feet). With all the repeater stations, you would think there would be good cell service up here—not necessarily. Try to phone home and describe the view. Then retrace your tracks down North Peak Access Road. **Option:** Explore some of the singletrack on the way down. Before barreling down a trail, walk ahead to check it out. Many of the trails are expert only.

7.4 Stay to the left as the narrower Old San Pedro Mountain Road heads north to Pacifica.

8.1 Turn right at the fork onto Old San Pedro Mountain Road.

9.1 Turn right uphill on the singletrack connector to Gray Whale Cove Trail. Veer left when the trail forks in about 10 yards.

9.2 Turn right up the coast on Gray Whale Cove Trail.

10.0 Arrive back at the parking lot.

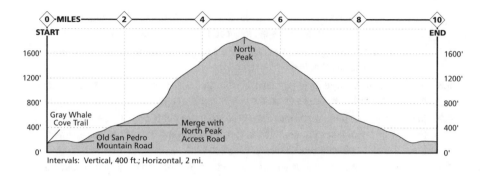

Intervals: Vertical, 400 ft.; Horizontal, 2 mi.

Ride Information

Local Information

Pacifica Chamber of Commerce and Visitor Center, 225 Rockaway Beach #1, Pacifica, CA 94044; (650) 355-4122; www.pacifica chamber.com.

Half Moon Bay Coastside Chamber of Commerce and Visitors Bureau, 520 Kelly Avenue, Half Moon Bay, CA 94019; www.halfmoon baychamber.org.

Accommodations

Half Moon Bay State Park Beach Campground, 95 Kelly Avenue, Half Moon Bay; (650) 726-8820; www.parks.ca.gov; reservations (800) 444-7275; www.reserveamerica.com.

Hostelling International Point Montara Lighthouse, Sixteenth Street at California Highway 1, Montara; (650) 728-7177; www.norcal hostels.org.

Restaurants and Java Jolts

A Coastal Affair Espresso Bar, 8455 Gabrillo Highway (CA 1), Montara; (650)728-5229.

Twinberry Cafe and Bakery, 107 Sevilla Avenue, El Granada; (650) 726-9775.

La Playa Mexican Restaurant and Cantina, 5460 Gabrillo Highway, Pacifica; (650) 738-2247.

Honorable Mentions

○ Windy Hill Open Space Preserve

This is a convenient and quick workout from Portola Valley. Bikes are confined to an out-and-back along the Spring Ridge Trail. The wide trail climbs nearly 3 miles from Portola Road up to Skyline Boulevard, gaining 1,800 feet along the way. The open grass-covered hill offers an unobstructed view of San Francisco Bay. Stick a portable kite in your pack—this preserve earns its name. There can be a lot of hikers and horses here, so follow the posted speed limits on the downhill run.

Take Interstate 280 to Palo Alto and exit onto Alpine Road heading west. Turn right onto Portola Road. There is a parking lot on the left in about 0.8 mile, or you can park at the Portola Valley Town Hall. Ride south on the town paths to the preserve and enter at Gate WH05. For those who can score a ride from the top, the drop-off spot is the parking lot and trailhead on Skyline Boulevard (California Highway 35), 2.3 miles south of La Honda Road (California Highway 84). For information contact the Midpeninsula Regional Open Space District at (650) 691–1200. An online map is available at www.openspace.org.

P Water Dog Lake Park

Encased in housing developments, this convenient backyard playground is the envy of stranded comrades who must porter their bikes to a trailhead. Water Dog Lake Park and the adjoining John S. Brooks Memorial Open Space provide the dirt, but dedicated volunteers provide the sweat equity for these trails. Blessings to the city of Belmont for letting the big kids build some trails. Enjoy switchbacks, pick a line through the ruts, grind the steep hills, watch out for traffic on the quick descents, brave the jumps, and guess the make and model of the buried car as you ride over it. There is something here for everyone; but strong technical riders will get the most out of the singletrack. The landscape is dry chaparral-covered hills, with the backdrop of the Bay. Watch this bike-friendly park evolve.

From U.S. Highway 101 in Belmont, take the Ralston Avenue exit and head west. Turn left onto Lyall Way (just past Alameda de las Pulgas). There is a trailhead near the intersection with Lake Road; park along the street. For your first time to the park, this 5-mile loop is a good place to start: Take the Lake Road path to the Hallmark Trail. Head south, following the perimeter trails around the park. At the paved parking lot at the bottom, ride along Carlmont Drive to where you began on Lake Road. If you want to keep exploring, head back up the hill on a different singletrack.

Once you get the lay of the land, park at the end of Carlmont Drive and head straight for the singletrack. The easiest way to gain elevation from here is to take a hard right up the first wide track before the creek. Until signs are in place, explore!

The city of Belmont manages this park; (650) 595–7441; www.belmont.gov/localgov/prec/trailmap.pdf.

Q Fifield–Cahill Ridge Trail

Riders have a long-awaited chance to experience the protected San Francisco Peninsula Watershed. Opened to the public in summer 2003, the 10-mile Fifield–Cahill Ridge Trail runs along the hills west of Lower Crystal Springs and San Andreas Reservoirs. Enjoy a guided ride through forests of Douglas fir and mixed hardwood. Sections of coastal scrub give rise to sweeping views of the watershed lands, Pacific Ocean, and San Francisco Bay. The trail is a wide gravel service road suitable for undaunted beginners and intermediate riders. The first 1.3 miles is a hefty climb, gaining 650 feet in elevation. Ironically, there is no water on the trail, so bring it with you.

Access is by reservation and with guided groups only through the San Francisco Public Utility Commission. Rides range from 4 to 20 miles. To arrange for a tour register online at www.sfwater.org (click on the butterfly logo), by e-mail at RidgeTrail@sfwater.org, or at (650) 652–3203.

From Interstate 280 near San Mateo, take California Highway 92 west. Drive 0.5 mile beyond Crystal Springs Reservoir and turn right through a silver gate to Skyline Quarry. The gate opens for the scheduled tours only.

The Art of Mountain Biking

Within the following pages, you will find everything you need to know about off-road bicycling. This section begins by exploring the fascinating history of the mountain bike itself, then goes on to discuss everything from mountain biking etiquette to tips and techniques for bicycling over logs and up hills. Also included are the types of clothing that will keep you comfortable and in style, essential equipment ideas to keep your rides smooth and trouble-free, and descriptions of off-road terrain to prepare you for the kinds of bumps and bounces you can expect to encounter.

The mountain bike, with its knobby tires and reinforced frame, takes cyclists to places once unreachable by bicycle—down rugged mountain trails, through streams of rushing water, across the frozen Alaskan tundra, and even to work in the city. There seem to be few limits on what this fat-tired beast can do and where it can take us. Few obstacles stand in its way; few boundaries slow its progress. Except for one—its own success. If trail closure means little to you now, read on and discover how a trail can be here today and gone tomorrow. With so many new off-road cyclists taking to the trails each year, it's no wonder trail access hinges precariously between universal acceptance and complete termination. But a little work on your part can go a long way to preserving trail access for future use. Nothing is more crucial to the survival of mountain biking itself than to read the examples set forth in the following pages and practice their message.

Without open trails, the maps in this book are virtually useless. Cyclists must learn to be responsible for the trails they use and to share these trails with others. This section addresses such issues as why trail use has become so controversial, what can be done to improve the image of mountain biking, and how to have fun and ride responsibly. You'll also find the worldwide-standard Rules of the Trail.

Mountain Bike Beginnings

It seems the mountain bike, originally designed for lunatic adventurists bored with straight lines, clean clothes, and smooth tires, has become globally popular in as short a time as it would take to race down a mountain trail.

Like many things of a revolutionary nature, the mountain bike was born on the West Coast. But unlike in-line skates, purple hair, and the peace sign, the concept of the off-road bike cannot be credited solely to the imaginative Californians—they were just the first to make waves.

The design of the first off-road–specific bike was based on the geometry of the old Schwinn Excelsior, a one-speed, camelback cruiser with balloon tires. Joe Breeze was the creator behind it, and in 1977 he built ten of these "Breezers" for himself and his Marin County, California, friends at $750 apiece—a bargain.

Breeze was a serious competitor in bicycle racing, placing thirteenth in the 1977 U.S. Road Racing National Championships. After races, he and friends would scour local bike shops hoping to find old bikes they could then restore. It was the 1941 Schwinn Excelsior, for which Breeze paid just five dollars, that began to shape and change bicycling history forever. After taking the bike home, removing the fenders, oiling the chain, and pumping up the tires, Breeze hit the dirt. He loved it.

His inspiration was not altogether unique. On the opposite end of the country, nearly 2,500 miles from Marin County, East Coast bike bums were also growing restless. More and more old, beat-up clunkers were being restored and modified. These behemoths often weighed as much as eighty pounds and were so reinforced they seemed virtually indestructible. But rides that take just forty minutes on today's twenty-five-pound featherweights took the steel-toed-boot-and-blue-jean-clad bikers of the late 1970s and early 1980s nearly four hours to complete.

Not until 1981 was it possible to purchase a production mountain bike, but local retailers found these ungainly bicycles difficult to sell and rarely kept them in stock. By 1983, however, mountain bikes were no longer such a fringe item, and large bike manufacturers quickly jumped into the action, producing their own versions of the off-road bike. By the 1990s the mountain bike had firmly established its place with bicyclists of nearly all ages and abilities, and it now commands nearly 90 percent of the U.S. bike market.

There are many reasons for the mountain bike's success in becoming the hottest two-wheeled vehicle in the nation. They are much friendlier to the cyclist than traditional road bikes because of their comfortable upright position and shock-absorbing fat tires. And because of the health-conscious, environmentalist movement, people are more activity minded and seek nature on a closer front than paved roads can allow. The mountain bike gives you these things and takes you far away from the daily grind—even if you're only minutes from the city.

Mountain Biking Etiquette

The Mountain Bike Controversy: Being a Responsible Trail User

Are Off-Road Bicyclists Environmental Outlaws? Do We Have the Right to Use Public Trails?

Mountain bikers have long endured the animosity of folks in the backcountry who complain about the consequences of off-road bicycling. Many people believe that the fat tires and knobby tread do unacceptable environmental damage and that our uncontrollable riding habits are a danger to animals and other trail users. Mountain biking does cause more damage than traveling by foot because the wheels are in contact with the ground all the time, and bicycle tracks can open channels that accelerate erosion. But by riding responsibly it is possible to leave only a minimal impact—something we all must take care to achieve.

Unfortunately, it is often people of great influence who view the mountain bike as the environment's worst enemy. Consequently, we mountain bike riders and environmentally concerned citizens must be educators, impressing upon others that we also deserve the right to use these trails. Our responsibilities as bicyclists are no more and no less than those of any other trail user.

Rules of the Trail

If every mountain biker always yielded the right-of-way, stayed on the trail, avoided wet or muddy trails, never cut switchbacks, always rode in control, showed respect for other trail users, and carried out every last scrap of what was carried in (candy wrappers and bike-part debris included)—in short, if we all did the right things—we wouldn't need a list of rules governing our behavior.

The fact is, most mountain bikers are conscientious and are trying to do the right thing; however, thousands of miles of dirt trails have been closed due to the irresponsible habits of a few riders.

Here are some basic guidelines adapted from the International Mountain Bicycling Association Rules of the Trail. These guidelines can help prevent damage to land, water, plants, and wildlife; maintain trail access; and avoid conflicts with other backcountry visitors and trail users.

1. Only ride on trails that are open. Don't trespass on private land, and be sure to obtain any necessary permits. If you're not sure if a trail is closed or if you need a permit, don't hesitate to ask. The way you ride will influence trail management decisions and policies. Federal and state wilderness areas are always off-limits to cycling.

2. Keep your bicycle under control. Watch the condition of the trail at all times, and follow the appropriate speed regulations and recommendations.

3. Yield to others on the trail. Make your approach well known in advance, either with a friendly greeting or a bell. When approaching a corner, junction, or blind spot, expect to encounter other trail users. When passing others, show your respect by slowing to a walking pace.

4. Don't startle animals. Animals may be easily scared by sudden approaches or loud noises. For your safety—and the safety of others in the area as well as the animals themselves—give all wildlife a wide berth. When encountering horses, defer to the horseback riders' directions and dismount on narrow trails.

5. Zero impact. Be aware of the impact you're making on the trail beneath you. You should not ride under conditions where you will leave evidence of your passing, such as on certain soils or shortly after a rainfall. If a ride features optional side hikes into wilderness areas, be a zero-impact hiker too. Whether you're on bike or on foot, stick to existing trails, leave gates as you found them, and carry out everything you brought in.

6. Be prepared. Know the equipment you are using, the area where you'll be riding, and your cycling abilities and limitations. Avoid unnecessary breakdowns by keeping your equipment in good shape. When you head out, bring spare parts and supplies for weather changes. Be sure to wear appropriate safety gear, including a helmet, and learn how to be self-sufficient.

Like the trails we ride on, the social dimension of mountain biking is very fragile and must be cared for responsibly. We do not want to destroy another person's enjoyment of the outdoors. By riding in the backcountry with caution, control, and responsibility, our presence can be felt positively by other trail users. By adhering to these rules, trail riding—a privilege that can quickly be taken away—will continue to be ours to share.

Soft Cycling

The term "soft cycling" describes the art of minimum-impact bicycling and should apply to both the physical and social dimensions of the sport. But make no mistake—it is possible to ride fast and furiously while maintaining the balance of soft cycling. Here are a few more ways to minimize the physical impact of mountain bike riding.

- **Stay on the trail.** Don't ride around fallen trees or mud holes that block your path. Stop and cross over them. When you come to a vista overlooking a deep valley, don't ride off the trail for a better vantage point. Instead, leave the bike and walk to see the view. Riding off the trail may seem inconsequential when done only once, but soon someone else will follow, then others, and the cumulative results can be catastrophic. Each time you wander from the trail you begin creating a new path, adding one more scar to the earth's surface.

- **Do not disturb the soil.** Follow a line within the trail that will not disturb or damage the soil.

- **Do not ride over muddy or wet trails.** After a rain shower or during the thawing season, trails will often resemble muddy, oozing swampland. The best thing to do is to stay off the trails completely. Realistically, however, we're all going to come across some muddy trails we cannot anticipate. Instead of blasting through each section of mud, which may seem both easier and more fun, lift the bike and walk past. Each time a cyclist rides through a soft or muddy section of trail, that part of the trail is permanently damaged. Regardless of the trail's conditions, though, remember always to go over the obstacles across the path, not around them. Stay on the trail.

- **Avoid trails that are considered impassable and impossible.** Don't take a leap of faith down a kamikaze descent on which you will be forced to lock your brakes and skid to the bottom, ripping the ground apart as you go.

Trail Maintenance

Unfortunately, despite all of the preventive measures taken to avoid trail damage, we're still going to run into many trails requiring attention. Simply put, a lot of hikers, equestrians, and cyclists use the same trails—some wear and tear is unavoidable.

But like your bike, if you want to use these trails for a long time to come, you must also maintain them.

Trail maintenance and restoration can be accomplished in a variety of ways. One way is for mountain bike clubs to combine efforts with other trail users (i.e., hikers and equestrians) and work closely with land managers to cut new trails or repair existing ones. This not only demonstrates the commitment cyclists have in caring for and maintaining the land, but also breaks the ice that often separates cyclists from their fellow trail mates. Another good way to help out is to show up, ready to work, on a Saturday morning with a few riding buddies at your favorite off-road domain. With a good attitude, thick gloves, and the local land manager's supervision, trail repair is fun and very rewarding. It's important, of course, that you arrange a trail-repair outing with the local land manager before you start pounding shovels into the dirt. They can lead you to the most needy sections of trail and instruct you on what repairs should be done and how best to accomplish the task.

We must be willing to sweat for our trails in order to sweat on them. Police yourself and point out to others the significance of trail maintenance. "Sweat Equity," the rewards of continued land use won with a fair share of sweat, pays off when the trail is "up for review" by the land manager and he or she remembers the efforts made by trail-conscious mountain bikers.

Rules of the Road

Occasionally, even hard-core off-road cyclists will find they have no choice but to ride the pavement. Laws vary by state, but outlined below are a few rules to follow no matter where you ride.

- Follow the same driving rules as motorists. Be sure to obey all road signs and traffic lights.
- Ride with the traffic and not against it.
- Wear bright clothing so you are more visible to motorists. Bright colors such as orange and lime green are also highly visible at night.
- Wear a helmet.
- Equip your bike with lights and wear reflective clothing if you plan on riding at night. When riding at night the bicycle or rider should have a white light visible at least 500 feet to the front and a red light or reflector visible at least 600 feet to the rear.
- Ride single file on busy roads so motorists can pass you safely.
- When stopping, be sure to pull completely off the roadway.
- Use hand signals to alert motorists to what you plan on doing next.
- Follow painted lane markings.
- Make eye contact with drivers. Assume they don't see you until you are sure they do.

- Don't ride out to the curb between parked cars unless they are far apart. Motorists may not see you when you try to move back into traffic.
- Turn left by looking back, signaling, getting into the left lane, and turning. In urban situations, continue straight to the crosswalk and walk your bike across the crosswalk when the pedestrian walk sign is illuminated.
- Never ride while under the influence of alcohol or drugs. DUI laws apply when you're riding a bicycle.
- Avoid riding in extremely foggy, rainy, icy, or windy conditions.
- Watch out for parallel-slat sewer grates, slippery manhole covers, oily pavement, gravel, wet leaves, and ice.
- Cross railroad tracks as perpendicular as possible. Be especially careful when it's wet out. For better control as you move across bumps and other hazards, stand up on your pedals.
- Don't ride too close to parked cars—a person opening the car door may hit you.
- Don't ride on sidewalks. Instead, walk your bike. Pedestrians have the right-of-way on all walkways and crosswalks. By law you must give pedestrians audible warning when you pass. Use a bike bell or announce clearly, "On your left/right."
- Slow down at street crossings and driveways.

Clothing

Just as the original mountain bikers headed off in their jeans to hit the trail, mountain bikers can and do wear just about anything to go riding now. There are a few things in the following list that are absolutely necessary and a few that will make your riding more comfortable and more enjoyable.

Be Prepared—Wear Your Armor

It's crucial to discuss the clothing you must wear to be safe, practical, and—if you prefer—stylish. The following is a list of items that will save you from disaster, outfit you comfortably, and most important, keep you looking cool.

Helmet. A helmet is an absolute necessity because it protects your head from complete annihilation. It is the only thing that will not disintegrate into a million pieces after a wicked crash on a descent. A helmet with a solid exterior shell will also protect your head from sharp or protruding objects.

Shorts. These are necessary if you plan to ride your bike more than twenty to thirty minutes. Padded cycling shorts provide cushioning between your body and the bicycle seat, protecting your derriere against serious saddle soreness. There are two types of cycling shorts you can buy. Touring shorts are good for people who don't want to look like they're wearing anatomically correct cellophane. These look like regular athletic shorts with pockets, but they have built-in padding in the crotch area for protection from chafing and saddle sores. The more popular, traditional cycling shorts are made of skintight material, also with a padded crotch. Cycling shorts also wick moisture away from your body and prevent chafing. Whichever style you prefer, cycling shorts are a necessity for long rides.

Gloves. You may find well-padded cycling gloves invaluable when traveling over rocky trails and gravelly roads for hours on end. When you fall off your bike and land on your palms, gloves are your best friend. Long-fingered gloves may also be useful, as branches, trees, assorted hard objects, and, occasionally, small animals will reach out and whack your knuckles. Insulated gloves are essential for winter riding.

Glasses. Not only do sunglasses give you an imposing presence and make you look cool (both are extremely important), they also protect your eyes from harmful ultraviolet rays, invisible branches, creepy bugs, and dirt.

Shoes. Mountain bike shoes are constructed with stiff soles in order to transfer more of the power from a pedal stroke to the drive train and to provide a solid platform on which to stand, thereby decreasing fatigue in your feet. You can use virtually any good, light, outdoor hiking footwear, but specific mountain bike shoes (especially those with inset cleats) are best. They are lighter, breathe better, and are constructed to work with your pedal strokes instead of the natural walking cadence.

Actual armor. If you ride on very technical trails you may want to consider buying some knee-and-shin guards and elbow pads to protect you from whacking your shins on your handlebars and your elbows on the ground.

Dress for the Weather

Layers. It is best to dress in layers that can be added or removed as weather conditions change. When the air has a nip in it, layers will keep the chill away from your chest and help prevent the development of bronchitis. A polypropylene long-sleeved shirt is best to wear against the skin beneath other layers of clothing. Polypropylene, like wool, wicks away moisture from your skin to keep your body dry. The next layer should be a wool or synthetic insulating layer that helps keep you warm but is also breathable. A fleece jacket or vest works well. The outer layer should be a waterproof, windproof, and breathable jacket and pants. Good cold-weather clothing should fit snugly against your body but not be restrictive. Try to avoid wearing cotton or baggy clothing when the temperature falls. Cotton holds moisture like a sponge, and baggy clothing catches cold air and swirls it around your body.

Tights or leg warmers. These are best in temperatures below 55 degrees Fahrenheit. Knees are sensitive and can develop all kinds of problems if they get cold. Common problems include tendinitis, bursitis, and arthritis.

Wool or synthetic socks. These may be helpful in cold weather conditions. Don't pack too many layers under those shoes, though. You may stand the chance of restricting circulation, and your feet will get very cold, very fast.

Thinsulate or Gore-tex gloves. We may all agree that there is nothing worse than frozen feet—unless your hands are frozen. A good pair of Thinsulate or Gore-tex gloves should keep your hands toasty and warm.

Hat or helmet on cold days. Sometimes, when the weather gets really cold and you still want to hit the trails, it's tough to stay warm. As our parents warned us, 130 percent of the body's heat escapes through the head, so it's important to keep the cranium warm. Ventilated helmets are designed to keep heads cool in the summer heat, but they do little to help keep heads warm during rides in subzero temperatures. Cyclists should consider wearing a hat on extremely cold days. Fleece skullcaps are great head and ear warmers that fit snugly over your head beneath the helmet. Head protection is not lost. Another option is a helmet cover that covers those ventilating gaps and helps keep the body heat in. These do not, however, keep your ears warm. Your ears will welcome a fleece headband when it's cold out.

All of this clothing can be found at your local bike shop or outdoor retailer, where the staff should be happy to help fit you into gear for the seasons of the year.

Be Prepared—Supplies and Equipment

The Essentials

Remember the Boy Scout motto: Be Prepared. Here are some essential items that will keep you from walking out a long trail, being stranded in the woods, or even losing your life.

First-Aid Kit

- adhesive bandages
- mole skin
- various sterile gauze and dressings
- white surgical tape
- Ace bandage
- antihistamine
- aspirin
- Betadine solution
- first-aid book
- antacid
- tweezers
- scissors
- antibacterial wipes
- triple-antibiotic ointment
- plastic gloves
- sterile cotton tip applicators
- syrup of ipecac (to induce vomiting)
- thermometer
- wire splint
- matches
- guidebook (In case all else fails and you must start a fire to survive, this guidebook will serve as excellent fire starter!)

Bicycle Repair Kit

- spare tube
- tire irons
- patch kit
- pump
- spoke wrench
- spare spokes to fit your wheel (tape these to the chain stay)
- chain tool
- Allen keys (bring appropriate sizes to fit your bike)
- duct tape

Water. Without it, cyclists may face dehydration, which may result in dizziness and fatigue. On a warm day, cyclists should drink at least one full bottle during every hour of riding. Remember, it's always good to drink before you feel thirsty—otherwise, it may be too late.

Food. This essential item will keep you rolling. Cycling burns up a lot of calories and is among the few sports in which no one is safe from "bonking." Bonking feels like it sounds. Without food in your system, your blood sugar level plummets, and there is no longer any energy in your body. This instantly results in total fatigue, shakiness, and lightheadedness. So when you're filling your water bottle, remember to bring along some food. Fruit, energy bars, or some other forms of high-energy food are highly recommended. Candy bars are not, however, because they will deliver a sudden burst of high energy, then let you down soon after, causing you to feel worse than before. Energy bars are available at most grocery stores and bike shops and are similar to candy bars, but they provide complex carbohydrate energy and high nutrition rather than fast-burning simple sugars.

Map and compass. Do not rely solely on the maps in this book. A GPS system is also useful (if you know how to use it).

To Have or Not to Have—Other Very Useful Items

There is no shortage of items for you and your bike to make riding better, safer, and easier. We have rummaged through the unending lists and separated the gadgets from the good stuff, coming up with what we believe are items certain to make mountain bike riding more enjoyable.

Tires. Buying a good pair of knobby tires is the quickest way to enhance the off-road handling capabilities of a bike. There are many types of mountain bike tires on the market. Some are made exclusively for very rugged off-road terrain. These big-knobbed, soft rubber tires virtually stick to the ground with magnetlike traction, but they tend to deteriorate quickly on pavement. There are other tires made exclusively for the road. These are called "slicks" and have no tread at all. For the average cyclist, though, a good tire somewhere in the middle of these two extremes should do the trick. Realize, however, that you get what you pay for. Do not skimp and buy cheap tires. As your primary point of contact with the trail, tires may be the most important piece of equipment on a bike. With inexpensive rubber, the tire's beads may unravel or chunks of tread actually rip off the tire. If you're lucky, all you'll suffer is a long walk back to the car. If you're unlucky, your tire could blow out in the middle of a rowdy downhill, causing a wicked crash.

Clipless pedals. Clipless pedals, like ski bindings, attach your shoe directly to the pedal. They allow you to exert pressure on the pedals during both the down- and up-strokes. They also help you to maneuver the bike while in the air or climbing various obstacles. Toe clips may be less expensive, but they are also heavier and harder to use. Clipless pedals take a little getting used to, but they're easier to get out of in an emergency than toe clips and are definitely worth the trouble.

Bar ends. These clamp-on additions to your original straight bar will provide more leverage, an excellent grip for climbing, and a more natural position for your hands. Be aware, however, of the bar end's propensity for hooking trees on fast descents, sending you, the cyclist, airborne. Opinions are divided on the general usefulness of bar ends these days and, over the last few years, bar ends have fallen out of favor with manufacturers and riders alike.

Backpacks and hydration packs. These bags are ideal for carrying keys, extra food and water, guidebooks, foul-weather clothing, tools, spare tubes, a camera, and a cellular phone, in case you need to call for help. If you're carrying lots of equipment, you may want to consider a set of panniers. These are much larger and mount on either side of each wheel on a rack. Keep in mind, however, that with panniers mobility will be severely limited. There are currently a number of streamlined backpacks with hydration systems on the market. Hydration packs are fast becoming an essential item for cyclists pedaling for more than a few hours, especially in hot, dry conditions. Some water packs can carry as much as one hundred ounces of water in their bladder bags. These packs strap on your back with a handy hose running over your shoulder so you can be drinking water while still holding onto the bars with both hands on a rocky descent.

Suspension forks. For off-roaders who want nothing to impede their speed on the trails, investing in a pair of suspension forks can be a good idea. Like tires, there are plenty of brands to choose from, and they all do the same thing—absorb the brutal beatings of a rough trail. The cost of these forks, however, is sometimes more brutal than the trail itself.

Full suspension bikes. Full suspension bikes help smooth out the ride and keep the wheels in contact with the ground. They have been around for a while, but the prices are now falling into a range that the average mountain biker can afford. There are a number of different designs intended for different activities, such as cross-country riding and downhill riding. Be careful when buying and test ride several bikes to determine just what you want.

Bike computers. These are fun gadgets to own and are much less expensive than in years past. They have such features as trip distance, speedometer, odometer, time of day, altitude, alarm, average speed, maximum speed, heart rate, global satellite positioning, etc. Bike computers will come in handy when following these maps or to know just how far you've ridden in the wrong direction.

Types of Terrain

Before roughing it off-road, we may first have to ride the pavement to get to our destination. Please don't be dismayed. Some of the country's best rides are on the road. Once we get past these smooth-surfaced pathways, though, adventures in dirt await us.

Rails-to-Trails. Abandoned rail lines are converted into usable public resources for exercising, commuting, or just enjoying nature. Old rails and ties are torn up and a trail, paved or unpaved, is laid along the existing corridor. This completes the cycle from ancient Indian trading routes to railroad corridors and back again to hiking and cycling trails.

Unpaved roads are typically found in rural areas and are most often public roads. Be careful when exploring, though, not to ride on someone's unpaved private drive.

Forest roads. These dirt and gravel roads are used primarily as access to forestland and are generally kept in good condition. They are almost always open to public use.

Singletrack can be the most fun on a mountain bike. These trails, with only one track to follow, are often narrow, challenging pathways. Remember to make sure these trails are open before zipping into the woods.

Doubletrack. These are usually old Jeep trails or small logging roads where two distinct trails exist parallel to each other. Doubletrack trail can be found almost anywhere and can be as exciting as singletrack.

Open land. Unless there is a marked trail through a field or open space, you should not plan to ride there. Once one person cuts his or her wheels through a field or meadow, many more are sure to follow, causing irreparable damage to the landscape.

Mountain Biking into Shape

If your objective is to get in shape and lose weight, then you're on the right track, because mountain biking is one of the best ways to get started.

One way many of us have lost weight in this sport is the crash-and-burn-it-off method. Picture this: You're speeding uncontrollably down a vertical drop that you realize you shouldn't be on—only after it is too late. Your front wheel lodges into a rut and launches you through endless weeds, trees, and pointy rocks before coming to an abrupt halt in a puddle of thick mud. Surveying the damage, you discover, with the layers of skin, body parts, and lost confidence littering the trail above, that those unwanted pounds have been shed—permanently. Instant weight loss.

There is, of course, a more conventional (and quite a bit less painful) approach to losing weight and gaining fitness on a mountain bike. It's called the workout, and bicycles provide an ideal way to get physical. Take a look at some of the benefits associated with cycling.

Cycling helps you shed pounds without gimmicky diet fads or weight-loss programs. You can explore the countryside and burn nearly ten to sixteen calories per minute or close to 600 to 1,000 calories per hour. Moreover, it's a great way to spend an afternoon.

No less significant than the external and cosmetic changes to your body from riding are the internal changes taking place. Over time, cycling regularly will strengthen your heart as your body grows vast networks of new capillaries to carry blood to all those working muscles. This will, in turn, give your skin a healthier glow. The capacity of your lungs may increase up to 20 percent, and your resting heart rate will drop significantly. The Stanford University School of Medicine reports to the American Heart Association that people can reduce their risk of heart attack by nearly 64 percent if they can burn up to 2,000 calories per week. This is only two to three hours of bike riding!

Recommended for insomnia, hypertension, indigestion, anxiety, and even for recuperation from major heart attacks, bicycling can be an excellent cure-all as well as a great preventive. Cycling just a few hours per week can improve your figure and sleeping habits, give you greater resistance to illness, increase your energy levels, and provide feelings of accomplishment and heightened self-esteem.

Techniques to Sharpen Your Skills

Many of us see ourselves as pure athletes—blessed with power, strength, and endless endurance. However, it may be those with finesse, balance, agility, and grace who get around most quickly on a mountain bike. Although power, strength, and endurance do have their places in mountain biking, these elements don't necessarily form the complete framework for a champion mountain biker.

The bike should become an extension of your body. Slight shifts in your hips or knees can have remarkable results. Experienced bike handlers seem to flash down technical descents, dashing over obstacles in a smooth and graceful effort as if pirouetting in Swan Lake. Here are some tips and techniques to help you connect with your bike and float gracefully over the dirt.

Going Uphill—Climbing Those Treacherous Hills

Shift into a low gear. Before shifting, be sure to ease up on your pedaling so there is not too much pressure on the chain. You can break your chain or bend your derailleur with too much pressure. With that in mind, it's important to shift before you find yourself on a steep slope, where it may be too late. Find the best gear for you that matches the terrain and steepness of each climb.

Stay seated. Standing out of the saddle is often helpful when climbing steep hills on a bike, but you may find that on dirt, standing may cause your rear tire to lose its grip and spin out. Climbing is not possible without traction. As you improve, you will likely learn the subtle tricks that make out-of-saddle climbing possible. Until then, have a seat.

Lean forward. On very steep hills, the front end may feel unweighted and suddenly pop up. Slide forward on the saddle and lean over the handlebars. Think about putting your chin down near your stem. This will add more weight to the front wheel and should keep you grounded. It's all about using the weight of your head to your advantage. Most people don't realize how heavy their noggin is.

Relax. As with downhilling, relaxation is a big key to your success when climbing steep, rocky climbs. Smooth pedaling translates into good traction. Tense bodies don't balance well at low speeds. Instead of fixating grimly on the front wheel, look up at the terrain above, and pick a good line.

Keep pedaling. On rocky climbs, be sure to keep the pressure on, and don't let up on those pedals! You'll be surprised at what your bike will just roll over as long as you keep the engine revved up.

Going Downhill—The Real Reason We Get Up in the Morning

Relax. Stay loose on the bike, and don't lock your elbows or clench your grip. Your elbows need to bend with the bumps and absorb the shock, while your hands should have a firm but controlled grip on the bars to keep things steady. Breathing slowly, deeply, and deliberately will help you relax while flying down bumpy singletrack. Maintaining a death-grip on the brakes will be unhelpful. Fear and tension will make you wreck every time.

Use your eyes. Keep your head up and scan the trail as far forward as possible. Choose a line well in advance. You decide what line to take—don't let the trail decide for you. Keep the surprises to a minimum. If you have to react quickly to an obstacle, then you've already made a mistake.

Rise above the saddle. When racing down bumpy, technical descents, you should not be sitting on the saddle, but hovering just over it or behind it, allowing your bent legs and arms, instead of your rear, to absorb the rocky trail. This will also help keep your weight back to avoid going over the handlebars. Think jockey.

Remember your pedals. Be mindful of where your pedals are in relation to upcoming obstacles. Clipping a rock will lead directly to unpleasantness. Most of the time, you'll want to keep your pedals parallel to the ground.

Stay focused. Many descents require your utmost concentration and focus just to reach the bottom. You must notice every groove, every root, every rock, every hole, every bump. You, the bike, and the trail should all become one as you seek singletrack nirvana on your way down the mountain. But if your thoughts wander, however, then so may your bike, and you may instead become one with the trees!

Braking. Using your brakes requires using your head, especially when descending. This doesn't mean using your head as a stopping block, but rather to think intelligently. Use your best judgment in terms of how much or how little to squeeze those brake levers. The more weight a tire is carrying, the more braking power it has. When you're going downhill, your front wheel carries more weight than the rear. Braking gently with the front brake will help keep you in control without going into a skid. Be careful, though, not to overdo it with the front brakes and accidentally toss yourself over the handlebars. And don't neglect your rear brake! When descending, shift your weight back over the rear wheel, thus increasing your rear braking power as well. This will balance the power of both brakes and give you maximum control. Good riders learn just how much of their weight to shift over each wheel and how to apply just enough braking power to each brake, so not to "endo" over the handlebars or skid down a trail.

Obstacles

Logs. When you want to hop a log, pull up sharply on the handlebars, and pedal forward in one swift motion. This clears the front end of the bike. Then quickly scoot forward and pedal the rear wheel up and over. Keep the forward momentum until you've cleared the log, and by all means, don't hit the brakes, or you may do some interesting acrobatic maneuvers!

Rocks and roots. Worse than highway potholes! Stay relaxed and let your elbows and knees absorb the shock. Staying seated will keep the rear wheel weighted to prevent slipping.

Water. Before crossing a stream or puddle, be sure to first check the depth and bottom surface. There may be an unseen hole or large rock hidden under the water that could wash you up if you're not careful. You should also consider that riding through a mountain stream can cause great damage to the stream's ecosystem. If you still want to try, hit the water at a good speed, pedal steadily, and allow the bike to steer you through. Once you're across, tap the brakes to squeegee the water off the rims and the guilt off your conscience.

Leaves. Be careful of wet leaves. They may look pretty, but a trail or bridge covered with leaves may cause your wheels to slip out from under you. Leaves are not nearly as unpredictable and dangerous as ice, but they do warrant your attention on a rainy day.

Mud. If you must ride through mud, hit it head on and keep pedaling. You want to part the ooze with your front wheel and get across before it swallows you up. Above all, don't leave the trail to go around the mud. This just widens the path even more and leads to increased trail erosion.

Sand. This can be one of the most challenging trail conditions. The basic technique is to get the weight off the front tire by pulling up on the handlebars, getting your weight behind your seat, and pedaling like crazy. Your front tire should float over the surface of the sand. If it dives in, you're walking.

Slickrock. Moab, Utah, is famous for its slickrock, but you may find small sections of exposed rock in many places around the country. Depending on the type of rock, slickrock is very rideable when it's dry but slippery when it's wet.

Curbs are fun to jump, but as with logs, be careful.

Curbside drains. Be careful not to get a wheel caught in the grate. This is a recipe for a pretzeled wheel and a broken collarbone.

Dogs make great pets, but they seem to have it in for mountain bikers. If you think you can't outrun a dog that's chasing you, stop and walk your bike out of its territory. A loud yell to "Get!" or "Go home!" often works, as does a sharp squirt from your water bottle right between the eyes.

Cars are tremendously convenient when we're in them, but dodging irate motorists in big automobiles becomes a real hazard when riding a bike. As a cyclist you must realize most drivers aren't expecting you to be there and often wish you weren't. Stay alert and ride carefully, clearly signaling all of your intentions.

Potholes, like grates and back-road canyons, should be avoided. Just because you're on an all-terrain bicycle doesn't mean you're indestructible. Potholes regularly damage rims, pop tires, and sometimes lift unsuspecting cyclists into a spectacular swan dive over the handlebars.

LAST-MINUTE CHECKOVER

Before a ride, it's a good idea to give your bike a once-over to make sure everything is in working order. Go through the following checklist before each ride to make sure everything is secure and in place.

- **Check the air pressure in your tires to make sure they are properly inflated before each ride.** Mountain bikes require about forty-five to fifty-five pounds per square inch of air pressure. If your tires are underinflated, there is greater likelihood that the tubes may get pinched on a rock, causing the tire to go flat.
- **Pinch the tires to feel for proper inflation.** They should give just a little on the sides but feel very hard on the treads. If you have a pressure gauge, use that.
- **Check your brakes.** Squeeze the rear brake and roll your bike forward. The rear tire should skid. Next, squeeze the front brake and roll your bike forward. The rear wheel should lift into the air. If this doesn't happen, then your brakes are too loose. Make sure the brake levers don't touch the handlebars when squeezed with full force.
- **Check all quick releases on your bike.** Make sure they are all securely tightened. To avoid hooking them on a stick or branch, quick releases should point toward the back of the bike. The front quick release lever should be on the left of the

bike and tightened so it runs parallel to the arm of the fork. The back quick release should be closed so it points toward the back of the bike.

- **Lube up.** If your chain squeaks, apply some lubricant.
- **Check your nuts and bolts.** Check the handlebars, saddle, cranks, and pedals to make sure that each is tight and securely fastened to your bike.
- **Check your wheels.** Spin each wheel to see that they spin through the frame and between brake pads freely.

Have you got everything? Make sure you have your spare tube, tire irons, patch kit, frame pump, tools, food, water, foul-weather gear, and guidebook.

Need more info on mountain biking? Consider reading *Basic Essentials Mountain Biking*. You'll discover such things as choosing and maintaining a mountain bike; useful bike-handling techniques; preparing for long rides; overcoming obstacles such as rocks, logs, and water; and even preparing for competition.

Repair and Maintenance

Fixing a Flat

TOOLS YOU WILL NEED

- Two tire irons
- Pump (either a floor pump or a frame pump)
- No screwdrivers!!! (This can puncture the tube.)

REMOVING THE WHEEL

The front wheel is easy. Simply disconnect the brake shoes, open the quick release mechanism or undo the bolts with the proper sized wrench, then remove the wheel from the bike.

    The rear wheel is a little more tricky. Before you loosen the wheel from the frame, shift the chain into the smallest gear on the freewheel (the cluster of gears in the back). Once you've done this, removing and installing the wheel, like the front, is much easier.

REMOVING THE TIRE

Step one: Insert a tire iron under the bead of the tire and pry the tire over the lip of the rim. Be careful not to pinch the tube when you do this.

Step two: Hold the first tire iron in place. With the second tire iron, repeat step one, 3 or 4 inches down the rim. Alternate tire irons, pulling the bead of the tire over the rim, section by section, until one side of the tire bead is completely off the rim.

Step three: Remove the rest of the tire and tube from the rim. This can be done by hand. It's easiest to remove the valve stem last. Once the tire is off the rim, pull the tube out of the tire.

CLEAN AND SAFETY CHECK

Step four: Using a rag, wipe the inside of the tire to clean out any dirt, sand, glass, thorns, etc. These may cause the tube to puncture. The inside of a tire should feel smooth. Any pricks or bumps could mean that you have found the culprit responsible for your flat tire.

Step five: Wipe the rim clean, then check the rim strip, making sure it covers the spoke nipples properly on the inside of the rim. If a spoke is poking through the rim strip, it could cause a puncture.

Step six: At this point, you can do one of two things: replace the punctured tube with a new one, or patch the hole. It's easiest to just replace the tube with a new tube when you're out on the trails. Roll up the old tube and take it home to repair later that night in front of the TV. Directions on patching a tube are usually included with the patch kit itself.

INSTALLING THE TIRE AND TUBE
(This can be done entirely by hand.)

Step seven: Inflate the new or repaired tube with enough air to give it shape, then tuck it back into the tire.

Step eight: To put the tire and tube back on the rim, begin by putting the valve in the valve hole. The valve must be straight. Then use your hands to push the beaded edge of the tire onto the rim all the way around so that one side of your tire is on the rim.

Step nine: Let most of the air out of the tube to allow room for the rest of the tire.

Step ten: Beginning opposite the valve, use your thumbs to push the other side of the tire onto the rim. Be careful not to pinch the tube in between the tire and the rim. The last few inches may be difficult, and you may need the tire iron to pry the tire onto the rim. If so, just be careful not to puncture the tube.

BEFORE INFLATING COMPLETELY

Step eleven: Check to make sure the tire is seated properly and that the tube is not caught between the tire and the rim. Do this by adding about five to ten pounds of air, and watch closely that the tube does not bulge out of the tire.

Step twelve: Once you're sure the tire and tube are properly seated, put the wheel back on the bike, then fill the tire with air. It's easier squeezing the wheel through the brake shoes if the tire is still flat.

Step thirteen: Now fill the tire with the proper amount of air, and check constantly to make sure the tube doesn't bulge from the rim. If the tube does appear to bulge out, release all the air as quickly as possible, or you could be in for a big bang. Place the wheel back in the dropout and tighten the quick release lever Reconnect the brake shoes.

When installing the rear wheel, place the chain back onto the smallest cog (farthest gear on the right), and pull the derailleur out of the way. Your wheel should slide right on.

Lubrication Prevents Deterioration

Lubrication is crucial to maintaining your bike. Dry spots will be eliminated. Creaks, squeaks, grinding, and binding will be gone. The chain will run quietly, and the gears will shift smoothly. The brakes will grip quicker, and your bike may last longer with fewer repairs. Need I say more? Well, yes. Without knowing where to put the lubrication, what good is it?

THINGS YOU WILL NEED
- One can of bicycle lubricant, found at any bike store
- A clean rag (to wipe excess lubricant away)

WHAT GETS LUBRICATED
- Front derailleur
- Rear derailleur
- Shift levers
- Front brake
- Rear brake
- Both brake levers
- Chain

WHERE TO LUBRICATE

To make it easy, simply spray a little lubricant on all the pivot points of your bike. If you're using a squeeze bottle, use just a drop or two. Put a few drops on each point wherever metal moves against metal, for instance, at the center of the brake calipers. Then let the lube sink in.

Once you have applied the lubricant to the derailleurs, shift the gears a few times, working the derailleurs back and forth. This allows the lubricant to work itself into the tiny cracks and spaces it must occupy to do its job. Work the brakes a few times as well.

LUBING THE CHAIN

Lubricating the chain should be done after the chain has been wiped clean of most road grime. Do this by spinning the pedals counterclockwise while gripping the chain with a clean rag. As you add the lubricant, be sure to get some in between

each link. With an aerosol spray, just spray the chain while pedaling backwards (counterclockwise) until the chain is fully lubricated. Let the lubricant soak in for a few seconds before wiping the excess away. Chains will collect dirt much faster if they're loaded with too much lubrication.

Ride Index

Listings are numeric for ease in locating the write-ups. Be your own judge on what is best; we each have our own ideas about paradise.

Coveted Singletrack

Great Technical Trails

Real Climbs + Great Views = Sweet Downhill

Major Peaks

Great Views without Long Killer Climbs

3. Angel Island Double Loop
30. Wilder Ranch Loop—Old Cove Landing and Ohlone Bluff Trails
33. Saratoga Gap–Long Ridge Loop

Best Long Rides

6. Deer Park–Repack Loop—Joe Breeze's Mega Ride to Mecca
8. Olema Valley–Bolinas Ridge Loop
19. Mount Diablo: Mitchell Canyon–Summit Loop
27. Henry W. Coe Park: Kelly Lake Loop
27. Henry W. Coe Park: Kelly Lake Loop—Coe Epic Enduro
31. Big Basin–Butano Loop

Good Winter Rides

Unless paved, give it a rest during periods of heavy rain.
1. Tennessee Valley–Golden Gate Loop
3. Angel Island Double Loop
4. Old Railroad Grade to East Peak Loop
5. The Lakes Loop
9. Wildcat Camp Out-and-Back
29. The Forest of Nisene Marks Out-and-Back
35. Skyline Ridge Loop
36. Old Haul Road Out-and-Back
40. McNee Ranch Out-and-Back
B. Bear Valley Trail
H. Coyote Hills Regional Park
Q. Fifield–Cahill Ridge Trail

Cool Summer Rides

2. Tennessee Valley–Green Gulch Loop—Muir Beach Loop
3. Angel Island Double Loop
5. The Lakes Loop
6. Deer Park–Repack Loop
7. China Camp Loop
9. Wildcat Camp Out-and-Back
14. Redwood Park Loop
15. Joaquin Miller Park
28. Soquel Demonstration Forest Loop

Whale-Watching Opportunities

Bicycle Councils and Clubs, Coalitions, and Racing Web Site

Councils and Clubs

★★★Three stars for the mountain bike advocates. Support these groups. They promote safe and responsible mountain biking, seek equal standing with other trail users, and work for increased trail access for bicycles. They are responsible for opening new trails to bikes, as well as maintaining existing trail access when challenged. Most of these groups sponsor trail maintenance projects—lend a hand.

Access4Bikes★★★
This is a political nonprofit group with a mission to establish equal access for bikes on the public trails of Marin County and beyond.
www.access4bikes.com

Almaden Cycle Touring Club (ACTC)
ACTC is a group of about 1,000 bicycle enthusiasts based in South Bay. Their emphasis is on fun, safety, and lots of riding for a wide range of abilities. While road riding dominates, they post two to three mountain bike rides per week. Riders can accumulate Billy Goat, Mountain Goat, and Grizzly Bear credits.
P.O. Box 7286
San Jose, CA 95150
(408) 446–2199
www.actc.org

Bay Area Roaming Tandems (BART)
This is a club for those brave enough to connect with another rider on the same bike. Although group rides are on the road, a few members have tandem mountain bikes. It's time to infiltrate.
www.bayarearoamingtandems.org

Bicycle Trail Council of the East Bay (BTCEB)★★★
BTCEB is the second oldest mountain bike advocacy group in the United States and one of the founding clubs of IMBA. They sponsor group rides, bike patrols, and skill clinics.
P.O. Box 9583
Berkeley, CA 94709
(510) 466–5123
E-mail: info@btceb.org
www.btceb.org

Bicycle Trails Council (BTC) of Marin★★★
This is the classic BTC, promoting safe and responsible mountain biking. They have successfully promoted access for bikes on several trails throughout Marin.
P.O. Box 494
Fairfax, CA 94978
(415) 488–1443
www.btcmarin.org

The Cherry City Cyclists
Club rides are social events, not races. Members share a love for cycling: road, mountain, tandem, and hybrid.
www.cherrycitycyclists.org

Delta Pedalers Bicycle Club

This East Contra Costa club promotes mountain and road biking, touring, tandems, and family rides for all levels of cyclists.
P.O. Box 2394
Antioch, CA 94531
www.deltaped.org

Different Spokes San Francisco (DSSF)

DSSF is the Bay Area's lesbian and gay bicycling club. Although they focus on road cycling, most members also have mountain bikes and use them often. There are a few mountain bike racers in the pack.
P.O. Box 14711
San Francisco, CA 94114
www.dssf.org

Eagle Cycling Club, Inc (ECC)

ECC is a diverse group of riders. They put on a mountain bike race each year at Skyline Park, along with the Cherry Pie road race and the Tour of Napa Valley century ride.
3335 Solano Avenue
Napa, CA 94558
(707) 226–7066
E-mail: info@eaglecyclingclub.org
www.eaglecyclingclub.org

Golden Gate Cyclists (GGC)

GGC combines camaraderie and cycling, listing weekly road and mountain rides for adults of all skill levels. Other club listings include hikes, camping, picnics, parties, and urban activities.
Golden Gate Cyclists
P.O. Box 656
Kentfield, CA 94914
www.goldengatecyclists.org

Los Gatos Bicycle Racing Club (LGBRC)

Although predominately a road and track racing club, the LGBRC has some very serious cyclocross and mountain bike racers. The club provides training programs, coaching, and social activities.
P.O. Box 2842
Saratoga, CA 95070
(408) 395–6611
www.lgbrc.org

Mako-Galaxy Granola Racing Team

This masters racing team has dominated the road and is ready to take over mountain biking.
2301 Kerner Boulevard
San Rafael, CA 94901
(415) 902–5658
www.mggracingteam.org

Mountain Bikers of Santa Cruz (MBOSC)★★★

These folks are dedicated trail workers and mountain bike advocates . . . and they have a lot of fun along the way. They sponsor group rides, trips, and the annual Tour de FAT.
730 Mission Street
Santa Cruz, CA 95060
www.mbosc.org

Nor Cal High School League

This cross-country racing league supports mountain biking as an organized school sport. What a concept!
Matt Fritzinger
5648 Oak Grove Avenue
Oakland, CA 94618
(510) 325–6502
www.norcalhighracing.org

Northern California Mountain Bike Association (NCMBA)★★★

NCMBA supports local mountain bike organizations in their advocacy efforts, with a vision to unify trail communities. www.ncmba.org

Responsible Organized Mountain Bike Pedalers (ROMP)★★★

ROMP is *the* mountain cycling advocacy and social group for San Mateo and Santa Clara Counties. Thank them for all the trails they have helped to open. Activities include trail maintenance, bike patrol, group rides, and goodwill on the trail.
P.O. Box 1723
Campbell, CA 95009
(408) 380–2271
www.romp.org

Santa Rosa Cycling Club

Although this is primarily a road bike club, many members have mountain bikes. They do schedule some off-road rides. Want to explore the wine country? These folks know it well.
www.srcc.com

Skyline Cycling Club

Whether road or mountain biking, they ride to eat—they eat to ride.
P.O. Box 60176
Sunnyvale, CA 94088
(408) 736–9858
www.sonic.net/~jps/skyline

Tam Valley Bike Club (TVBC)

TVBC hosts mountain bike rides every Sunday morning and on full moon evenings in the Marin Headlands and on the slopes of Mount Tamalpais.
(415) 388–6393, ext. 19
www.tamvalleybikeclub.com

Team Wrong Way

These mountain biking folks race, ride, advocate, help maintain trails, and generally give back to the community. Their whole point is to have fun doing it.
www.teamwrongway.com

Valley Spokesman

While their emphasis is on road cycling, they do post some mountain bike rides. Rides are for a range of abilities.
P.O. Box 2630
Dublin, CA 94568
www.valleyspokesmen.org

Women's Mountain Bike & Tea Society (WOMBATS)

WOMBATS is a network of women of all ages and abilities who share a passion for pedaling.
P.O. Box 757
Fairfax, CA 94978
Hotline: (415) 459–0980
www.wombats.org

Bicycle Coalitions

These coalitions advocate safe bicycling for everyday transportation and recreation. Among other activities, these groups support bike access on regional connector trails.

East Bay Bicycle Coalition

P.O. Box 1736
Oakland, CA 94604
(510) 433–7433
E-mail: info@ebbc.org
www.ebbc.org

Marin County Bicycle Coalition
P.O. Box 35
San Anselmo, CA 94979
(415) 456–3469
www.marinbike.org

Peninsula Bicycle & Pedestrian Coalition
539 Hillcrest Drive
Redwood City, CA 94062
(650) 291–7343
E-mail: info@penbiped.org
www.penbiped.org

San Francisco Bicycle Coalition
1095 Market Street, Suite 215
San Francisco, CA 94103
(415) 431–2453
E-mail: sfbc@sfbike.org
www.sfbike.org

Silicon Valley Bicycle Coalition
E-mail: svbc@svbcbikes.org
www.svbcbikes.org

Racing Web Site

Northern California/Nevada Cycling Association
The Web site provides a listing of mountain bike races in Northern California and Nevada.
www.ncnca.org/mtn

About the Author

California native Lorene Jackson came to the Bay Area to attend graduate school in environmental health at UC Berkeley—and she never left. Gradually moving up the ranks of cross-country bicycle racing, she has won the expert division for her age group at the National Off-Road Bicycle Association (NORBA) national races. She lives in San Rafael, California, and is now training for mountain bike triathlons.